THIS BOOK IS FOR

C000196857

- you've ever encountered work - well, anywhere really
- you've lived a life
- you are still working on perfecting your adulting skills
- you've been through a failed relationship, coercive control or damaging interpersonal experiences - and questioned if it's you, not them
- you like to laugh
- you've felt shame
- you've ever had any kind of self doubt/low self-esteem/lack of self-worth/perfectionism, etc.
- you kinda like Bridget Jones, but you want something with a bit more grit
- you've endured loss
- you've ever taken the blame for someone else's bad behaviour
- you're ok with crying
- you heard the alarm bells ringing and saw the red flags waving, but ignored/hid/shunned them until it was almost too late
- you'd like to know that you're not alone with the messiness of life
- you find the word 'twat' funny

What happens when you so deeply believe something you were told as a child that it becomes the driving force behind almost every thought, feeling and action for the rest of your life... until you decide to take complete control and change your life entirely? For decades, successful HR and transformational change expert, Carolyn Hobdey, believed she was 'trouble' and if she wasn't 'nicer' she'd spend her days alone and unloved.

All The Twats I Met Along The Way tells the tales of crappy boyfriends, sickening sexual encounters, manipulative men, love triangles, unsupportive and unsupported medical diagnoses... and that's just in the first few pages. From porn-addicted boyfriends who rapidly go from total fitties to owners of 'dad bods', to car crashes and boob jobs. Marriage to a lover who became more like a brother (and who had been hiding a deep secret throughout their 15 year relationship) and later a relationship with a man and his 'ready-made family' that exposes a damaging case of coercive control and narcisstic personality disorder. Carolyn's story exposes the unrelenting pull of the child-parent relationship – even in adulthood – and all the messiness and confusion that can cause. As she writes, "I didn't want to be the trouble-maker, the one to cause my parents concern, anymore."

All The Twats I Met Along The Way is a story many women will be able to identify with, from teenage heartbreak to a series of dangerous relationships; battles with internal thoughts and feelings versus external perceptions and reputations. Fans of Bridget Jones and Amy Schumer's The Girl With The Lower Back Tattoo will appreciate the candour, humour and raw honesty about heartbreak, adulting, domestic abuse, premature menopause, childlessness and personal tragedies.

ABOUT THE AUTHOR

www.carolynhobdey.com

Despite 20 years of building a successful corporate career, working for some of the world's largest employers, Carolyn Hobdey's personal life has been a self-confessed mess... until now. So, she began to write about the reality behind her successful career because there are so many 'successful' people out there struggling in one way or another. Carolyn's progressively more senior roles had earned her a seat at the boardroom table leading internationally recognisable brands where, whilst specialising in Human Resources, she was required to operate across all business disciplines. Having gained a BA(Hons) in English & Creative Studies at Portsmouth University, Carolyn went on to support her practical work experience with a post-graduate qualification in HR at Leeds Metropolitan University, where she won the Chartered Institute of Personnel & Development (West Yorkshire) Student Award. Later followed a Masters in Lean Operations gained at Cardiff University, where she was the first HR specialist in the 13 years of the course and became the winner of the inaugural Sir Julian Hodge Prize for Logistics, Operations & Manufacturing. Carolyn is now founder and CEO of MayDey Ltd where she is an expert in identity, confidence and change. Carolyn is passionate about helping people to successfully transform from self-loathing to self-love.Living in North Yorkshire, Carolyn loves to box & weight train, enjoys latin & ballroom dancing and is a car enthusiast.

ABOUT MAYDEY LTD

http://www.maydey.co.uk/

Navigate through change.
Discover what matters.
Find what's missing.
Sort what's not quite right.
Define YOUR happy.

MayDey is a supportive community of people, led by Carolyn, who feel like something isn't 'quite right' in their lives, but know that they only have one chance in this world and want to make changes.

It's unique Fathom Framework, is MayDey's 9-step 'How To' guide to discovering what you really want in life and reconnecting with who you really are. It helps identify what 'happiness' means to you and provides techniques, plans and the support network to ensure you achieve it..
If this sounds like you, then join the MayDey Crew!

ACKNOWLEDGEMENTS

I want to try to acknowledge all the people that helped me write this book, starting with those people who ensured I was here to write it; there have been a couple of points where that almost wasn't the case.

I will be indebted forever to Peter Callendar, the kindest of souls, who, despite my constant insistence, is too humble to take credit for saving my life. So I'm saying it here for everyone to read, Peter: what you did that day was totally selfless. The alternative outcome doesn't bear contemplation.

Similarly, I owe so much to Gillian Farr: my best friend, my partner in crime, and the only one who really understands some of the events documented here because she had a ring-side seat. You've held me through all the lows and celebrated every high. You loved me when I thought I was unloveable and then taught me how to turn that love on myself.

To my parents who bought me here in the first place. I know I have not made the journey easy, but I hope the laughs have in some way compensated. I'm trying my best to make it all worthwhile in the end. I hope you understand that I had to get out there and do things my way.

To my sister, Rachel Hale. For standing up for me and to me when I needed both. Through every twist and turn you have been steadfast. Thank you for helping me to feel less out of place. For providing our family with the most wonderful thing that I was unable to do: children. I truly learnt what love was when they joined our lives. Thank you to the unique Mike for making them possible and showing up to help me whenever I needed it.

David Hobdey. This book would be shorter without you, but my life would have been so much less if you'd not come into it. You have always been my cheerleader; thank you for extending that to your patience with this book. I love you - not in the way I imagined, but forever nonetheless.

My friends: my 'other' family. You look out for me, guide me, love me, and help me embrace life. For their part in getting this story out, I particularly must thank:

The Choir Girls, especially Lynda Johnson, who recognised my suffering and provided a place of safety; you and Simon helped me to locate the disparate pieces of my life. Thank you also to The Ivy League, The Hayward Ladies Trio and The Gavin & Stacey Superfans. To the beautiful Maria Spooner, Simon Robinson (who I am a little bit in love with, obvs), James White for helping me to dance my way through and Lewis Borlase for listening whilst training my body! Haydee Cochrane for guiding me through the exploration of my life that made this an inevitable output.

Cliff Sewell at 15ten15 - you've pushed and been brutally honest to improve me. Despite my kicking and screaming, it's been hilarious.

To DD: for reading the first draft of the book. For your enthusiasm, enhancements and encouragement. Especially for the absence of judgement. You made me believe that I could go all the way. Always 'Yours x' at 02.14.

For the practicalities I've been supported by some incredible people. Kelly Tyler at Speaker INsight for putting structure around my ideas. For connecting me with Samantha Houghton, who's skill in getting the story out of me was invaluable. To ThinkSmart Marketing, especially the endless patience of Clare-Marie Taylor. The enthusiasm of Chris Day at Filament Publishing, who gave me confidence in the title (and Anthony Downes for teasing that out of me!). In getting the book out there, my gratitude goes to Helen Lewis at LiterallyPR for believing in my story.

Finally (and with sincerity), I want to thank everyone who has ever hurt, harmed or hated me; you've made the road challenging and treacherous, but awesome. If I hadn't been through those experiences I wouldn't have written this book. I am who I am because of and despite you and today I like who I am. You are twats and I am indebted to all of you.

DEDICATION:

FOR MY FAMILY WHO MADE ME.

FOR GILL AND PETER WHO SAVED ME.

ALL THE TWATS I MET ALONG THE WAY

CAROLYN HOBDEY

Published by
Filament Publishing Ltd
16, Croydon Road, Beddington
Croydon, Surrey. CR0 4PA
+44 (0)20 8688 2598
www.filamentpublishing.com

© 2021 Carolyn Hobdey
ISBN 978-1-913623-33-3

Printed in the UK by 4Edge

TABLE OF CONTENTS

PROLOGUE

*T*he little girl sat on the step outside the house feeling the sun on her translucent skin; the freckles were practically popping up one-by-one on her arms as she picked at the remnants of a scab on one knee of the skinny legs that stuck out from her cut-off denim shorts.

Looking up at the adult next to her, she squinted against the bright light as she peered through the fringe of her neat 'page-boy' haircut; it was no wonder that she sometimes got mistaken for a boy. She hated that; the feeling of embarrassment burned inside. Occasionally it made her cry. Often she had strong feelings that she didn't have words for yet; the frustration of these erupted sometimes and meant she could be trouble.

"If you don't learn to be nicer then no-one will love you or want to be with you. You'll end up on your own", said the adult.

The words cut through the silence as her heart pounded. She bowed her head so that her chin was almost on her chest and stuck out her bottom lip, which had started to tremble. As the hurt swelled up inside she fumbled with the loose threads around her shorts pocket. The little girl didn't want to be alone. There was nothing for it, she must learn to be nicer.

ONE:

BELLY LAUGHS & BELLBOTTOMS

Laughter. That was the predominant sound of my home life. It created the magnetic pull that meant our little bungalow was always full with friends and boyfriends, even though the nucleus of just the four of us was so strong that we didn't need anyone else. My mum's unwavering energy and great food, although less so her singing (never the right words and only occasionally in tune), my dad's quiet kindness and infectious chuckle, and my sister, Emma's, hilarious quick wit and beauty. My role? I was the impersonator. My parents always said that when they attended school events or parent's evenings (in those days, only parents went whilst children remained anxiously at home) they knew who everyone was before they were introduced based on my enactment of them at home! Oh, and I laughed hard and easily - mum once said that she loved that I laughed however rubbish her jokes were. Our collective humour would best be described as 'dark'; we didn't laugh at others' expense or suffering, but we found the general state of the human condition really funny. Observing the adversity and dysfunction of life was our thing, fuelled by copious amounts of the comedy genius of Victoria Wood; if you didn't know her body of work then you probably couldn't follow a conversation around our dinner table because it was peppered with a unified chorus of her characters' sayings.

Don't go picturing an expansive house with plenty of room for all these visitors. Ours was a little bungalow, with the loft converted into a further bedroom that over the years Em and I went through phases of sharing (not always because we had to, sometimes because we just wanted to), and the only dining space in our kitchen - so cue lots of "emergency chairs" (we also loved the comedy of Peter Kay) and makeshift beds on the floor for sleepovers; I think I spent the majority of my teens sleeping on our lounge floor at weekends. The endless sheet changes and laundry must have driven my mum mad!

I was the scrawny, plain one. Emma, in contrast, had the archetypal blonde hair and blue eyes and blossomed into a beautiful, curvy young woman with a lovely nature to match. Two and a half years my senior, I always admired her and felt so fortunate that she looked out for me - heaven help anyone who crossed me (although that also entitled her, on occasion, to give me the usual sibling hiding!). My mum was right when she told me that Em was the nicest person she knew.

It took me well into my teens to even begin to mature, significantly behind the curve(s) of my friends; I was mortified that I hadn't grown taller or developed through puberty and still looked like a little girl even at 15. In my 16th year, however, things started to change a little and I helped them along by at least trying to look a bit older. Thanks to the combined hairdressing prowess of my mum and Em, I sported the wavy perm and blonde highlights that every self-respecting teenage girl wore in the eighties-finally, something about me was the envy of my friends.

Naturally introverted, in the true sense of the word, this meant that much of my thoughts and processing went on quietly inside my head. Despite the connection and love I felt within my family, I also had a distinct sense of separateness and of not being understood; somehow I didn't quite fit in with their chilled vibe-I owned a feisty streak accompanied with a big heart. They would describe it as making me difficult and stroppy; these labels served only to fuel my frustrations further. It hurt deeply in a way that I found hard to explain and if I did, I feared being ridiculed, because when the 'strops' happened, they laughed. I loved and respected them, so I accepted their opinion of me.

My parents instilled a strong work ethic into Emma and I. Every day Dad set out early, working 7 days a week as an electrician in a local factory; he was practical-minded, brilliant at building and fixing things that go wrong with hard-working hands and a set of tools about which he was very precious. Dad was my hero (although that description made him blush), exactly what every daughter wants her father to be; a quiet, shy man who loved his 3 'girls' and would happily have spent his time only with them.

My beloved childhood teddy bear was named after him; Dad and I had a special bond over that bear.

Mum ran our home like clockwork whilst trying to earn a bit of money herself to support the household coffers; her honed organisational skills were enviable, but meant she rarely sat down and was always up on her 'enormous' feet (they are not big, but she'd grown up thinking they were) - there was always something else to do. It was a behaviour that I learned. Growing up there seemed to be a perpetual diet, even though she was tall and had a great figure and awesome cheekbones, but appetite suppressant cubes were big business back then, so that was the latest fad. My favourite memory of my modern mum was when she rocked bellbottom jeans teamed with a figure-hugging red Coca Cola t-shirt. And boy did she cook and bake - you've never seen a Victoria sponge cake rise so high; delicious aromas constantly filled our house.

Despite not having a lot of money behind them, my parents' loving, happy marriage was the cornerstone of our home; they said that they could not wait until they retired so they got to spend each day in one another's company. Our annual holidays were really fun times, even though we couldn't afford the foreign trips that some of my friends enjoyed, our times spent in the seaside resorts of Cornwall or Wales meant that not once did I feel like I missed out. We'd use the lengthy car journeys as an excuse to play word games or there we'd be, motoring along the winding roads singing made-up lyrics (usually 'rude') to the tune of well-known pop songs, stopping off at services for frequent loo breaks – mum was known for needing a wee only half an hour into the journey. There we'd eat our homemade picnic to save money; whilst mum was a great cook, her sandwich-making was notoriously awful. Emma and I would joke about the sweaty cheese and gag at the smell of thermos coffee. Those annual two-week breaks were all we ever got, so they were a massive deal and we always made the most of them.

During our teens, my sister's best friend joined us on those holidays on several occasions. She practically lived with us, staying at ours sometimes during the week and most weekends, and becoming one of our family. My parents saw her as another daughter, and it was like having a second older sister, she was always really good to me even though it could have been so easy for her and Em to exclude me. When it came to those holidays, my parents gave her the same pocket money that they'd carefully saved up for us; we were treated equally because that was the right thing to do. It worked for us all.

The practice of welcoming people into our little home continued when Emma had her first serious boyfriend; over time he replaced my sister's friend in living with us too and developed the same close relationship with my parents. It brought about a keen awareness of other families and their dynamics; over the years it struck me how understanding my parents were of other people's difficulties, demonstrated by their kind and tolerant attitude and generous behaviour to those that needed refuge. I saw that in technicolour when my sister's boyfriend's dad committed suicide. Em's boyfriend was at my parent's house when he received the call to say that his father was missing. The following day I was the only one home when Em's boyfriend called to say that they'd found him dead. In all fairness to him, despite his grief, he tried to protect me from the news by asking if he could speak to someone else, which said everything about how kind he was to me. Instead, I took the message, went to find my mum who was helping out at the local hotel and then walked into town to tell Emma, who was at work. We all matured a bit that day.

It was some time before, amid the flashing lights and a sticky dance floor of a local disco, that I had met my first serious boyfriend; it was a party night that Em and her best friend used to frequent a few years prior. They'd been allowed to go to the one that happened on a weekday evening (and used to go home from school a few hours early the afternoon before to get some sleep. Being the studious one I was never permitted that privilege!). At the disco, I'd recognised Pete vaguely and it turned out he had been in my sister's form group back when she was at school. He was shy and quiet, but good looking and a couple of years older (what any teen girl wanted); he'd left school and was an engineering apprentice, the blend of his practicality and reserved nature reminded me of my dad.

Friends referred to us as 'Kylie and Jason' (I had the tiny frame and big hair for god's sake!) from the hugely popular Aussie soap, Neighbours. We would regularly be seen zipping around in his dad's bright blue van once

Pete passed his test, or we'd get ourselves admitted into the local nightclub (who were not overly stringent as we were both under age), along with some of our friends. I was not much of a drinker; my parents had allowed us to have a small amount of alcohol with our Sunday lunch for many years, so it didn't hold much mystery or adventure to me. Pete would sometimes get drunk and, emboldened, there occasionally was a stand-off with another male if he thought they were paying me attention. He once slept outside in the van because he didn't want to risk being sick in my parents' house! Usually, however, we'd creep back through the front door in the early hours trying hard not to make any noise, which wasn't easy in the confined space of our bungalow. The following morning mum would be eagerly waiting to hear all about the previous night's adventures, willing us to get up from our lie-ins and then interrogating us for details of who had done what, whilst simultaneously tending to one of her amazing Sunday roasts.

Unsurprisingly Pete also ended up living at our house a lot of the time, crammed into our bungalow, with Em's boyfriend and his various mates. Mum loved the extra company, whereas Dad tended more to tolerate it for the sake of his girls; what was lovely was that our boyfriends became like the sons they never had.

In those early stages, we all used to hang out in a way that was comfortable and fun.

My periods arrived somewhat later than all of my friends, but they certainly made up for their absence; they were dreadful from the word go, leaving me washed out, and on several occasions causing me to cry with pain at night. Unlike some of the girls at school, I was in no hurry to lose my virginity, desiring it to be a special occasion. Despite meeting Pete when I was just 14, I was nearing 18 when I felt like I was ready to have sex. We'd been away for the odd night here and there before, but this time we went for several days to the North England coast - whisked away by this stage in Pete's own car. We were staying in a classic, somewhat rundown B&B with its well-trodden hall carpet and dining room full of residents old enough to be our grandparents; it made us both cringe and giggle simultaneously. We strolled along the long promenade in the bracing wind, tasting the salt from the sea on our lips in sharp contrast to the sugary candy floss. We wandered in and out of the amusement arcades, losing money on games and slot machines, but laughing beneath the neon lights and over the pounding music.

That night, we got dressed up and went to one of the large nightclubs in the town - it was a huge place with an amazing light display and a crowd that seemed to move as one to the music as I looked at them from one of the many balconies. I loved to dance, but Pete was less keen, although he would indulge me a little to keep me happy. I longed to be in amongst that throng feeling the freedom that came with dancing - it was one of the things I wished I'd been able to learn as a child, but it was never a desire I'd felt able to articulate at home. I wasn't sure they'd understand. Back in our room Pete and I got ready for bed and, I have to admit, I felt like it was now or never with regards to having sex with him. That perhaps sounds less emotional than I was in reality, but I'd just rather do it with him, who I liked, than be subjected to one of the drunken, regrettable encounters with a stranger that haunted some of my friends at school. I did feel a nervous excitement, but as we'd known each other for over 3 years our relationship had inevitably progressed physically over that time so this felt like the natural next step rather than a huge leap of faith. I was aware that I was giving myself to him, though, and that it was not something I would get to repeat with anyone else again with quite the same significance. It was what we both wanted and I believed I was ready. It felt right. It wasn't some great revelation, nor was it the disappointment that I'd feared. If anyone had asked me, I'd have said it was 'nice'. The unexpected mess of the aftermath was the only shocker - none of my friends had talked about that!

The next morning, I woke up and understandably felt a little different; that I'd crossed a boundary into being more grown-up. Pete was quiet, which wasn't unusual for him, so after breakfast, we checked out and decided to spend the rest of the day in the town as there was no rush to get home. I was happy.

As the day progressed and we wandered souvenir and rock shops, however, I began to realise that I was doing the talking for both of us. Pete had barely said a word to me. This wasn't 'usual' quiet; it was moody quiet. The thoughts I'd been ruminating upon about a shared experience that had brought us closer together, began to evaporate. My mind started to race and I quickly concluded that the night before must have been really bad for him. I didn't dare ask; I didn't want to know that answer. My stomach was churning as I sneaked a look at his expressionless face; he was giving nothing away. The deafening silence filled the car on the long drive home in the darkness; in the end, I fell asleep with the exhaustion of maintaining my composure in the face of my hurtling mind. Why was he being like this? It had to be my fault. I'd displeased him. We arrived home in the early hours of the next morning; I was massively relieved to escape the tension of the car and it was tacitly understood to be too late for any kind of conversation. We curled up uncomfortably in my single bed.

∽

TWO:

THE GHOST OF CHRISTMAS FUTURE

Having embarked on our physical relationship I felt like I had given myself to Pete because I loved him. I so admired my parents' marriage and, due to his reserved nature, I thought he was like my Dad. Unlike my Dad, though, sometimes the quiet times were masking an underlying moodiness; it was the same brooding aura that had accompanied us on the journey back in his car, and about which I had been too afraid to enquire in case the response I got confirmed my fears: that I was rubbish in bed and the sex had been a disappointment. I often wondered if my topsy-turvy hormones brought this out in him, so I tried hard to make it up to him and be a good girlfriend in all other respects; he certainly didn't seem averse to keep giving the sex a try. As such he was often on my mind and my world was dominated by our relationship. It was the following Summer that we went on holiday for a week to the south coast with my parents. Emma was working and wanted to save her holidays to use with her boyfriend, so she stayed behind to house-sit and feed our cats.

Mum and Dad settled into the double room of our holiday apartment, which had great views of the coastline, whilst Pete and I made our home in the twin room for the next seven days. It was exciting to go away together, and we were currently blessed with a stretch of glorious weather so I had in mind time on the beach (in the shade for me), lovely cliff-top walks and meals out. Good times ahead.

It was the first morning after our arrival when I woke up and was momentarily disorientated by my surroundings, but as I remembered where I was I broke into a big smile and immediately checked the weather outside through a chink in the curtains; I was greeted by uninterrupted blue sky. Pete was still asleep, so I jumped into the shower (because, as I was often reminded through the door of our sole bathroom at home, I took ages to get ready). I went back to our bedroom with two cups of tea that Dad had made us, to find Pete awake and sitting on the top of his bed; the sheets crumpled underneath him. After a brief exchange where he seemed a bit grumpy, I got dressed, made my bed and left him to it; I didn't know what was behind the current mood and I decided not to prod for a reason.

I joined my parents for breakfast, determined to have a good day and relax into the break together. When he emerged from the bedroom Pete still seemed a little distant, but I was getting used to that at times and I appreciated that going away with your 'in-laws' might take a bit of adjusting to. Often I couldn't quite put my finger on a description of his behaviour - it was inexplicable to me: moody, difficult…but these were words that my family used about me weren't they? So I thought it must have been a response to how I was with him and tried my best instead to appease him, although I had to admit that occasionally it ignited my more fiery side, which always incurred the wrath of my parents. Whilst his sulking did make me tense up sporadically throughout the day, mostly because I was a bit embarrassed in front of mum and dad, we did have a good day, finishing up having an excellent fish supper out at a restaurant in the harbour.

Retiring to the apartment after a brief walk, I let Pete use the bathroom before me because I required greater preparations to get ready for bed (I was raised to religiously cleanse, tone and moisturise my skin at night), meaning more moans about how long I took! I sat idly chatting to mum and dad discussing the agenda for the next day before wandering through to the bedroom; I was surprised to find Pete snuggled down in my neatly made bed. To begin with, I laughed, "What are you doing? That's my bed!" He pointed to the messy heap of sheets and the blanket half hanging onto the floor and said that his bed wasn't made properly so he couldn't sleep in it. The partial smirk on his face and cold tone of his voice puzzled me, but I could tell that he wasn't joking. My heart began to pound as I experienced that familiar uncomfortable feeling in my gut; this wasn't the first time I had been treated as though I had done something wrong without knowing what it was.

Sometimes he was genuinely just messing about, but sometimes he was just plain hurtful like he was on that horrible road trip. There was never an explanation. I felt a flare of anger for a moment, but I quickly pushed that down, not wanting to get into an argument with my parents next door and conscious that my spiritedness got me into trouble with them. I felt a tinge of guilt that perhaps this was me over-reacting as usual and that I needed to quickly squash how I felt. I swallowed hard and got a grip on myself; forcing a smile I reluctantly made his bed before climbing into it and switching off the light. "Goodnight", he said. I could hear the victory smile on his face. I lay in the dark wondering what it was that I did that made him behave that way and resolving to stop doing it immediately.

The next morning, he was different again, climbing into the bed next to me, greeting me with a good morning cuddle and a mischievous grin. I was relieved not to be faced with the previous evening's behaviour, albeit a bit confused. Had I upset him yesterday to make him act like that? Was it my fault? I couldn't resolve it, so I decided to brush all doubtful thoughts aside and get on with the day.

It turned out not to be an isolated incident. Not necessarily the bed-making thing, but an undercurrent of unkindness across several scenarios: money, how I looked, what we did and, not that I would have told my parents, with overspill into the bedroom. A couple of times sex seemed a little...cruel. He bit me, but in a way that felt like it came from a place of harm rather than passion. In my inexperience I struggled to know if that was 'normal' and who could I possibly ask?! Yet in-between times, he was his funny self - getting on with my parents (he went to the beach alone with them when I had to stay in the apartment due to heat rash) and all seemed fine. I probably was just over-sensitive and being awkward, so I put it down to me needing to try harder to chill-out and get a sense of humour.

It was shortly after the end of the holiday, however, when mum apologised. Initially, I was confused - sorry for what? She explained that she and dad had picked up on Pete's moods and for the first time they had seen that he could be "difficult". In fact, she admitted that they had always thought spats between him and I were my fault, but the time spent together on holiday had shown them a different side to him; they said it was no wonder that I reacted in the way that I did. I was stunned, but also relieved; perhaps it wasn't just me that irritated him and caused the bad behaviour. It inevitably made me look at him through a slightly different lens, but as ever the world continued to turn, he could often be lovely and he was always welcome at our house, spending lots of time with Emma and her boyfriend in particular, even when I was working at my part-time job. Pete often came to pick me up or was there when I got home. The demands of A-levels and a local musical production I was involved with, which I loved, but was taking up quite a bit of my free time, meant at times our relationship became more fractious. He didn't understand the requirements of my studies and my personal insecurities meant that the time we were spending apart was playing on my mind. When we were together I felt a mixture of the need to placate him, but also slight suffocation; everything in my free time seemed to revolve around the two of us and my sister's relationship. Don't get me wrong, we did some lovely things together, but occasionally what I wanted was some time to myself.

I was warier of his behaviour since my mum's comments following the trip away and I had started to be concerned that his eye might have been wandering due to the time we weren't getting to spend together. It hurt. At the same time, I became close to a guy in my sixth form; he was, funny, smart and ambitious, and was arguably more of a match for my desire to go to university. I relished the positive attention he gave me and it was a badly kept secret amongst our peers that he liked me. Inevitably when Pete and I went out we would bump into some of my school friends, and it was fair to say there was some testosterone-fuelled tension between these two.

The idea of going to university had been sparked by my English teacher when I was 12 years old; no-one in my family had ever had the opportunity to study at this level before. Nothing was going to deter me from achieving that goal, but it certainly felt as though Pete tried his damnedest to derail me; he was unsupportive of my studying generally and, as my exams got closer, it seemed as though he thought nothing of upsetting me to watch me unravel before him. The pressure escalated and it took its toll on my health as I became very run down both physically and emotionally. In my head, I knew that it was wrong to be around him anymore as he repeatedly crushed my feelings, but in my heart, I felt this pull to please him, to keep him happy. They were emotions that I couldn't rationalise, but I needed to ensure he didn't leave me, no matter what. I couldn't 'fail' at this relationship.

We continued in this push-pull scenario for quite some time. Me, drawn by the intellect of someone else, but unable to extract myself from the emotional pull to Pete and the significance of him being my first serious relationship. One night at his parent's house we'd been squabbling again, but he wanted to have sex. I felt 'disconnected' from him and let my reluctance be known; it felt wrong to be intimate when I was this unhappy. He was persistent, despite my distress, and with his parents downstairs I didn't want to make a fuss, so we had sex anyway; I failed to contain my feelings and I cried throughout, but he was undeterred. It felt completely invasive, but also the only way to keep him happy.

Not long after, he ended our relationship. My emotional unravelling gathered speed; I was heartbroken that I couldn't make it work, that I couldn't be enough for him to love me. In the weeks that followed, I went through all the angst about whether he was seeing someone else and what was it that wasn't good enough for him. I cried constantly, wishing we could get back to being as happy as I romanticised that we once had been. I wondered where I had gone wrong and was bereft without him; he'd been such a huge part of my life for nearly 4 years.

My feelings for Pete dragged on and I found it challenging to completely let go; I wasn't eating or sleeping properly as the knot in my stomach seemed to continue unabated. He had been my first love and, regardless of his nasty behaviour, I was struggling to believe that it could be over. My parents had a happy marriage. My sister remained with her first serious boyfriend. I needed to tell him the depth of how I felt, so I wrote him a card to him and decided to hand-deliver it; I'd hoped to catch a glimpse of him, but he was out, which only served to fuel my anguish that he had found someone to replace me. His mum said she would pass the card on to him, but by the time I got home she'd called my parents to tell them I'd been there; I never had liked that woman! Mum and Dad were not at all impressed and told me to stop crying, give it up and move on. They strengthened their determined attitude and forbade me to see him; it felt cruel and I didn't think they understood how desperate I was. Here I was single, alone and a failure - how could they understand how that felt?

The very last time I spoke to him was when he rang on A-Level results day to see how I'd done. I was frustrated hearing his voice, recalling how he hadn't cared this much when I was trying to revise. Why was he bothering with me now? I told him straight, fuelled by my anger at his audacity to show any interest now. I'd not got the grades I should have, which meant I'd missed out on my preferred university places: "Are you happy now you got what you wanted?!". I couldn't help feeling that how he'd treated me in the run-up to my exams was borne out of jealousy of my world at school and desire to go away to study. There was not much he could say in response.

჻

'So the adult was right', thought the little girl as she picked at the scab on her knee. She would get left. Be alone again. She can't have been nice enough. Good enough. Otherwise, he would have stayed and she wouldn't feel this sad. Lonely. How could she have been so silly? But then she had been told before that she was "too sensitive". Maybe other grown-ups didn't feel like this.

She needed to get better at hiding her feelings. She needed to do better.

Try harder.

That was it. Next time she wouldn't get it wrong.

჻

Mum and I clashed on the back of my exam results; she thought I should go out and get a job, but I was determined to go back and resit English as I'd set my heart on studying that at the next level. I was single-minded over this in a way I should have been over the prior year; I dug my heels in. My confidence had taken quite a hit, not just because of Pete, but I'd found some of the bitchiness of teenage girls in the sixth form rather wearing as they jostled in a social hierarchy that I didn't much care for. However, I got a part-time job in a local café to earn some money whilst I went back a year and to give myself time to get emotionally back on my feet.

Rejoining the sixth form for some classes with what had previously been the year below me was hard, but I was so fortunate that the gentleman that once said that I should study English was to be one of two teachers for my resit. I knew I had done the right thing when he burst into the room with the results of our first essay and declared to the room that I had got an 'A'; there was no mistaking he was doing that for my confidence and so that the rest of the room didn't think I was a dunce.

As happened every year, my sixth form hosted a black-tie Christmas party; it was a highlight for every student and time was spent eagerly planning ballgowns and cocktail dresses. It was on this evening that Alistair came into my world; I remembered him because he'd attended the same school four years ahead of me. I recalled that he used to turn up at school in his cool car; he was now studying at a major city university. It felt like serendipity that I should be there due to my resits and he was only there on behalf of friends that ran the venue to help ensure that things went off without incident. A group of teenagers drinking and having a party, I mean, what could possibly go wrong?! He charmed me from the outset with his charismatic chat and confident manner that came with his additional years of maturity; as we kissed I felt a surge of endorphins that I'd not experienced in a while. We spoke on the telephone after that evening (the world before mobile phones, eh?) and I got to know him a little more. The attraction was obvious and mutual when we 'happened' to bump into each other a couple of times in our local town whilst he was home for Christmas. In the days before New Year's Eve, I was aware that we'd not been in touch for a few days, so I decided to be ballsy and call round to his family's home. He'd told me where he lived. By then I was driving and had my own car.

As his mother fetched him downstairs to speak to me, it turned out not to have been one of my best moves - his past girlfriend, who was still a good family friend, was already there, and his more recently 'ex' girlfriend was also inside, as it turned out, trying to engineer a reconciliation. My timing could not have been worse. He explained all as we stood outside in the cold with him feeling mortified that he'd not told me this in our earlier conversations, and me feeling like an idiot for innocently showing up. His family later referred to this as the 'A Christmas Carol' incident, with the [girlfriend] ghosts of past, present and future all present at once - genius! I got in my car and swiftly left, focussing instead on getting ready for the night out ahead of me with one of my best friends.

In a small town there were limited places to go, and even fewer in which to be 'seen', so it was probably inevitable that I spotted him across the room despite how crowded the pub was. He'd obviously seen me too, and soon made his way over; my friend looked at me and raised an eyebrow as if to say, "are you ok with this?". I felt incredibly calm actually, whatever had gone on had been his issue, not mine. He was profusely apologetic and explained that his relationship with her had been over, but as I knew could happen, sometimes the ending is not always an entirely clean edge. She'd tried to reconcile things, but my visit itself had raised questions and he confessed he had met someone else (I didn't know that was where we were, but hey!). He'd seen her out earlier in the evening and explained his slightly less-than-usually manicured appearance on the fact that she'd thrown a pint over him. Ouch. I couldn't help but laugh and it broke any tension between us; he stayed chatting the rest of the night, walking home with us after we'd seen in the New Year.

That evening was the start of our budding romance and we soon fell into a relationship. He knew how to treat a girl - it was a whirlwind of adventures, fast cars, gifts and lovely gestures all the time. He'd write me love letters, draw me pictures and constantly plan surprises; I felt like the luckiest girl alive - totally adored. My broken heart was mended.

❧

THREE:

GRAND HOTELS & WARNING BELLS

His attention continued unabated. If anything it became more intense when he told me he was in love with me. At one point Melissa, my best friend from school and constant confidante said, "I wonder what he'll do next to impress you". He always had something carefully planned to sweep me off my feet.

I didn't have long to wait; on the night before I left for university he asked me to marry him. Whilst I was a bit unsure what my parents would say, I was also nervous about the life-changing experience I was about to embark on. Knowing that he wanted to remain with me and wanted that forever was very reassuring; the start of university was often a testing time for any teenage relationship. I was hugely flattered; it was an excited "yes" from me.

I settled into university life (studying English of course!) with the usual combination of enthusiasm and home-sickness that most new students experience. I juggled my coursework, meeting and socialising with new friends, and fending for myself for the first time. I mostly spent my weekends with Alistair, however, using the small flat he shared as our base as he took me to quirky restaurants and for lunch in fancy hotels where I would look incongruous in my student 'uniform' of red duffle coat and Doc Martens. I had loved the architecture and vibe of London since my childhood when my grandfather used to take us sightseeing around all the usual tourist haunts. Within weeks of going away, Alistair made things official by asking my parents if he could marry me. They weren't entirely happy (I later discovered) due to my age, but they entertained the idea and embraced it; they liked him. He was well mannered, from a good family and respectful to them.

It was hard to pinpoint exactly when the warning bells started to sound. I guess that's the thing though, they don't start as bells do they? Small 'incidents' that can be explained or rationalised, or, as was very much the case with me, things that I took accountability and blame for. They started to chime a little louder when I got a call from mum demanding to know why I was going to quit university once I was married; she was particularly displeased that she and dad had heard about it from Alistair's mum, who was a lovely lady and not predisposed to lies or exaggeration. Even she had expressed surprise at the news considering how I'd set my sights on a degree and seemed to be enjoying the course. I was as astounded as mum, considering Alistair and I had discussed nothing of the sort. Why on earth would he have given her that impression? How did he conceive that idea in the first place? After a few minutes of calming mum down, she accepted what I was saying about it being a big misunderstanding somewhere; I was sure I just needed to talk to him.

When I did, he played it down and explained it away: he and his mum had just spoken about possible future scenarios, especially as he had suggested perhaps getting married during one of the holidays (he'd talked about how it would be good to have my graduation certificate in my married name). There was nothing for me to worry about he assured me, he had it all in hand. Instead, I had a strong talk with myself, saying that I needed to trust in my fiancé and show myself as well-chosen wife material, after all, he was perfect and I didn't want to lose him. I knew how it felt to fail at a relationship and I didn't want a repeat of that heartache.

I understood that he may feel a bit threatened by me living away and all the new people I was meeting; back home he'd known all my friends. I resolved that I need to ensure that he was happy and secure; it pleased me to please him, so I needed to do more of that. I even went along with some of his more controlling tendencies - he liked to take the lead, decide what we would do and where we'd go. Whilst it made me rather uncomfortable, I even stayed quiet when he chose what I'd wear, everything from my underwear outwards, especially when we were going out somewhere; I'd get out of the shower and find my clothes laid out on the bed for me. I didn't object to him going through my things, but it was how something made me feel when I wore it that mattered to me; the same thing could feel very different on consecutive days. Having my clothes chosen for me was akin to telling me how I should feel. Yet I pushed aside my feelings and said nothing; I was probably just being silly and selfish - after all, he did it because he loved me and I think he thought it was sexy.

In time though, it didn't stop with my clothes as he started to try to coerce me into performing sexual acts I didn't want to. He thought it was adventurous, whereas I just found his suggestions a little odd, but I accepted that he was more experienced than I was and tried, for the most part, to go along with them. When he accidentally cut me internally, probably just with his nail the A&E nurse said, he did ease off for a while. I, however, felt ashamed for causing a fuss and knew I had to try to be more resilient to satisfy his needs.

In other respects I was enjoying the sense of freedom that living away gave me; exploring my independence, learning new things and meeting different people. I'd struck up numerous friendships, and one in particular with a guy on my course, Scott. He was kind, introverted and intellectual, quite intense and thoughtful. Being around him was the opposite of having all the decisions made by Alistair. He was interested in my opinion and welcomed some debate; it was a compliment that someone was stimulated by my mind rather than my body. Over the months of the first year of my course, we spent more time studying together, both on campus and off as part of our assignments. It was almost inevitable that we grew closer; his relationship naivety was a welcome antidote to what felt like the runaway train in other parts of my life.

Alistair had purchased an engagement ring for me, which he insisted I wore at all times, and the more claustrophobic that became, the more Scott became a haven away from the invisible prison I felt I was caught up in. I was totally confused. I loved Alistair, right? He was amazing and our future was all mapped out. That should be reassuring. How could I be attracted to anyone else? Perhaps this was just a deep friendship and I was struggling to distinguish the two types of emotion. It seemed an impossible situation on many levels so I took Scott home one weekend to meet my family because I had talked about him so often. I think I needed their opinion. They saw the depth of our feelings for each other immediately and were uncomfortable and not at all pleased with me. I received such a telling off from them for bringing him to the house; they felt that Alistair was such a nice guy and couldn't comprehend why I would I treat him this way. To be honest, I didn't know either, I was so baffled by it all. So I quashed my emotions and kept quiet. I didn't want another bollocking or questions to which I felt unable to articulate answers; I didn't think I could get mum and dad to understand. I'd got myself into a pickle that only I had to get myself out of.

I was delighted, therefore, when out of the blue Melissa got in touch and invited herself to stay with me one upcoming weekend. I not only missed her like crazy since we'd left the sixth form and had gone our separate ways to different universities, but I was desperate to see her and talk about the increasingly stressful Alistair/Scott triangle - if that indeed was what it was. Melissa was the one person I felt I could talk to: she never judged me, instead offered sound advice because she had her head screwed on; she always seemed to understand where I was coming from. Our friendship history meant that I could say much more than I was currently able to with my 'new' friends at university. Right now she was exactly what I needed. She told me what time she'd be arriving on Friday evening and I excitedly made plans in my head about what we could do for two whole days together – just like the good old days! The last time she'd been to stay had been lovely. There would be lots of gossip to catch up on, comparisons about our new lives away from home and you could guarantee lots of laughs; she too had a wicked sense of humour.

On that Friday I longed for the day's lectures to be over and rushed home to get myself ready for Melissa's arrival. Food and drinks at home that evening (well, maybe a quick trip to the lovely pub across the road), before heading out to the student bars and clubs the following night - quite a contrast from the quiet neck of the woods we came from. It was going to be great and I could already feel the relief of getting some much-needed stuff off my chest! The doorbell rang, she was bang on time, and I almost squealed in delight at the anticipation of seeing my best friend standing on my doorstep. I raced down the two flights of stairs with a huge grin on my face ready to give her the biggest of hugs; whilst I had some great new friends, I had really missed her. I flung the door open wide and froze. OMG. I felt the grin slide off of my face and be replaced by a forced smile, my throat felt tight as I swallowed and I steadied myself against the doorframe. In the dusky light cast out of the doorway stood Alistair. Fuck. Fuck! FUCK! I glanced over his shoulder, desperately hoping Melissa was behind him – surely we'd at least get a bit of girly time together so that I could seek her counsel? As I quickly scoured the street outside it sunk in that she was not there. What the hell was going on?

The walk upstairs back to my room felt like the longest 30 seconds in history. There was no Melissa. There was Alistair. He proceeded to tell me how he'd arranged this 'surprise' with the help of my best friend as the cover story. Despite the lump in my throat, I managed to make the right noises about how clever he'd been, and how lovely it was to receive such a wonderful gift of time together. I could barely breathe as I waited for my moment to escape to the bathroom. As I perched on the side on the bath a sob escaped; I grabbed the hand towel and covered my face to prevent him from hearing me. I was unnervingly devastated. He was the last person in the world I wanted to see right now. I was desperate to see Melissa and wished I'd told her just how much. I tried to pull myself together and flushed the toilet to buy myself another minute to check my teary face in the mirror. I picked the clogged mascara out of my lashes and patted my cheeks with cold water to ease the blotchiness. With a deep breath, I went back to my bedroom where he was sitting on the bed wearing a satisfied grin.

From what I was able to take in during the following minutes, Alistair announced that his arrival wasn't my only surprise. He was taking me away for the weekend; we were going to the coast to stay at a beautiful hotel on the seafront. Rewind a year, six months even, maybe less, and this invitation would have thrilled me; it struck me how so much could change in such a short space of time. I felt like a caged animal, incapable of engineering any kind of escape. It was compounded by the sudden loss of the freedom I had expected that weekend; a rare opportunity to shed the anxieties I'd been carrying and get some perspective. Instead, I was now in turmoil whilst wearing a mask of calm and happiness. I tried to just go with the flow whilst my mind was on fire. The situation felt unexpectedly out of control and to have taken on a life of its own. I decided that I just needed to get through the weekend with the minimum amount of fuss and regroup after Alistair had left to travel home. Maybe then I could call Melissa and get her advice about what to do next.

The feeling that I couldn't deny though, was that it was now blatantly obvious to me that I did not want to be with Alistair. My disappointment at Melissa not being there was masking the horror that he was. That evening I went through the motions, numbly doing as I was told, as Alistair instructed me on exactly what to pack to go away with; he choose every item that I placed in my overnight bag as if I were some kind of puppet with no will of its own. I despised how passively I was behaving, it was not the real me - what had happened to the ballsy, strong me? The opinionated woman who was her mother's daughter? The one borne of a family where men and women were equal? I felt at a loss as to what other action I could take; my whole being was dialled down with someone else pulling the strings to make me function. The next morning we set off early in his car, with a single thought dominating my mind: he would expect to have sex with me. I didn't want to. I flat out didn't want to. The idea of it was repulsive. I wasn't just a bit turned off. I didn't want him anywhere near me; the thought of it made me shudder. I was at a loss to know what I should do. I tried to run through my options, but other thoughts failed me. I was incoherent. We checked into the hotel as he smiled proudly at what he had managed to pull off here; it was lovely and there was a time when I would have felt so giddy that someone thought I was worthy of such an experience. I gave my best performance in trying to look pleased for him, but I felt so bereft that some of my unhappiness was bound to be leaking out; holding it together was proving to be exhausting. He knew I wasn't right, that was why he was here. He knew we weren't right, that was why he had brought me here. And one glaring fact in this whole awful situation remained: I was engaged to him. All of his actions yelled that in my face in a way that made me want to squeeze my eyes shut. The weighted inconvenience of that fact felt in that moment as though it was holding me to ransom and was ripping away any choices I had. I felt so guilty for having these thoughts; he loved me, and I should be so grateful for that. As he turned the key in our bedroom door, I could hardly breathe. The tears stung behind my eyes at the inevitability of what was coming next. I didn't want it to happen. He knew I didn't want it to happen. I uttered "no", but we both knew that any resistance was pointless. Despite my body being rigid and unwelcoming, it was forced to yield to him.

"Will you just fucking relax!"

He hissed the words aggressively next to my ear as I lay on top of the covers on the end of the bed. Most of my clothes were still on, but my skirt was roughly hoisted up, my breasts exposed; my knickers had been pulled off and were on the carpet somewhere near his feet. He was only a slight guy, but I felt the weight of his frame on top of me, one of his arms planted firmly across my chest bone holding me down. I was shaking with the hideousness of how powerless I felt. I tried to go elsewhere in my mind, to shut down and hide until it was over, but it was futile; I was destined to experience every moment in the technicolour that comes with the heightened consciousness of horror. I heard his fast, heavy breathing and felt it against my turned cheek, shuddering with the effort of clenching my jaw. Waiting. I was dying inside, an agonisingly slow death, with no hope of being saved. Time stood still until he rolled off me and lay panting in a sweaty heap on the other half of the bed. I couldn't move. Frozen to that spot on the bed as if I was nailed down. I was terrified, partly because if I moved it might stir him to come back for more, or that the shift would allow the agonising wail that was building inside me to escape unchecked. I trembled beneath the surface of my skin in shock and revulsion.

Eventually, he moved. My reflexes caused me to flinch. He got up and began to explore the room, revealing with a flourish the bathroom's centrepiece, a huge Jacuzzi bath; he turned on the taps and declared we should climb in and enjoy it. How romantic. I sat next to him in the warmth and bubbles feeling grubby despite them and wanting to wretch each time his skin brushed against mine.

He'd announced that we were booked into the restaurant for dinner. It was a spectacular room, filled by other diners with a bustle that was unable to drown out the cacophony in my head. I was speechless that he expected that I could sit across the table from him and eat after what had happened, but as it sunk in that he thought this was entirely normal, I realised that he thought what we'd done - he'd done - was ok. For me, it was excruciating. Appalling. Fraudulent almost. His arrogance now seemed astounding, but then, he didn't think anything unusual had happened. The voices in my head got louder, screaming at me: what the hell just happened there? Was it my fault? How could I have let that happen? Why didn't I stop it? Fight? Did I just give in? This was not how I understood relationships to be, especially not one between prospective man and wife; my parents' marriage, I was certain, did not operate under this kind of dynamic. As such, I was completely unprepared for the prospect of needing to 'defend' myself.

As the evening dragged on with me pushing a meal around my plate that I couldn't even contemplate consuming, and drinking more wine than was usual on my empty stomach, the venomous thoughts seeped further into my brain. What did happen? I braved a look at him. He was the picture of calm. For him, everything was in order. I was his fiancée, we were away on a weekend together and we'd had sex. So why was my body screaming at me with indignation? Had I got it wrong? Did I just need to quieten it down? But the word that kept ricocheting around my mind to describe that incident was unavoidable. I tried to dismiss it every time it appeared, feeling a potent shame that I was applying such a description to the actions of the man whom I was meant to be marrying. And that was my point: we were engaged, so did the fact that I'd not wanted to have sex with him even count? And I'd told him 'no'...I had said that. I did say it, didn't I?

But those words that he'd used, his vicious tone, his manner; that was undeniable.

For years his words and my subsequent questions silently haunted my soul.

৵

As the little girl sat alone in her bedroom, she thought about what she must have done that was very wrong to make him so angry with her. Make him want to hurt her.

A noise from elsewhere in the house, made her jump; that was happening a lot these days. She wished she could stay in her room, where it was familiar. Safe. Her skinny body wasn't designed to fight.

She was confused. She'd tried hard to be nice, even when being nice hadn't felt very good. Sometimes she'd had to try hard not to cry. She'd swallowed down her tears. Tried not to be sensitive.

She'd done it to make him feel happy. Then he would want to stay. Doing that was being nice. She was doing what the adult said.

∂

FOUR:

CARPET SWEEPING

You've finished with him and you did it by letter?! How could you? He's wonderful to you, he clearly loves you and you'd have had a lovely life with him, but you've thrown it all away!".

The tone was accusatory and filled with disappointment; her voice slightly shaky. Any doubts my parents had felt about Alistair and I getting engaged seemed to have evaporated; mum was furious and once again I'd got it wrong.

I never wanted to see him again after that hideous weekend. I could not have bared to see his face nor speak a word to him; the very thought of being in proximity to him made me shudder. As much as I had tried to fiercely push away the thoughts and images that tried to claw their way into my head, they sometimes won their invasion and I would find myself reliving the horror of that weekend. My self-blame about what I did to allow it, or doubts about whether I did enough to prevent it, meant I also oscillated between not sleeping well as distorted versions of events played out in my dreams and sleeping constantly as a way of hiding from what had happened; either way I woke as exhausted as when I went to bed. So I made my excuses to Alistair to end the relationship; I'd put it all in a letter and sent it to him. The cowards way out, but it the only thing I felt like I had the energy to do. Inside I was recoiling, just getting up each day and functioning whilst I held all of this in was all I could do.

I'd spoken to Melissa, not telling her what he'd done, but just about the fact of his appearance, which of course she'd known about due to her part in his 'surprise'. She was so profuse with her apology - she'd known that I'd wanted to have a chat with her. I told her she had nothing to be sorry for, and I meant it, I knew exactly how persuasive and single-minded he could be; she'd have been manipulated into doing what he wanted.

This backlash hurt though because it was assumed that I was in the wrong; causing problems (again) and filling my parents with disappointment. What I thought, how I felt, was invalid; the searing pain of that was overtaken only by the guilt I felt at those disrespectful thoughts. As people they were so incredibly kind - they would go out of their way for anyone. My mum repeatedly demonstrated how she'd been more than a beautician to her clients; she dealt with compassion with everything they brought to her: illness, bereavement, relationship problems. She had an emotional endurance that went well beyond the endless hours on her feet. There were times when she'd been poorly, but she'd battle on, tell them she was "fine" when they politely inquired how she was (she always said that few were genuinely interested in her answer). If life had afforded her the opportunities she'd have made an amazing social worker.

Yet somehow, for reasons I couldn't understand, they didn't know how to cope with me, my actions and my emotions. I was uncomfortable for them. Different. An anomaly. I wanted desperately not to have to sweep the depth of my emotions under the carpet. I longed to pull up that bloody carpet and shine a light on everything that I felt was lying on the cold floor underneath. What would happen then? It was the consternation behind the answers to that question that kept me quiet, but it fuelled anger that burned inside and isolated me further. Why was it such a challenge to understand me? Why was it so hard to be me?

The tension mounted within me, the huge injustice of these allegations towards me. It was threatening to explode through every vein in my body as I paced around my kitchen with an agitation that was becoming increasingly hard to control. In my head I was begging myself not to show myself as trouble: the 'stroppy teenager' they thought I still was. Don't prove them right. I failed. I couldn't contain it a second longer. I shouted down the phone, "You really want to know what happened? He raped me!". I slammed down the receiver. I stood there staring at it, my breathing short; I was shaking.

I waited for it to ring.

Silence.

It was never spoken of again.

࿇

FIVE:

A KNIFE, A FORK & A SPOON

I continued to shut down, burying any shard of the pain each time it attempted to pierce the protective wall I had created. Depression ensued, my penance for shoving down into my soul what I could not bear to acknowledge. The darkness, the shattering sadness, the nothingness that took over in response to disowning my feelings.

I knew enough to recognise that I needed help, so I was referred by my GP for counselling. After half a dozen sessions where I managed to speak to the male therapist I'd been assigned about what had happened with Alistair, he went off to review my case with a panel of colleagues (this was standard practice apparently). The verdict he returned the following session was staggering - it would've been laughable had the circumstances not been so dire. "I think you're a bit of an airy, arty type," he said, "quite sensitive; you might struggle to handle the world". I mean, really??!! I was a 19-year-old assault case! Like, WTF?! He went on to add that it was worth asking myself whether I might have felt how I did about what happened because perhaps I was confused about my sexuality - had I considered whether I might be a lesbian?

Now, let me just say I consider there to be nothing

wrong with being a lesbian and, believe me, I have actively tried to contemplate it as an alternative path for me over the years (keep reading to discover why!), but despite my best attempts to conjure those feelings, I can place my hand on my heart and say it isn't for me. I accept I didn't know much at 19, but I did know that. I was horrified that my feelings about my ordeal would be considered a reaction to doubts over my sexuality. It was another 25 years before I stepped back through a counsellor's door (and no, that still wasn't because I was in denial about my sexuality!).

In the meantime, I'd been prescribed anti-depressants by my GP, but after two weeks I gave them up. I just stopped, which I know is NOT what you're meant to do, but I just couldn't bear them any longer. The physical side effects were awful for me; I was already struggling to eat (my default response whenever I was upset), but they suppressed my appetite to the point that I was gagging even when I drank water. I am absolutely supportive of anyone who finds medication helpful in their fight against depression, and I know that the medication itself has evolved greatly over the years, but I vowed to myself when I stopped taking those pills that I would never go down that route again.

By this point, I was embroiled in a relationship with Scott. He too suffered from depression and, whilst he knew what it was to live as a very intense person, in all honesty, it probably hindered me more than it helped; we were swimming in the same soup - like two addicts trying to keep each other 'clean'.

I was juggling, not always successfully, my coursework and, at one stage, two part-time jobs as the usual financial pressures of university began to kick in. I'd also been handed a diagnosis of Myalgic Encephalomyelitis (M.E. - also known as 'Chronic Fatigue Syndrome') due to the intensity of the physical responses I was having: lethargy, sleeping for extreme periods (sometimes up to 20 hours a day), perpetual brain fog and the ongoing lack of appetite became my new 'normal' state. I don't think I would have been classed in official terms as anorexic, but I understood that mentality well. If everything around me was out of control then I controlled what I could and that was my food intake; it gave me some of my power back and the hunger provided clarity of thought that I believed was allowing me to keep my head above water. I must have looked terrible.

I found myself trekking backwards and forwards to see doctors and visiting the hospital for a multitude of blood tests. The medics didn't seem to know what was wrong with me so the M.E. label stuck because I didn't fit into any other box. I took the diagnosis because I wanted answers as to why I felt so awful, but I didn't believe it was M.E. anymore then than I do now. What was manifesting itself were physical symptoms of a diabolical emotional state. The nightmares recurred often when I slept: being unable to move whilst I was attacked, my body heavy as lead and the sheer panic of being helpless.

I'd push back out through the iron blanket of sleep to find myself drenched in sweat, panting with exhaustion and my heart pounding with panic.

Yet, somehow, inexplicably, I kept going. This immense pull to keep moving forward, keep trying, to work, to struggle on, to achieve, to not let anyone down, to battle. I'm not sure where the resilience came from; somewhere deep inside failure was not an option and it presented as a determination to prove that I was okay.

I graduated with a 2:1, which was pretty incredible in the circumstances; the last eighteen months had been hellish. My parents seemed pleased. I'd not had the energy or headspace to do the rounds of career fairs, nor was I inclined to apply for a corporate graduate scheme. They seemed to only offer a cookie-cutter approach to development and somehow that just didn't feel right for me. On the other hand, I had no firm idea of what I wanted to do, so when Scott landed a proof-reading job it felt like a potential solution. It was an 'out'. A direction. It was based in the North - a stark contrast to where I had been living. I decided to join him; it was comforting, not being alone for the next phase of life and meant I didn't have to return home to see all the same faces in the pub week-in, week-out that had driven me to want to escape three years prior. A new location offered me a fresh start and an opportunity for Scott and me to forge a new life together. It was another place to escape to.

I found a temping job, which was okay, but nothing to write home about - the fact that it wasn't exactly mentally taxing was probably what I needed whilst I regrouped. Money was very tight, however, and our rented place wasn't pleasant - cold and damp. Conditions that I didn't fare well in. Compounding this, Scott quickly discovered that he hated his new job; life as post-graduates didn't feel particularly rosy. His depression returned and it made him rather disagreeable. I didn't seem to be able to do anything right, no matter how hard I tried (which in itself just irritated him more); this just increased my insecurities and our relationship died a painful death. He moved away shortly after. I dug in and stuck it out. I found myself a new home with lovely landlords, persevered at my job and managed my heartbreak throughout; it was tough going, but in reality, I felt ashamed that my new life had fallen apart so soon. Going home wasn't an option; I had to make a success of myself, come what may, so that I didn't cause my family any more worry.

A year down the line, now feeling a little more settled, my job had been made permanent; this time at one of the company's other locations and with some additional responsibility, which made it a little more interesting. I started to date a guy from work, who I discovered was related to one of the company's directors. That wasn't ideal, but I liked Chris - he was nice looking and friendly, so there didn't seem to be much harm in it. Life was moving forward again and after a while of doing the commute to the new site, I decided to move closer; I'd rather spend my money on rent than petrol. I'd enjoyed the shared house I'd lived in, but living life mostly out of one room was starting to drag, especially as, over time, Chris began to regularly spend the night with me. I wanted my own space, a little corner of the world to retreat to when I wanted time out. That proved impossible to achieve, however, as despite telling Chris's mum about my intentions, she quickly seized the opportunity that this presented and after some skilful engineering he ended up living at my place. I sat there wondering how on earth that came about, but I liked him so, hey, was it really so bad?

It was only a few weeks until I began to comprehend why his mum and stepfather had been so keen for him to vacate their lovely home: disorganised, untidy, selfish and utterly hopeless with money were just some of his qualities. He was also a dreamer, a fantasist to be more precise; whilst he'd talk the talk - big goals and ambitions - none of it came to fruition. I gradually became more unhappy as his issues became my issues: bank cards spat out at cash points due to insufficient funds were swiftly followed by requests to use my card (no, I wasn't THAT daft!). Always living beyond his means and prioritising buying car magazines and microwave meals over anything that he should have been using his money for. His growing inertia each evening, coupled with a junk food habit, soon led to a gathering affliction of 'dad bod'.

There was me supporting him like a surrogate mother, even though I had my own stuff to deal with, like trying to pay off my student loan and grappling with my increasingly volatile menstrual cycle! There was also the issue of his pornography habit, which he indulged in alone or when his mate came over; this was critical to our physical relationship fizzling out, leaving my self-esteem affected as he obviously preferred the online girls to having sex with me. And bluntly, no woman gets turned on by picking up her partner's soiled pants off the bedroom floor! This lack of attentiveness hit an all-time low when he bought me a steering wheel lock for my car on my birthday and then proceeded to leave the receipt for it next to the telephone, which informed me that he'd been and bought it on his way home from work (it was about the only shop in the vicinity, so it had clearly been purchased out of desperation, not affection!). I was growing ever-more resentful.

My family never warmed to him, feeling he was all take, take, take. One of their most vivid memories was of him helping himself to food at my parent's home when we visited. He never contributed anything (always the last to the bar) and didn't think it could be considered cheeky when he went into the pantry to help himself - on one occasion he even scoffed some of the ingredients for mum's recipe for the next day's dessert! Unbelievable! He seemed to never stop eating.

Patience with him wasn't only running low on the domestic front. It became apparent that our employers wanted rid of him, and one way to do that was to get rid of me, so I became collateral damage. I was fired after being accused of sharing information with Chris that he should not have been party to (for the record, the information was widely known amongst his peers), but my lack of employment service meant they could do as they wished and I found myself out of work. I decided not to worry my parents with the news of my failure, but set about finding a new job instead as quickly as possible.

After a bumpy few weeks, I finally had my lucky break, a really lucky break, as I landed a much better job and my first proper Human Resources position at a massive company. It rewarded me with an increased salary and gave me the chance to buy a newer car, which was needed for the much greater daily commute. For a while we moved to a much improved rental home on a new estate in a village near our previous house; we had a lovely garden and countryside views. Somehow I hoped this might help us (well, him) to pull it together to have a better life in decent surroundings and with more money coming in. His mum had donated an old sofa to us in the previous house (some kind of compensation for also donating her son?), but with my new job I was able to replace it along with just about every other piece of furniture and household appliance from a bed to the kettle over several months. Chris, meanwhile, contributed the only two things that mattered to him - the tv and his computer. Don't get me wrong, it would probably have been the microwave if it wasn't already supplied.

My hopes of improvement were very short-lived as I was often subsidising his half of the rent that he'd assured me he'd be able to afford. On top of the costs of the longer commute, I had ended up working harder, but having less money. I was sick of his lazy, self-centred ways, so I decided to move and not take him with me. I soon found a flat much nearer to my work, so I sat him down to tell him about the change. He was surprisingly upbeat, but I soon realised that as Chris didn't live in the real world (and, dare I say, wasn't the brightest bulb in the box) he wasn't processing what was happening under his nose.

Now, I know you might be thinking that perhaps he was just really pleased to be getting rid of me, but it was when my parents came to help me move that it became clear that he hadn't understood what I'd said. He'd hired a van and was willing to drive it with my belongings to my new place (the first time he'd been helpful in a long while!), but it was whilst he was piling boxes inside and talking about our future as well as chirpily telling our neighbours that I was just moving to be nearer to my job, that we realised that he wasn't comprehending that I was leaving him too. Witnessing this, my mum swore blind I hadn't told him and, shockingly, started to feel a bit sorry for him. We'd never seen him work hard before so I think we were all in shock. At one point, as we were struggling to make everything fit in the van whilst the two cars appeared to be bursting at the seams, it was mum who suggested we make two trips. I took her to one side and exclaimed there was no way; we were doing this in one go if it bloody killed me!

"Don't you think you should leave him something? I feel a bit sorry for him."

"Really mum?! No, he's financially bled me dry."

"But he doesn't even have any cutlery."

"Mum, I'm leaving him with absolutely everything that he's contributed."

Her look meant I begrudgingly left him one of each knife, fork and spoon from our six place-settings cutlery set - the popular type back in the day with dark green plastic handles. This annoyingly left me with an odd number of everything, which my mild OCD struggled with (they did eventually get reunited and order was restored). This meant that his tv and computer now had some company. Even the bedsheets and curtains were mine, although I graciously relented by not taking down my curtain poles. As I gathered them up and packed them away, he declared cheerily that he was fine; he went into the garage and produced, from the little that was left in there, his new bed. As he proceeded to blow up a tropical fish-shaped lilo from our only foreign holiday, I had mixed emotions. Part of me was fighting not to collapse into a fit of giggles at the absurdity of the scenario playing out in front of me. The other part was consumed with the absolute irritation he had evoked on that holiday where he'd spent the entire time idly floating around the bloody pool on that brightly coloured plastic mass, frying in the sun and failing to observe that the filthy apartment he'd booked for us was making me miserable. Now here he was putting that lilo on the lounge floor and repeating that he'd be fine. If I'd needed any other symbol of why it was right for me to leave him, that lilo screamed it out in rainbow colours.

Just as I'd intended, we made the journey and shifted the lot in one fell swoop. Unloading it at the other end and carrying it all up to my second floor flat was a hard slog, but the joyous end was in sight: a new life, a better one. Chris then had to drive the hire van back to be returned the next morning, which meant, (shock-horror) that he had to pay for it! We were collectively stunned. He climbed into the driver's seat as mum, dad and I stood on the kerb waving him off. As he turned out the end of the road Mum looked at me with her forced grin still on her face and said, "And I hope I never fucking see you again!".

Mum never swore.

◦

SIX:
LET'S (NOT) TALK ABOUT SEX

My lovely boss at my latest job was conscious of my youth, the fact that I was living far from home, and of my occasional lack of self-confidence, so he enrolled me onto a 12-week development course, held in the evenings. The programme's focus was on developing an individual's general confidence and public speaking skills, with aspects of the modules requiring us to stand up and present 2-minute talks to the group at least twice each session, which was daunting.

On one session, several weeks into the course, the aim was to deliver a presentation about the most difficult thing you had ever coped with. That was it for me – I decided I had to talk about the rape. I searched my brain for the alternatives, but there were none. It was singularly the worst experience of my life. Once I made the decision there was no going back, I needed to say what had happened out loud, even though the thought of doing so made me shudder. At the start of the course we'd been separated into small groups each with a team leader to support us between sessions, so I explained to mine that I had something significant to talk about and that it was the first time I'd ever spoken about it; I was relieved that he arranged for me to speak last that evening.

As I stood in front of the rest of my cohort the usual prompts from the back of the room to keep the speakers to their allotted time slot never came; there was total silence in that room and I have no idea how long I spoke for. My heart felt like it was going to pound its way out of my chest, but I knew it was my one chance to get the words out. I owned that talk with my heart and soul, it was a huge relief to speak my truth and release some of what I'd been holding onto, which was doing its best to pull me apart inside. Hearing those words leave my mouth, it was almost as though it wasn't me saying them; it was surreal, but at the same time it gave me a little acceptance. I was unaccustomed to the feeling and I relished it; it freed me and was better than therapy. The people in that room were so supportive: no judgement and it was a safe space for us all to speak candidly. The stories shared by everyone that night were very inspirational, powerful and humbling.

Each week the group had to vote for the best talks and I was honoured to win that night; for the first time, I felt believed. One of the course attendees, John, came up to me at the end of the evening and congratulated me on how courageous I'd been to speak about my ordeal; he said he understood what it must have taken to stand up and share what I had, and that something similar had happened to his sister. I was so touched that he'd felt able to share that with me; it certainly created a deeper connection between us for the remainder of the course.

At the end of the programme, everyone shared their contact details and John emailed me to ask for them as he'd lost them. Remembering how we'd seemed to click, as I sent them over I found myself gently flirting as I followed it up with a, not so subtle, request for assurance that my details were at the top of his list. There was a spark between us, he felt it too and subsequently asked me out for lunch.

I'd discovered on the course that John was Managing Director of a medical services business – articulate and intelligent, and always smartly dressed in a suit. Subsequently, I'd learned that he was 11 years older than me, which I confess was less than I'd originally thought, but I guess that at 24 most people in their 30s seemed 'mature'! Our lunch date took place at an Italian restaurant he particularly liked because it was located on the riverside and the view was amazing. He wasn't wrong, but when we arrived it wasn't the view that caught John's eye, in the practically empty restaurant it was immediately obvious that sitting at one of the tables was someone he knew. A gentleman was waving furiously and beckoning us over.

Far from just a casual acquaintance, this was an old work colleague with whom John had a long history, both corporately and socially, so when this gentleman insisted that we join him for lunch it was impossible to refuse. This 'tour de force' of a personality was a member of the aristocracy and with it came exceptional confidence; he wasn't picking up any of the signs of John's discomfort or recognising that our friendship was still very much a fledgeling. As they fell quickly into a discussion of their shared contacts and experiences, I instantly felt out of my depth as I struggled to follow the conversation or, at times, make sense of this guy's extremely 'far back' posh accent. I would consider myself fairly well-spoken, and John was even more so, but this gentleman had a timbre to his voice that I could barely understand. I sat there most of the time hoping he wouldn't ask me a question for fear that I wouldn't understand what was being said.

He indicated that he was expecting company and, just moments later, a woman approached the table looking distinctly frosty; judging from her expression, she obviously wasn't particularly pleased with this arrangement. Her presence seemed to increase John's unease, the reason for which became apparent when she informed him that she had spent the previous evening with his estranged wife. Oh, so they were friends. The fact of our date would, naturally, be communicated straight back. It was fortunate (if you'd call it that) that John's wife had left him and not the other way around as at least their separation was her choice, although I was acutely aware that it may not make the fact of him dating much more palatable. John had already explained that with regards to their marital home she was a little like a boomerang and periodically came back to live in the spare room when circumstances suited her.

It was post-lunch that John confessed that he had once snogged this frosty lady at a work Christmas party so no wonder I'd been getting the daggers - bizarrely marking her territory whilst defending that of John's estranged wife. And as for her relationship with the other gentleman at our lunch table...well, the plot thickened...

Keen to salvage the rather disastrous lunch, John took me on to a nearby town; it was a beautiful sunny day, so we wandered for a while enjoying the pretty park before stopping for afternoon tea. Finally getting to talk more easily to him I saw how John had a great sense of humour and a lovely laugh, the kind of chortle that you would find yourself laughing along with. He admitted it was not how he had anticipated our date to be. It certainly had not been the most auspicious of starts to a relationship, but it certainly left us with an interesting story to reminisce about. Not least, as he was to remind me sometime later, my response when he'd apologised as we'd left the restaurant: "It's ok, you can tell a lot about a person by the company they keep". Ouch. He said he knew then that he needed to rescue it and to be fair to him he did. He was a proper gentleman that afternoon; I liked how that felt.

He turned out in the weeks and months that followed to be a wonderful mix of both protection and promotion for me. His work role meant I often became his 'plus one' at dinners and events, which required me to be able to hold my own in the company of those significantly more senior than me in both years and career.

Yet he was always there to look out for me - guiding, encouraging, caring. It grew my confidence in myself and my admiration for him.

Within a short space of time, I thought John was the sun, moon and stars. He treated me well versus his predecessors: kind, thoughtful and respectful. Not long into our dating, we both felt smitten and, despite a friend of his who claimed I was just after his money (for the record, I wasn't), we were engaged within nine months of meeting. His separation became a divorce, which sadly turned nasty when his ex-wife realised that he was finally moving on and her ability to rely on him as a crutch to her life would no longer be there. Ultimately, she would only agree to a divorce if John accepted it on the grounds of his adultery. I was furious; we'd met way beyond their separation and she'd been the one to have had an affair! John was more pragmatic. He just saw it as a means to an end, with that end meaning we could get married. So that was what we focused on. We purchased a lovely house that we were able to make some improvements to, located in a great area, and got married at the start of the new Millennium in a stunning castle setting with our friends and family around us. It was a wonderful, happy day. I felt settled. Safe.

Yet things never seemed to stay the same for long; I'd been enjoying my job, but change was underway in the company I worked for. I'd just gained my professional HR qualifications and saw my future in a leadership role in a generalist setting; I was ready to take the next step in my career. I began to look elsewhere for my next challenge and soon enough, thanks to the great foundation this role had given me, I found my next position. It was a promotion, offering me greater responsibility and something new to get my teeth into at work.

At home our marriage was good, we were a perfect match intellectually, he was affectionate and loving, and my family adored him. Our sex life, however, had taken a bit of a nosedive. His first wife hadn't wanted children and their sex life had fizzled out after the first 18 months John said. She'd been a cold, difficult woman, which was also my experience of her. John told me that she hadn't enjoyed sex, but as my mum pointed out one time, "she liked sex with someone else!". I learnt that he found it impossible to discuss our physical relationship and given the combination of our busy jobs and my horrifically heavy periods, which left me both drained and feeling less than desirable, re-igniting our sex life became awkward. It soon became easier to accept things as they were because, in every other respect, we were really happy together. The hotel where we'd married had invited us back for a complimentary first-anniversary dinner and overnight stay. What should have been a romantic occasion, (and to be fair, John tried to instigate sex) wasn't, as I was not feeling it in the slightest - somehow it felt forced. Staged. He got a little cross with me, which was out-of-character given his usual placid self.

I hoped that a holiday to Italy with my parents would boost my energy levels and put the spring back into our marriage, but I spent a lot of the trip feeling worn out and in a dark place. Mum asked me what was wrong, but I couldn't seem to snap out of it, it reminded me of feeling particularly hormonal as a teenager: moody and upset without logical explanation. Small things were a cause of irritation. John's biggest challenge was his job, and on that holiday, in particular, he was hugely stressed; it did place a further negative dimension on our time together that was hard to escape - it was clear at times that it weighed heavily on him.

He left that role eventually to join a firm of accountants as a partner, but to be honest that didn't make him happy either. It began to get quite wearing as he was never satisfied and content in his work, which dragged us both down at times. My role was extremely demanding, so I eventually ran out of positivity, encouraging words and ideas of how to make things better for John.

At one point there was a potential gear-change when John was going to accept a job that would have warranted a move to Singapore; it would have meant a tough call for me as my career was starting to flourish and the possibility to work out there as an ex-pat was very limited. It didn't come to fruition in the end through no fault of John's, but it left us restless and we decided to move house - I think we'd emotionally left the one we were in whilst he was searching for property abroad for us.

We found our absolute dream house, especially in John's eyes. A stunning converted barn in a hilltop hamlet, it boasted incredible views of the countryside and development potential in the form of outbuildings that required conversion. It was a larger project than the one we'd undertaken at our last home, but our vision for what it could become brought us together in an exciting shared goal. It was a project outside of our working lives and this home was our little patch of escapism. A longer commute for both of us seemed like a decent price to pay for our slice of utopia.

Yet after we moved, and as his job ramped up its intensity, John started to show signs of feeling financially pressured by taking the lion's share of the responsibility for our mortgage. I was determined to push on with my career so that I could help out more.

౨

SEVEN:

LITTLE PRICKS & BLACK BALLS

After a couple of very intense years in my previous role, I moved jobs again. This one was back in the south of the UK. I couldn't turn down this role; it would be fantastic for my career. It was an international assignment and took me out of manufacturing, which was a conscious choice as my last place meant I'd had my fill of that for a while! It was a fabulous position to be in at barely 30; I'd worked hard for this and there was room for progression in the wider business. Behind the obvious great career choice, I was also conscious of the pressure John had felt financially for some time as the major earner. He was still unhappy at work, which continued to be a worry. It meant that we'd been more cautious than we originally planned in making the improvements we'd imagined for our home.

Initially, I naively thought that if I earned more we'd be able to keep our beautiful home that he loved, so I rented a flat near my new company and lived between the two properties. I travelled into Europe every week for work; it was then usual for me to travel north for the weekend. On Sunday evenings it was customary for me to drive back south ready for the working week to begin. The reality was that my two homes were a long way apart. In fairness to John, he was hugely supportive of my career, but we both had to accept that there was nothing for it other than to brace ourselves for another house move; we were turning house moving into an art form. I was heartbroken about leaving our home, but as John continued to speak of the pressures he felt under at work we knew that we needed to make some changes.

One weekend, in particular, he'd said that he couldn't keep doing his job as it was; I was very concerned because he'd seemed in an unusually bad way. It wasn't like him to be quite so explicit about such things as he often would try to shield me from the worst of it and soldier on. The Monday morning following that discussion I reached the office just before 8.30am. As was typical, I arrived with an overnight bag in my car because I was flying out to Sweden later that day. I was just walking into my office when my mobile phone rang; it was John's office number (he'd always been an early bird), so I quickly dumped my stuff down and answered the call.

I was slightly taken aback when it wasn't John's voice on the other end, but instead that of one of the other partners from his accountancy firm. I immediately sensed the urgency at the other end of the phone line; the serious tone and measured speech. They'd received a call from our local hospital as John's vehicle was registered with them as it was a company car; he'd been in an accident. As they were not next of kin, not much information had been given to his office; they needed me to call the hospital myself. As I thanked them for calling, my heart pounded and my stomach lurched as a hollow whooshing sound filled my ears. My hands had started to tremble as I called the hospital switchboard; the world had suddenly gone into slow motion.

"How soon can you get here?"

The nurse was calm, kind, but gravely serious; they were telling me they thought he was going to die.

I was three hours away.

I went into autopilot. I went calmly to speak to my assistant and then to a fellow manager to explain the call I'd received. I couldn't believe the words I was speaking out loud. With my colleague's urging, I grabbed my bag as I then left the office as if I were running for my life. Except it was John's life.

The nurse's words haunted me throughout my journey, which stretched before me like a nightmare of time; that familiar route, usually surrounded in happiness that I was heading 'home', was now an instrument of torture.

I put my foot down on the accelerator. What I wanted was for the police to stop me as I somehow imagined they would clear me a path through the traffic when they heard the reason for my speed. That didn't happen. I don't recall how I made the journey, but the three hours turned into two and a half. I switched between having the radio blaring out mindless tunes as I couldn't bear the silence in the car, and not being able to tolerate the radio either; everything else in the world suddenly seemed so meaningless and banal. The same colleague of John's who had called me with the initial news rang me en route to ask what they could do to help. I had one fear and had to voice it: I couldn't bear the thought that he would die surrounded by strangers. I asked them to send someone he knew and make sure they saw him. I had no idea if the worst happened that he would ever know they'd been there, but I couldn't take the chance. They told me to consider it done. Then I did what most of us do: I became a 'conditional believer'. Into the road noise inside the car, I said aloud, "God, please let me get there. If he's going to die, please let me get there in time so he knows I was with him".

I called my parents. Selfish really. They were too far away and there was nothing they could do but sit and worry - about John and about me driving in that state. A problem shared is a problem halved, but sometimes it is just involving others in your shit so that you're not the only one suffering. After I called them I felt that guilt. What had telling them even achieved other than creating more worry? And yet they would want to know.

As I reached the hospital I could barely contain my frustration at the 'pay and display' parking system; I had hardly any coins on me, but, hey, give me a ticket and I'd argue it later. I dashed into the reception and made myself known at the desk. I needed to know whether he was alive or not. I was desperate to know yet terrified of hearing the answer. I caught sight of one of the other partners from John's work. Somewhere inside I momentarily smiled - they'd sent the one person he complained about the most! I know that must seem like an awful thing to say, not least because the gentleman in question was incredibly kind that day, but I knew that John would have found that funny.

I was relieved to be told that he was alive. He was badly injured, but had regained consciousness and was having a scan. I just needed to see that for myself. Luckily I didn't have long to wait. It was a sight no-one can prepare you for. He was wearing a hospital gown and temporary dressings; he was otherwise covered in dried blood as the priority for the hospital staff had just been reaching his wounds and stemming the flow. He could barely see me through the only eye that was functioning, but he knew I was there and reached out his hand. The first of my prayers had been answered at least. He'd been exceptionally lucky. Despite having multiple injuries, his consciousness was a good sign.

My next priority was to speak to my parents to tell them I'd arrived and that for now at least we were both safe. I went outside, inhaled some deep breaths of cold fresh air and stood in the entrance to call and let them know he was alive. Hearing their familiar voices, a loud sob broke out from my throat and I wept, hardly able to get the words out to tell them; the tension of the journey released alongside the relief that he hadn't died. Feeling weak, my legs began to buckle.

Out of nowhere a paramedic appeared, placed a chair underneath me and gently sat me down; I didn't know who that angel was and I never saw him again.

John couldn't recall any of the accident, which was a good thing as it had been a near-death event. He remembered that he'd been driving to work on the country lane near our home that he travelled daily; the police confirmed that it hadn't been icy when he'd overtaken a car. That was his last memory. He had come off the road some way after a gentle bend; no-one else had been in sight or involved. The car he'd overtaken came across him shortly afterwards; he'd left the road, hit a low-level drystone wall that had catapulted his car from end-to-end. The investigators could tell us this because they found damage on the adjacent tree 10 feet up, which they said was from where the backend of the car had hit it. The car then landed on its side and rolled over several times before finally coming to rest on its roof with John hanging upside down and bleeding profusely from two nasty head wounds - one across the back and the other demolishing his eye socket. As fate would have it, two of the people who stopped to help were trained first-aiders who stayed with him whilst he was cut out of his car whilst still upside down; it rendered me speechless with gratitude when they subsequently tracked us down at the hospital to check he was ok.

The particularly horrible eye wound was from where the tree he hit crashed through the windscreen directly into his face, breaking his nose and eye socket, slicing his face up and coming within a millimetre of his eyeball. He'd been very lucky not to have lost his eye, but he needed to be transferred to a specialist surgical unit to undergo four hours of facial surgery. He'd crashed at around 7am. He went into surgery at 9pm. It had been a very long day, he was in agony and it was terrible to helplessly witness. By this time his family had been and gone and I sat alone in the vast reception area of the hospital. It was late at night in a city-centre hospital; ironically it was very inhospitable.

It was at that moment that I sat and cried; big, silent tears rolled down my face as the enormity of the day sank in, and it wasn't over. I sat there and contemplated what John's body had endured, the agony he had been in, the extent of his injuries and the underlying stress he was already experiencing. Now my fear had shifted to whether, after all this trauma, his body could cope with the surgery. As each hour ticked on and the adrenaline I'd been running on segued into exhaustion, I began to panic again that he wouldn't survive theatre. I'm ashamed to say I prayed again; it had worked earlier in the day, so perhaps I was on a roll. I was hoping for John that my luck had not yet run out.

The operation was a huge success; the eyelid that they thought he'd lost (which resulted in a plan to stretch his lower lid and stitch it above his eyebrow as a temporary measure to protect his eyeball - how I held onto my stomach as they told me that I'll never know!) had reappeared - albeit severed in two - when they had removed all the tree debris from his face.

The staff were delighted and keen to show me the bits of tree and the photographs like they were Summer holiday snaps. I was unbelievably appreciative for what they had done but declined their offer. I was, by then, a wreck. Knowing he was safe once again and desperately needing rest, I decided it was time to retire to the nearby hotel that his firm had already arranged for me. They had dropped off my overnight bag and moved my car to their company carpark; they had been extraordinarily kind that day and I couldn't imagine how much worse it all would have been without their support.

When I couldn't face going to recover his belongings from John's car, as seeing the state of the vehicle was too upsetting, one of the other partners from the firm went. He met with the same recovery truck guy who attended the accident scene with the paramedics. He said that as was often the case he arrived whilst they were still cutting John out of his car. The conversation that John's colleague had with that guy brought home to us the severity of what had happened and just how fortunate he'd been; the recovery guy couldn't believe it when he was told that John had survived. Having attended a lot of those kinds of incidents he said that the medics at the scene definitely thought they would lose John that day. It was sobering news.

Many months later John and I drove past the spot of his accident as we had numerous times since it happened. Yet on this occasion, a matter of metres further down the road, we suddenly came upon a carpet of flowers wrapped in cellophane on the verge. My hands shot to my face as I whispered, "Oh God. Oh no, no, no". John took my hand as I started to cry. Someone else had received that phone call. Someone else hadn't been so lucky.

John had remained in the hospital for 5 days; it was a miserable experience on numerous levels. With one eye completely out of action and the other rendered almost useless due to the absence of his trademark glasses (destroyed in the crash), he was bored and tired from the lack of sleep due to the bruises all over his body. Combined with the relentless noise of a shared hospital ward, he craved the familiarity of home. When we were told on the Friday that the ward closed on weekends and he would have to be moved elsewhere, we begged for John to be discharged. We said and did all the right things to satisfy the medical staff such that they allowed us to leave the hospital together that evening. It was the first of many traumatic journeys we made for a while with John as a passenger; whilst he remembered nothing of the accident, his body obviously recalled a 'feeling'. Despite my expert driving (we all think we're great drivers don't we?), every time we went around a bend in the road John tensed and took a sharp intake of breath. I did everything I could to try to ease the stress, but it was something that only he was going to be able to come to terms with.

We had a diary full of outpatient appointments to attend, alongside nursing John's smashed up face, his bandaged, glass-filled hands, and the angry laceration across the back of his head that meant his thick hair was still filled with dried blood and nuggets of glass; it took copious amounts of baby oil and patience to resolve the latter! Putting him back together was just going to take time and a team effort. My employer was brilliant as I took another two weeks off work whilst we attended medical consultations and tried to fathom John's current capabilities, but despite this, he began holding work meetings at home the following week; his craving for some normality was strong.

I needed eventually to return to work, however, so we organised that John could work (gently!) from my rental flat where I could look after him and go home at lunchtime to check he was ok and make him some food (I have to confess that my lack of culinary ability was a greater risk to him than the accident had ever been!). So we shoehorned all six foot one of him into my little two-seater sports car along with our bags and off we went on another scary drive.

His recovery progressed remarkably well, so eight months later we decided to cement his return to health with some sunshine and R&R on a luxury holiday abroad. It was an opportunity for reflection as that February's events had left us both with much to consider; staring death in the face without warning we needed to take stock of everything in our lives and feel gratitude for life itself. My sister was about to give birth to her second child within days of our return. It led me to share with John on holiday that in the days after his accident I'd realised that had he died I'd have nothing to show for our life together - no legacy of 'us'. I'd realised that I wanted a baby. He was delighted.

Even though our sex life had continued to be pretty non-existent, understandably not helped by John's accident and injuries, I did recognise that having a baby required us to actually have sex. It felt strange to stop taking the pill after all of these years; it was a bit of a relief. At 32, I'd been on every contraceptive pill you could imagine in an attempt to control my heavy, painful and constant (as in daily, not just monthly) periods. Wherever we'd lived, I found myself backwards and forwards to the doctors trying to find a solution; losing blood every day of the month bar one, left me feeling pretty unwell most of the time. This had gone on more or less the entire time that John and I had been together. No medical assessment I'd been through ever really pinpointed it to anything specific or followed it up, and no-one had ever suggested coming off the pill completely. Now I'd stopped, I wondered what would happen. The answer? A big fat nothing. Literally nothing. My periods stopped dead overnight. After all the years of battling them, it was quite a relief and a bit of a novelty, but my school biology told me that this also wasn't a good sign in the baby-making process! I left it for a few months believing my body would need time to sort itself out and adjust back to a less synthetic rhythm. Still nothing.

We'd not made the full transition to life down in the south, so I saw a doctor at my registered surgery back near our northern base. She was a locum in her 50s and, rather oddly, seemed uncomfortable and embarrassed as I spoke about the mechanics of the female body. Blood tests were performed and I was told to call in a week for the results. When the doctor's receptionist gave me the news that my tests had "all come back negative", I was relieved; I sat back and waited for nature to take its course. A few months later and no periods appeared, so I decided to take matters into my own hands and try an alternative approach - don't ask me why or how I settled on acupuncture having never tried it before...let's just go with the fact that I thought it was worth a go.

There I was, on my lunch break, lying on a treatment couch, stripped naked from the waist down apart from my knickers (thankfully) and a blanket to protect my modesty. A rather quirky looking man, who's only discernible qualification appeared to be his possession of a white lab coat, had stuck needles all over my lower abdomen before leaving me alone to "relax". After a couple of minutes of not relaxing in this rather stark room I looked down at my semi-naked lower half with needles protruding from it...how long would he be gone for? Would be ever come back? How long did I think I ought to wait like this before seeking help? The ludicrousness of this scenario suddenly struck me as I pictured how I must currently look. I craned my neck looking for any possible hidden cameras that may be recording this 'joke', but all I could see in the sparse room were anatomical posters detailing acupuncture points. I started to shake with the giggles; I put my hands over my mouth to try and hold it in just in case the guy decided his tea break was over and came back. My laughter made the needles hurt slightly, the irony of wanting to get pregnant involving having a body full of little pricks was not lost...

The acupuncturist said he'd helped other women before with fertility issues, which was promising, and I left that day feeling more positive to be doing something other than 'waiting'. It wasn't the only thing I left with; he'd also given me a bag full of tiny black balls - the size of the silver dragées used to decorate cupcakes. He told me to swallow 20 of the bitter-tasting pills in one go twice daily. They smelt dreadful. They tasted even worse. I didn't know what they were (or whether they were legal), but I did what I was told. I decided to stick with it though. It was during another session he explained that before the needles were inserted, he was going to heat them, once they were in my skin, to stimulate the points further than just the usual tweaking alone. Okay! It was then that he took out what I can only describe as a fat cigar-looking thing; he lit it, let it burn a little, and then blew it out...and then proceeded to place it on the end of each needle to heat them. It created a weird sensation on my skin and through each needle; it wasn't entirely unpleasant, more of a mild 'electric' tingling feeling. I had no idea if this was making a baby, but it was certainly making me laugh! Endorphins are good for you though, huh? Yet credit where credit is due, a few sessions in (and many hundred weird black balls later), I had a period. Not much of one, but a period nonetheless; the kind man in the white coat had done what he'd promised and I didn't go back. From there I was only looking forwards.

ॐ

EIGHT:

WHO DO YOU THINK YOU ARE?

That period turned out to be a false dawn; it was the last one I had. So I went back to my GP. Whilst only in my early thirties I was conscious that time was passing and my menstrual history didn't reassure me that this was going to be easy. My sister joked that mum had only had to iron our dad's trousers to fall pregnant, but Emma had endured several miscarriages and had finally required surgery to laser her out a womb space and rid her of endometriosis. I was aware from my research that there was a likelihood something similar would need sorting for me.

This time I saw my regular GP. I went through the details of my menstruation history (yet again - this had become a recurring theme and I had my story off pat) for that year and about the blood tests from six months ago. As she listened she brought the test results up on her computer screen.

"Oh".

Her face fell. The discernible change accelerated me from mild concern to worried. My physiological response was to click into high alert. My body awaited its 'fight or flight' instruction. My hormone levels were not as they ought to be, she said. Across the areas they'd tested; oestrogen, progesterone, testosterone (yep, it was news to me that us ladies need this one too!), FSH, DHEA...words and phrases I'd never heard of, she informed me that mine were all depleted. Significantly. I was confused and, to be honest, instantly cross with myself; I'd had a niggle that something wasn't right even after the receptionist had told me my results were okay. After everything I'd experienced since puberty I knew things weren't right, but I'd been raised to respect the medical profession, that doctors were the experts, so I'd placed my trust in them.

My GP advised that a referral to see a specialist would be the right next step; fortunately, my private medical insurance through my work would speed up the process. I made the short walk to John's northern base (we'd bought a small flat when we sold our house) in a blur, trying to fathom how to articulate to John what had just occurred and what label to put on what was the matter with me. I tried to explain the conversation that I'd just had, but the place was full of workmen delivering furniture and John was further distracted trying to get to grips with how his new 'PDA' (the precursor to the smartphone) worked; I was irritated that he wasn't paying attention to what I was saying; even though I wasn't exactly sure what I was trying to convey to him I felt it was important. I had a work appointment to attend, so I left in a huff and cried in the car.

I received a consultation appointment within a couple of weeks; I could tag it onto another weekend back at the flat. The day before the appointment John and I sat in a café and the anticipation of it meant the conversation inevitably turned to what the specialist might say. We contemplated that we might need intervention to conceive, discounted that it was anything 'serious' (no-one ever wants to utter the 'C' word) otherwise they'd have been seeing me sooner, and I shared that my worst-case scenario was that I was going through the menopause; we both laughed, "is it me or is it hot in here?". Since joining my family John had also been indoctrinated into the comedic genius of Victoria Wood. Whatever it was, we knew we had to face facts, something was amiss and, by this stage, the not-knowing was driving me mad.

Having reversed our living arrangements by selling our house in the north and purchasing one in the South near my job, the appointment was in the city where John still worked. I got the train into the city to meet him at his office and walk to the consultant's premises. On my way to the station, I called into my GP surgery to collect a copy of the earlier test results; I'd requested them so that I was equipped with the relevant data. I opened the envelope on the train and looked at the contents with curiosity. What I was presented with shocked me to the core. Typed, amongst the myriad of data, it stated plainly that I was in the menopausal range. I immediately felt the tears pricking in my eyes as I lowered my head to avoid the stares of the commuters in the busy carriage. I was devastated and furious in equal measure. I was 32 when those tests were done. 32 when the receptionist had told me that all my results were "negative". What the hell had she been thinking? How could the incongruence of my age (my date of birth was on the sheet) and those results not have been picked up on? I struggled to take it in, trying to process what this meant. By the time I reached John's office, I looked pale and felt numb; I had anticipated that there was some issue, but never seriously expected this. I showed John the results. He cuddled me and, being characteristically pragmatic, said, "let's go and see what the specialist says".

We sat silently in the consultant's waiting room, which was excruciatingly full of pregnant women and children; further words seemed superfluous. When we were called in we were met by a gentleman in his fifties; he was pleasant as he greeted us and we were invited to take a seat on the other side of his desk that stood between us. I endured the usual endless round of questions about my medical and menstrual history. Why did clinicians never read your notes?! Why did I have to trawl through these details every time I sat in front of them? Why did it always feel like a menstrual memory test? They appeared to have no idea how upsetting it was to keep having to go over the same issues time and again.

He was very matter of fact as he confirmed my referral from the GP and that he had seen the test results, a copy of which I still clutched anxiously in my hands.

"So you've gone through the menopause", he stated matter of factly.

No softening of the message. No words of comfort. No comprehension of the incongruity between my age and this diagnosis. As far as he was concerned this was just another clinical situation to be managed. Having delivered the news he proceeded to write a prescription for Hormone Replacement Therapy, which he slid across his desk. I picked up the piece of paper he'd proffered. I was completely stunned. By the news, the delivery style, and the fact that I was being treated like a fifty-something-year-old woman for whom the menopause had arrived at the appropriate juncture. No emotion, no care or trace of empathy nor, as it transpired to be of paramount importance to me, any explanation of why this may have happened.

Looking as though that was the appointment coming to a close, I enquired as to what I could do to help myself in this situation. If I'd thought the appointment couldn't deteriorate further, I was mistaken. "Not really", he said. I think perhaps my face told him that wasn't a satisfactory answer. He paused for a moment, thinking.

"Ermm", followed by, "Well your body mass index is very low, so I suggest you eat the occasional chip butty".

That was the extent of his advice. Delivered in an entirely perfunctory manner. Even I knew that the lack of hormones would have had a detrimental impact on my body, and I knew enough that gaining weight through the consumption of unhealthy food was ill-advised in any scenario. 'Appalled' didn't even come close to how I felt. I was obviously not a textbook case, but clearly, all he had to rely on were textbooks; the upshot was that he didn't know what to do with me.

I think it was John who asked a question about having children; this was handled in much the same manner. "Adoption or egg-donation", his response. Now that obviously was the end of the appointment; he got up from his seat and extended his hand for us each to duly shake before departure. That suited me because I couldn't get out of his consultation room fast enough. Outside the hospital building as we rounded the first corner I couldn't hold myself together any longer. The huge, all-encompassing sob that I'd been suppressing since he'd first delivered the news erupted from me. John put his arm around me and guided me to where his car was parked; I sobbed hysterically all the way home. He tried to find the upside and made the mistake of saying it could have been worse.

"Worse!" I yelled. "How could it possibly be worse?! I'm not just going through the menopause, it's already happened! It doesn't GET any worse!".

I'd thought the worst case was that I was going through the menopause. It turned out there was a nightmare beyond that; that the menopause had already been and gone. No getting used to the idea, no time to grieve what was coming to an end, no time to harvest eggs, no opportunity to reduce the impact on my body. There'd been an even more awful scenario, and now I was living it.

I cried that night until it felt like I physically couldn't cry anymore. Even when Emma rang to see how we'd got on I was too distraught to speak to her; John relayed the turn of events to her in hushed tones in an adjacent room. Exhausted, I slumped into bed, but as distressing thoughts continued to come in relentless waves, my body found more tears. Eventually, I cried myself to sleep on a soggy pillow with tissues strewn across the bedroom floor and found a few hours' reprieve from my devastation.

The next morning I awoke and, for a split second, everything was okay until the crushing realisation hit me again. John hesitated briefly waiting for my consent that he should head to work despite the situation; I knew that asking him to stay would only serve to add to his pressure. I took a similar approach. After all, I didn't know what else to do. Whilst that day I had the benefit of being able to work from home so that I didn't have to face the world, I did just that - I gave myself a good talking to about people who were worse off than me and then pulled myself up by the bootstraps and got stuck into work. The only grace I allowed myself was to text my closest colleague and tell him it hadn't been good news and that, whilst I would be working, I'd appreciate not having to speak by phone that day.

My way of coping was to push the emotions away, down deep inside of me. I told myself that there were lots of problems going on in the world, real problems, and no-one wanted to hear me banging on about my health and heartache. It was heartache. I felt as though my heart had actually broken. An empty void where it used to be and an actual pain that I couldn't explain. Yet there was another feeling that it took me a while to label, but over time I found the name for it: it was called 'shame'.

I realised that I was extremely embarrassed that I had gone through the menopause. I wasn't sure if because of my age I just wasn't aware of conversations about the menopause, or because they just didn't happen. Did menopausal women talk about the menopause? I realised I had no idea, but, for me, I was experiencing what I could only describe as humiliation.

One of my biggest problems was that I had no-one to identify with who had been through what I now had to face. It was a complete unknown and, even though I had John, I felt dreadfully alone. He was wonderful at listening to me and he cared for me on a practical level so well as he always had, but that was the limit of his ability; he couldn't understand this on an emotional level or how to respond to me. For my part, I couldn't articulate my emotions either. I felt isolated with this barrage of feelings and thoughts that I couldn't make sense of.

A huge challenge was my identity: I didn't recognise myself anymore as what I'd known had vanished. It felt like who I was had been taken in a single moment. Staring in the mirror I wondered who the hell was looking back at me. The reflection I recognised - the hair, the features of a familiar face - but beyond that was a vacuum of nothingness where my soul had been ripped out. The essence of me was gone. I felt guilty that my grief should have been for the lost children I'd never love, but the truth was that, whilst I was crushed that they would never be realised in my life, they were secondary to the grief I felt at the loss of me. The woman who thought she had choices, the one who'd believed she could decide, the womanly woman, the one with femininity, desirability, with youth, a whole life to live – the person who I thought I was, had gone.

My whole identity shifted – I still looked the same on the outside, but my body believed it was at least 20 years older. It aged me overnight. So I dealt with it the only way I knew how. Logic took over as I plunged into knowledge mode to regain some control over my life. I'd been taking folic acid one day, then furtively buying menopause supplements over the counter the next. How exactly did you adjust to that? I refused to take the prescribed HRT, not for now anyway; I had spent years taking different contraceptive pills prescribed by various doctors who it now felt had had little regard for my wellbeing. I was compelled to do something to contribute to improving the state of my health. I knew it couldn't be fixed, but I wasn't about to give up and do nothing. I didn't know what I'd do, I felt dreadfully lost, but kept searching for whatever it was going to be. I was offered some counselling to deal with the childlessness, but that wasn't the pain that was driving me right now (that part came later), it was the vast grief at losing myself. Where did I now belong in the world? Talking to my family was agonising as I didn't know what to say or how to explain how I felt because everything I said in my head sounded ludicrous; we seemed to end up in this awkward 'dance'. Absolute credit to my mum who said: "One thing I'm never going to do is talk to you about my menopause as what I experienced was at the right age and was nothing like what you're going through". It helped so much to have her say that, a validation of my painful feelings and that this wasn't 'normal'. But what then did that leave us to say about it? There was no anchor point in any of this, I was adrift and without any sense of on which shore I may be washed up. I hated that. I felt deeply unsettled by it. I didn't lie to people exactly, but I honestly struggled to get the words to come out. Saying that I couldn't have children somehow seemed easier; it was the 'acceptable' face of what had happened and people could better understand that at least. However, I lost count of how many well-meaning stories of hope about others' childlessness that I had to smile my way through; all the while I was dying inside. I didn't realise that feeling would become so literal.

I scoured for books that might hold answers for me, but there was virtually nothing available. I eventually went into a larger bookshop and one title stood out to me. The cover made me recoil, but it was the very aptly titled "Premature Menopause". Looking around to check that no-one I knew would see me buy it, I took it home in my bag in the hope of some enlightenment and, more importantly, some comfort that I wasn't as isolated as I felt. It was by an American writer and the style made it challenging to relate to - a bit too self-indulgent for my liking because, after all, I was in control of my emotions! Yet the real-life stories it contained made me sob in private. It helped insomuch as it shone a light on the emotional impact these women faced, but that in itself meant I stopped reading - I realised I wasn't ready to deal with feelings outside of my own. What it did highlight was the explanation all these women had for the physical reasons for what they had gone through. There was a reason for their early-onset symptoms; they had some comprehension of why it had happened to them. I was desperate to understand why my body had so catastrophically failed.

I moved on with my reading and started to swot up about hormones instead. I learned how, far from just serving a reproductive purpose, as we are commonly led to believe, our hormones are the cornerstone of our whole physiology. They play a major role in keeping our vital organs safe, especially our heart. As I read on I began to comprehend how my chances of cancer, dementia, heart problems and major organ failure were all increased as a result of the lack of hormones I'd had in my body during my life. As I cast my mind back across the issues I'd suffered throughout my teenage years and twenties, I began to understand that I'd probably never had the correct combination of hormones or certainly not for long enough for them to perform their function. It was terrifying to read the details and I was frightened wondering what it all meant for me. As I read more about the signs and consequences of the menopause I tracked back through my medical history and had a dawning realisation: my menopausal symptoms had begun when I was about 24 years old. Holy shit. Whilst none of what was happening currently made a lot of sense, quite a lot of how I'd felt in the past began to fall into place.

I was struggling with the lack of explanation as to why this had happened to me in my early twenties and what long-term damage may have been caused. All of this swirled around in my head especially as I felt I had no way of obtaining answers about what was happening inside my body. Was I just a biological ticking time bomb? The more I read, the more afraid I became - the list of repercussions for the lack of hormones throughout my life seemed to grow into a catalogue of 'nasties' that may be lying in wait for me at any time. My mental concept that I was 'trouble' had now taken on a physical manifestation. I suddenly felt on constant 'high alert' about my body, looking out for every change, every nuance or pain; I was about to get to know my body a whole lot better, with 'listening' to it becoming my specialist skill.

How did I even begin to communicate this? I would sound like an idiot if I told people that I now believed I would die early, that mine wouldn't be a long life. That is exactly how I felt as all indicators were that my body was one almighty, epic fail. It had already grown old prematurely, and now I needed to accept that may well be the trajectory I was on. No-one could tell me if it was, but no-one could tell me that it wasn't.

What I had throughout this was John to care for me; his kindness in the face of the constant maelstrom of emotions, bad news and appointments. He looked after me the best way he knew how: he fed and watered me, and kept living 'normal' life. He provided safety and security whilst I was tossed about in my internal storm.

Yet what I needed in reality was for someone to remind me that I was still a woman; to drag me around the bedroom by my hair (metaphorically!), to tell me I was sexy, and remind me I was still young and alive.

What John said about our childless state was, "we have to look on the positive side.This means we can live a life where we go out to dinner and have trips to the theatre when we want".

Inside my head, I was screaming: "I want it to mean that I can fall out of a nightclub drunk!".

What I had was a brother; what I needed was a lover.

&

NINE:

SPERM & SEEDS

Not wanting to settle - I use that word loosely as I felt anything but settled - I accepted every test and investigation offered that may provide me with some answers. What followed was an internal ultrasound to assess what, exactly, was - and had been- going on. Not pleasant at the best of times, I would imagine, but here I was faced again with the same 'chip butty' consultant who had unfeelingly delivered me the devastating menopause news.

We found ourselves at a different hospital location, this time courtesy of the NHS. The environment matched my mood - it was a dingy, barren room with a small examination area barely concealed behind a pale green, three-quarter length curtain. A nurse 'chaperone', whose presence was necessary due to the intimate nature of the forthcoming procedure, stood quietly in the corner and offered me a weak smile.

The consultant sat at the cluttered desk whilst I perched on a hard plastic chair beside it.

"How's it going on the HRT?". His perfunctory manner was consistent with our previous meeting.

"I've not taken it yet", I replied.

He looked at me like I'd just defecated on his desk. His whole demeanour towards me changed, clearly unimpressed that I had not followed orders. In clipped tones, he questioned my reasons.

I remained level as I responded. "I spent many years taking various types of contraceptive pill and trusting the advice I was given. I've now been handed yet another prescription for another different type of hormone and before I start just blindly taking it I want to do some research. I don't know whether all those other pills may have led me here".

In the brief silence, the room temperature dropped.

Like a child being scolded by their parent, my apparent insubordination was met with a lecture. He rudely reminded me of the risks of osteoporosis and heart disease. I stared straight back at him determined that he wasn't going to see the tears of anger that were threatening just below the surface. Straight-talking I could accept, but lack of humanity I could not.

The exchange over, I was invited to remove the bottom half of my clothing behind the curtain (yes, a recurring theme as a female and often, as here, requiring the skills of a circus contortionist!) and get onto the couch. There was a very tired-looking blue blanket on the bed that I was instructed to place over my nakedness; as I lay and waited for the next part I had the opportunity to consider how many people had laid under that blanket. It looked as though there had been many. I wondered if it had been washed in between. It didn't look like it. I lifted my head and semi-scoured it for evidence and then thought better of it and placed my head back on the miserly pillow. I momentarily sniggered in my head as I recalled another Victoria Wood sketch - the one where she works in the supermarket and says she wraps herself in her dog's blanket to keep her warm when she works in meatpacking. I thought how odd the brain is with what it recalls...and then contemplated that perhaps it was just mine.

My random thoughts were interrupted as the consultant appeared. His displeasure with me undoubtedly translated to the physical examination; the best word to describe it was 'rough'. Not just the usual discomfort associated with this type of procedure, but deliberately unpleasant, authoritarian. I bit my lip in an attempt to block out the degrading invasiveness and to control the involuntary shaking that threatened to consume me. His manner triggered something, it was the injustice at having to stay quiet and take my medicine in the face of his positional power. The repressed need to scream at him to get off me was making me perspire. So much for the chaperone who'd remained mute in the corner.

Back out to the waiting room, I met John, who had meanwhile been giving a sperm sample as part of their routine approach to our fertility issues. We were both confused given the absoluteness of my diagnosis, but John had obediently done as he was told. He began telling me how dreadful an experience it had been... if looks could have killed! As we grabbed our coats in the hurry to leave, I hissed at John that I never wanted to see that dreadful man again.

My fractured trust in the NHS was now totally shattered. John's career background meant he often worked with clients within the medical arena and shortly after my diagnosis he attended a seminar where, as serendipity would have it, he met a female surgeon who specialised in the menopause. Perfect timing. He confided in her about my situation; she was very understanding and offered to see me at her clinic on Harley Street in London. It was such a relief to speak to someone who understood in detail what had happened to me but also was of a similar age and therefore could appreciate the emotional impacts as well as the physical. Of greatest comfort was her appreciation of my experience within the NHS - she'd trained as a doctor with them and said that she'd found their coverage of the menopause to be scant and horribly outdated. It led her to self-educate when her mother had a particularly troublesome menopause and was receiving no help. As shocking as it was to hear her views, it did reassure me that my expectations of what should have happened versus my experience were not unrealistic. After all, every woman everywhere goes through the menopause with symptoms to some degree or another - that's 100% of about 50% of the world's population - and yet our knowledge, dialogue and treatment of it still seemed stuck in the dark ages! As I was oft heard saying, we'd managed to put a man on the moon, but we still hadn't found a way to conduct cervical tests with dignity or understand the menopause. Let's be clear, I'm not a man-hater (far from it!), but you get the point of my frustration.

This expert turned out to be brilliant, recognising that knowledge was one of my ways of coping with what had happened, so she recommended some books and gave me the confidence to start using some natural hormone creams that she was able to prescribe.

Other tests were recommended and that's when I learnt that I had to gird my loins (excuse the pun!) for endless rounds of bad news about my health. Rolling forward, it was 13 years before I received any good health news related to the impacts of my premature menopause. My first bone scan (I have to fight for these to be done via the NHS because, as it turned out, I "don't fit the criteria") revealed the next concern, that I had osteopenia. No, I didn't know what it was either! More reading revealed that it meant my bones had thinned and it was the lesser-known pre-cursor to osteoporosis, which is when the bones become brittle and have a high risk of breaking - yep, the one you associate with old ladies who fall over.

As news of each health shock began to sink in, I still grappled with the feeling of being 'lost' as a person; I no longer had any sense of where I fitted in and was permanently discombobulated. Learning ever more about how what I had gone through was very unusual at my age and, in particular, as there had been no trigger (significant illness, hysterectomy or chemotherapy being typical explanations), I felt disconnected from my peer group who had, or were planning, children. Instead, I felt middle-aged. What I truly felt was self-loathing. I looked in the mirror and didn't know who I saw. My body looked the same, but inside it was completely changed; it had let me down and that was totally outside of my control. I was angry, frustrated. I felt ashamed of this new version of me and of the fact that I hadn't spotted it was happening. No opportunity to adapt to the change or chance to mourn. To the outside world, I looked like I'd picked myself up and carried on, but inside I was dying - emotionally and physically I felt like I was rotting; decaying at the speed of a piece of fruit observed through a time-lapse camera.

From then onwards I hated Mother's Day. I still find it a challenge. Just saying that makes me feel bad because I love my mum and would never wish to deny any woman the joy of motherhood. It wasn't something I could control with logic, it just was how I felt.

I was restless. I wasn't comfortable within myself, so I couldn't settle to anything; it was like a constant electrical charge. I was looking to escape from myself. The German-owned company I worked for were bought by a large American corporation and this became the catalyst of my next job hunt; I'd learnt a lot in my current role and I was ready for a promotion. Besides, throwing myself into a new challenge would give me focus and meaning again.

An opportunity came onto my radar for a perfect-sounding job; it would mean a return to the food industry (so time was a healer on that score!), but it was also a Director role, so my first step up to that level. The position required another relocation, but this time it took us closer to my family, and somewhere in my mind I wondered if that might be helpful if we decided to go down the egg donation or adoption routes the consultant had mentioned - not that I seemed able to find the emotional energy to contemplate either.

I was interviewed for the role by various members of the small board of directors and the Group HR Director over several meetings. Amongst those was an interview with the Purchasing Director, Jennifer (Jen). She was glamorous and self-assured in a way quite contrary to the others I'd met thus far; there was an instant warmth that emanated from her. The new Operations Director who should have been present had been delayed in traffic, so the interview began with just the two of us.

"I've never interviewed an HR Director before", said Jen in a strong West Country accent (I loved it), "but what I have is a list of questions that I use for interviewing purchasing people [peeepol - brilliant, it instantly made me smile] so what I'm going to do is just take out the word 'purchasing' in each question and replace it with 'HR' and see how we get on. Is that ok?".

I burst out laughing and she joined me, a lovely full-bodied laugh; she's the woman for me I thought! I now wanted the job because of her.

I got it. I was delighted and determined it was going to be a new start after the trauma of the last year or so. John had been unhappy in his work since before his accident and that near-death experience had crystallised his thinking about wanting to set up his own business. We'd been planning that for a while, and this was the push he needed. We hit the housing market at the height of the property boom, so we managed to sell our home to the first person who viewed it. It finally felt like perhaps some things might be going our way and this move was bringing together our two lives; we'd been plodding along, going through life's motions. We'd been perfectly happy with each other, but being apart had often been hard given how much we enjoyed each other's company.

Whilst we sorted the house sale, I moved to the South-West by myself at first. Initially, I lived in a local B&B before moving into a holiday cottage for a while. John came down at weekends and our time was consumed by looking for a place of our own.

After viewing several houses, we found a gorgeous cottage situated on a village green about 25 minutes through gorgeous country lanes to my work. It wasn't the largest house or the prettiest, but my mum was quite right in saying it occupied the best position in the village. It didn't have much of a kitchen, and needed some renovation work, mostly to modernise it and bring out some of its lovely features, but the basics were all in place and we weren't afraid of the work involved. We both instantly fell in love with it and were excited by this new project as well as the prospect of a change of job for both of us.

Somehow this felt like putting down some roots and getting the life together that we wanted, especially since the accident and my diagnosis.

I officially began my job at the end of May and was still settling in when the team of Directors gathered along with the MD's PA for dinner at a local hotel to meet our new MD. The dinner was an icebreaker for us all as I was still quite new and it was early days in my relationship with all of them. I made my way into the small wood-panelled room as directed by the receptionist and observed that the MD's PA was already sitting on a bar stool with a drink in her hand. Standing near her was a guy who from his air of confidence I instantly concluded was the new MD. He looked up as I entered the room and greeted me with a thousand-watt smile and eyes that bore straight into my soul. A sensation hit me like a thunderbolt; it was an electric energy that knocked me sideways, taking the air out of my lungs and causing me to catch my breath. It was an entirely alien feeling, something different that I couldn't decipher; my brain was scrambling to stabilise and my body was some way behind trying desperately to catch up. The force of the emotion caused me to feel instantly coy and self-conscious; the feeling was rather uncomfortable. Luckily, somewhere within me, the HR professional kicked in, I put out my hand to shake and managed to introduce myself. I held my breath as he held my hand. He introduced himself as Brad. I guessed that he was a few years older than me, shorter than John and broader in build, more athletic; he had an assuredness in his stance that made him attractive even though he wasn't conventionally 'good-looking'. He held my gaze in a way that made me certain he could detect my internal free-fall and a slight amusement danced on his face that oozed testosterone.

He seemed phased by nothing. He could hold the crowd; a magnetic personality that made us all laugh. It made for a hilarious evening. Jen and I were on fire - bouncing off each other like a double-act; the current MD jokingly apologised that they were, "still getting used to" me. It was the biggest compliment he could have paid me and it cemented my relationship with Jen; we now both knew we were not like them, but we were each other's kind of woman. It was one of those evenings that doesn't turn out at all how you anticipated - sprinkled with fairy dust and secured in the annals of history.

I'd never been much of a drinker, and this evening had been no different, but as I sat in the taxi home I felt intoxicated. As the driver wound silently through the country lanes, my hair gently brushing my face as it floated on the warm evening air streaming through the slightly open car window, I began to come down from the high. For a while, I'd forgotten about the menopause. I'd felt young again. Funny. Engaging. Attractive. That last one made me cringe. I'd not been raised to think it was ok to see myself like that so maybe that was taking it too far…but in those precious few hours I'd not loathed myself at least. It was unfamiliar, like a distant memory you weren't certain hadn't been a dream. It was like a chink of light in the darkness. As the taxi drew closer to my temporary home the light began to dissipate. I crept inside the cottage because John had arrived whilst I was out and would be in bed. In my head I kept asking myself why I was desperate for him not to wake and enquire how my evening had been; every time the thought appeared I pushed the question to one side.

As I stood looking at myself in the bathroom mirror I tried to hold onto the evening's feelings; they were evaporating, but there was no denying that some indelible mark had been left on me that evening. In all the emotional decay that perpetually sat rotting inside me, a seed had germinated in that chink of light.

༄

TEN:

COCKTAILS & WATERMELON

Back at work the following day we were all on high alert, 'standing by our beds' as our new Managing Director visited the site for the first time for the customary factory tour and introductions to key personnel. As Directors, each of us from the previous night's dinner had a one-to-one scheduled with him in the afternoon in the boardroom - a very grandiose title for a tired-looking room with 1970s throwback decor.

Having not been with the business long, I arrived at the meeting with my CV so that I could talk him through my background and experience, and, more importantly, to demonstrate that the antiquated ways he would be witnessing on the site were not what I thought were acceptable standards. Whilst the site was making a small profit, its parochial 'family-business' mentality was disguising a much greater opportunity in mine and Jen's collective experience; I was looking forward to understanding what he had in mind and to working together to bring about some much-needed change. I placed my discombobulation from the previous evening to one side and entered the room as the consummate professional I had always been. I instantly sensed a very different mood; the perfunctory greeting was as though we'd never met and the charisma had been replaced by a machismo that turned the session into a challenging interview. I came away slightly confused by the two different men I seemed to have encountered and concluded that the previous evening had been the charm offensive before the true intent was revealed today. In short, I was certain that he didn't like me (my mind was running back through the previous evening trying to work out how that had happened) and that I'd have to work hard to convince him of my capability.

A few weeks later Brad started with us. He immediately began to assert his authority and the out-going MD pragmatically stepped aside to let him through. In his first week, we had a small leaving party for the retiring MD with the site's senior management team; we were heading back to the same hotel and, once again, the transport was laid on. As Brad was also in the process of relocating to the area with his wife, the proximity of our temporary accommodation meant that we were designated to share a taxi; it felt far from ideal. As I got into the back seat beside him I could feel the tension between us, but as he began to make small talk he was once again a softened version of the man that I experienced in the office. Certainly, once we reached the venue he was charm personified with the gathered guests; he radiated the kind of social authority that meant you always knew exactly where he was in any room. With a glass of Champagne in one hand, I quickly located Jen, who was like a colourful oasis in the desert of my nerves (work social events had never been my thing); she looked, as ever, voluptuously fabulous. Out of nowhere, Brad joined us and immediately complimented her on how lovely she looked; without hesitation, I joked, "well he didn't say that to me!". Still finding him difficult to judge, I instantly wondered if I'd overstepped the mark, but he laughed amiably so Jen and I joined in, although the look she and I shared said, "thank fuck for that!".

There was no let-up in my discomfort as I found on the table plan that I was seated next to him for dinner; it was starting to feel like a setup. His interview style transferred to this setting, but this time on a more personal, non-work basis. Whilst he spent a polite amount of time speaking to the person sitting to his right, his focus was undoubtedly on me; his questions incisive, but never rude. There was a strange kind of chemistry, it was a compelling sense of being played with, but being powerless to prevent it; it was as though he was gently taking the piss out of me. I continued to respond to his questions with a straight bat. It amused him. That same playful smile from our first meeting never left his lips as the unrelenting questions gave me no respite. In the taxi to our respective homes, I fought to retain my composure as my skin felt electrified by his presence just inches away from me; part of me was indignant about his constant need to want to get one over on me, another was excited to go toe-to-toe with my tormentor.

With him now firmly at the helm of the business, Brad kicked off with an exciting start - lots of 'state of the nation' speeches, big plans were made, and everyone was running around to be seen to be executing his commands. He was ruffling plenty of feathers with his opinionated manner and need for change, which was anathema to many of the loyal employees who had only ever served under the leadership of the previous MD. Yet to temper the forthright style, he was also sharp and funny, which you couldn't help but enjoy. As a small board of Directors, we spent a lot of time together, building plans, listening to his views, and answering the (often questionable) enquiries he made about our personal lives - responses to which I did my best to avoid.

He set his stall out early on with regards to standards from the team by bringing in an interim Technical Director, whom he'd worked with before, and removing the current FD (the last board-level bastion of the old regime). It was decided that the directors would meet her replacement over dinner, although this time we changed venue to a hotel in the town nearest to where John and I had had now moved into our beautiful cottage. I assumed this meant, for me at least, that I would get a taxi for the short ride home, but I was told in no uncertain terms by his PA that Brad wanted us all to stay over. No debate. There was to be a meeting the next day to discuss our strategic plan; we would use one of the meeting rooms at the hotel instead of travelling to the site. This was a rouse, I realised, for an evening of drinking.

I checked into the hotel late afternoon; I had a report I

was writing, so I decided to sit quietly in my hotel room with a cup of Earl Grey and a gorgeous view out of my bedroom window. As I got ready in my room I felt a sense of apprehension, which I sensed wasn't entirely due to meeting our new colleague for the first time.

Dinner went smoothly; not the kind of laughs we'd had when we'd met Brad, but we weren't in a private dining room this time so consciously not too raucous. True to form, I didn't drink much, ensuring a glass of wine was slowly sipped. I noticed that Brad wasn't drinking much either, although he was generously topping up the drinks of the others.

The new FD, another female, seemed ok on an initial pass; she threw herself into the evening and the wine, although stated that she wanted to ensure she made a good first impression. Jen and the interim Technical Director got stuck into the drinks as the evening wore on, such that in the end, we were the last men (and women) standing in the residents' bar; the staff had long since gone home. By this time things had gone way past the hilarity of that first meal with Brad; aside from some usual childish antics, we were getting the night porter (who was vacuuming the restaurant carpet) to make jugs of cocktails using recipes that Brad was Googling on his phone. As I was not a cocktail drinker, I was passing my glasses of Long Island Iced Tea along the table in front of the sofa to Jen, who was refusing none of them.

It was well past midnight when the new FD said she had

to call it a day as she had quite a journey back to her current job the next morning. The interim Technical guy, who was about as wide as he was tall and the second most inebriated, proceeded to help up Jen who was on all fours on the floor having tried, unsuccessfully, to get up from the sofa. He placed his hands under her armpits and hoicked her unceremoniously to her feet, although she seemed to remain strangely bent from the waist like a blow-up doll with a slow puncture. Given her state I was slightly stunned when Brad asked the new FD if she'd mind ensuring Jen got back to her room safely, his reason being that they were heading in the same direction. I should have said something given that this woman had only just met us, but there was the usual air of authority in his tone that meant I remained silent; the decision was already made and they obediently headed off down a corridor.

As I made my way towards the main staircase Brad fell in step beside me. "It looks like we're heading in the same direction", he said. Something about his statement sounded strangely stilted and for a moment I couldn't determine if he felt as awkward around me as I did around him. The age of the hotel meant there were numerous, shallow steps for us to climb, which, in my heels and the presence of my boss, I was navigating carefully. We turned the corner to tackle the second steep flight, Brad broke the tense silence: "What's your room like?". That was an easier question than the usual soul-baring interrogations I was starting to grow accustomed to. "Umm, it's lovely. It has a separate seating area with a desk, which is nice", I replied, grateful that this seemed like safe territory. We both stopped at the top of the stairs; it turned out our rooms were facing each other. In a single movement he stepped towards his door and threw it open, "Mine has a four-poster bed", he gestured inside, "take a look". Feeling very awkward I took a couple of small steps over the threshold and surveyed the room. I looked at him and smiled, "It's really nice". I tried to sound politely enthusiastic, "The rooms here are all quite individual". I wasn't sure what else to say. All I could think was that this was where my boss was going to sleep, have a shower, get dressed...and that somewhere in his bag that sat on the floor next to the wardrobe was probably his clean pants for the following day. I stifled a laugh and instead, a nervous giggle escaped; it felt clumsy. "Are they?", he asked as he stepped towards my bedroom door, "let's see then". It was uncomfortable, but I felt as though I couldn't refuse; he was my boss and I couldn't seem to articulate a good reason why not that wouldn't come back and be used to tease me at work. Thus far he'd taken pleasure numerous times at poking fun at what he saw as my naivety.

As I turned the key in the door I frantically tried to remember how I'd left the room many hours earlier; I'd not got ready in a hurry and I was naturally tidy so I didn't expect that it would be a mess, but I did have a long-established habit when I stayed in hotels of putting my clothes out ready for the following day. This often included laying out my underwear; it wouldn't be uncommon to see my underwear over the back of a chair. I winced as he confidently stepped into my room, walking around slowly and taking it all in. I stood by the end of the bed with an arm around one of the corner posts feeling like a spare part and waiting for this to be over. He turned around from where he stood by the window and walked back nearer to the centre of the room; he stopped and adopted his customary assured stance whilst looking at me. Whatever pleasantries he'd been espousing about my room ceased and there was a momentary silence. I smiled in a 'right, that's that then' kind of way to give him an out to leave. He was a master of eye contact, but this was totally unwavering. I suddenly felt a surge of adrenalin; my grip on the bedpost tightened involuntarily and my palm was damp. This is where he tells me that I'm not working out in my role. I braced myself for the bad news. He began speaking as he walked towards me, "so you'll have noticed how I feel about you". He was being very level. My brain was whirring, but no words came out. I needed him to keep talking whilst I ploughed my energy into remaining composed. "You must be able to see that I can't concentrate when you're around", he continued. I couldn't fathom the expression on my face, but it must have looked puzzled. "I can't stop looking at you when you're in the room", he said more softly as he stepped nearer, getting very close to me now. There was a pause before I burst out laughing.

"But you don't like me!", I blurted out, thinking I was now getting his joke.

He stepped back slightly. "Why would you think that?!", he looked stunned.

For a few seconds, all my mind could muster was 'Oh'. "I just didn't think that you liked me", I said rather weakly, shaking my head in my confusion.

He stepped further forward. "I can't get you out of my thoughts".

I wasn't sure I was still breathing. Every fibre of my being felt like it was on fire, whilst simultaneously I went numb. I couldn't speak any more.

He put an arm around my waist and pulled me towards him. My breath escaped in a gasp with the force of my body hitting his; the heat of such intimate contact had an intensity that I'd long forgotten. He was breathing hard as he cupped the base of my skull in his other hand, bent his head and kissed me hard on the mouth. A tremor swept through my entire body as, beyond reason, I lent into him and responded to the kiss; I wrapped my arms around his neck, surrendering to the unfamiliar riot of dopamine. As passion consumed us, it was like a weird out-of-body experience. I was completely powerless against the magnetic pull of the moment; the rest of the world went on pause.

We pulled apart as he relaxed his hold on me a little; I recovered enough strength to take my own weight again. We stood in silence for a few seconds, he held me so that our faces were just inches apart, looking at each other and listening to our shallow breathing. He smiled at me as he took a sharp breath in and stepped back; he went back to small talk about the room. I tried to join in, although all that was going on in my head was, "Oh my fucking God, my boss just snogged me!".

He went and sat in the lounge area by the desk, clearly not intending to leave anytime soon. He was filling time with idle chat as I re-stabilised; the smirk that played on his face belied the bland content of his words. He stopped abruptly, reached out and grabbed my arm and pulled me to him, sitting me on his lap. "You must know how attracted I am to you", he said with a composure that staggered me; it was in complete contrast to how I was feeling. "You can't say this stuff to me, they've started fitting my new kitchen today!". Oh my word! I'd just had my Dirty Dancing 'I carried a watermelon' moment! What kind of an idiot must I sound like? What was wrong with me?!

He was undeterred. We talked, we kissed. We spent the night lying semi-naked in my bed discussing the insanity of the situation, whilst he told me all the things that had attracted him to me. For the first time in what felt like a very long while, that night I felt desirable and I didn't want it to end. It was like a drug; he had an allure that I couldn't pull away from. It should have felt wrong, but it didn't. It felt long overdue.

In the early morning, he kissed me for the last time as he crept across the creaky floorboards back to his room to get showered and dressed for the meeting ahead. We next met at the breakfast table. How the hell should one behave in these circumstances? I buttered some toast and found it disproportionately difficult to swallow. Brad was bordering on perfunctory, which was a bit of a surprise, but I took it as the decision to maintain a professional front as we waited for our colleagues to join us. Scraping in at the end of breakfast service, the Interim Technical Director joined us; he was showered and changed but bore every hallmark of a severe hangover. We knew that the new FD was leaving early, so she was accounted for. There was no sign of Jen. "Have you heard from Jen?", Brad directed at me. I checked my phone again. "No, nothing". "Do you think you better check she's ok?". It wasn't really a question. I dutifully got up from the table and made my way up to her room and knocked on the door. Nothing. I knocked a bit harder, hoping I wasn't going to need to get someone from reception to let me in. I heard movement and then, "who is it?". "It's me". I hoped she recognised my voice. The door opened and the stench of sick hit me instantly; I tried not to let my face tell Jen that. She stepped back into the gloom of the room as I held the door open. "I just wanted to check that you're ok", I said, although her matted hair, last nights' clothes and make up smeared across her face told me the answer. She'd not choked on her own vomit, so that was a start. "Yes, yes, I'm fine!", she replied breezily, "I'll just get myself ready and I'll join you". I wasn't sure if she wasn't still a bit drunk. "OK, we'll be in the meeting room across the courtyard", I said in case she couldn't recall where to go. I left her to pull herself together. I wasn't sure what Jen's alcohol tolerance or hangover 'norm' was at this stage, so I made my way to my room to gather my things and try to get my thoughts in order.

It soon became apparent that the meeting was, as I'd imagined, a bit of a non-event. Not just because we were staying over really just to meet the new FD, but now because 50% of the attendees could barely keep their heads off the table. Brad decided to keep going by setting out the need for a strategic discussion, but as he talked in his chipper tone and with a smile permanently on his face, it told me that he was deliberately making this torturous for them. I was struggling to suppress a giggle - part tiredness, part delirium about the previous evening's events, and part in response to the scene that was playing out in front of me. Jen and the Technical guy took it in turns to reach for various imagined sources of comfort: water, tea, coffee, squash, mints. Nothing was cutting it as the Long Island Iced Tea inflicted its worst.

After a while of not getting very far, Brad suggested we take a break. I leant towards Jen and asked whether she wanted some paracetamol from the first aid kit I always kept in the car. She looked at me like I was offering her diamonds, so I headed out to the car park. I returned a few minutes later with the packet in my hand, just in time to see her pushing open the door to the ladies toilet; I understood how bad she felt when I watched her starting to projectile vomit on the floor before she could even shut it behind her. I hung back so that she wouldn't know I'd witnessed her and rested my back against the wall as I tried to get the convulsions of laughter under control.

The meeting broke up by lunchtime as our boss

relented and let everyone go home to get some rest. I was absolutely shattered, but sleep was the last thing I could do; my head was wrecked. My husband was due home that evening. I needed to get a grip on myself. I loved him. We had a great life. We were happy, weren't we? I'd just been caught up in the moment, flattered by the unexpected attention and relieved I hadn't been about to get fired. The entire situation felt surreal, as though it were all happening to someone else and I was an observer. I tried to put it down to exhaustion, but there was a frisson in my body that was undeniable and about which I couldn't manage to feel bad.

ELEVEN:

SPIRALS & SPELLS

My dad's heart surgery loomed large; we were all on tenterhooks as he went for his pre-op only for it to be cancelled; he was showing symptoms of a cold. Having psyched herself up for the worry, Mum was more floored by this news than Dad. He was given a revised date of December 20th, which meant he was inevitably going to be in the hospital for Christmas Day. We all had to get our heads around that.

It wasn't just production that was ramping up in the pre-Christmas rush – things were getting increasingly heated at work between Brad and I. Between flirtatious conversations, secret texting and a few stolen moments alone, I had no trouble being motivated to get up and go to work. My office hours got longer as not only was there so much to do in the business, but it turned out there was so much business to do. He'd ring me on my way to work and during the journey home. We couldn't get enough of one another such was the intoxicating chemistry between us; he spoke frequently about 'us' and our future. Jen sensed what was going on. She told me that being around us was amazing, enthralling! It was wonderful to feel on fire like that every day -

to feel so alive when I'd felt so...dead. This time I was off my food with the sheer giddiness, and against the backdrop of the worry about my dad...my weight was starting to drop.

The day before dad's surgery John and I went to my parent's house and drove him and mum the nearly 2 hours to the specialist hospital to get dad settled in. This time we felt a mixture of relief that he was well enough for the surgery to go ahead and terror that the surgery was definitely going ahead. John had been amazing up until this point - his knowledge and connections in this arena of medicine were the reason dad was having this particular type of heart surgery rather than that which the NHS had tried to oust onto him, which would have condemned him to a life on medication and managing their life-altering side-effects.

John tried to reassure us as it came to the time to leave dad there, looking small and vulnerable. We knew that being in a room full of strangers was a nightmare for his shyness, but being dad, he made no fuss and got on with it quietly. His biggest concern was my mum and how upset she was to say goodbye knowing the operation he faced. We'd been told that the duration of the surgery meant that there was no point going up to the hospital and waiting the next day; they'd call us with news and only if it was early enough in the day would there be any benefit in us trekking to see him. The harsh reality that none of us could bear to utter was that this was risky, if routine, surgery; it was a big operation and there was a chance that he wouldn't make it through.

We just had to go home and await their call.

When we got home mum did what she did best and started preparing us dinner. When I told her that I didn't feel at all well and was going to lie down, she was suitably irritated - quite rightly, this wasn't about me. Yet I really didn't feel great and lying down was the only thing I had energy for; a quick nap after all the adrenalin of the day and I'd feel better.

About an hour later I awoke and swiftly felt distinctly worse. Suddenly my only option was to rush downstairs to the bathroom; I nearly got the door closed before I vomited severely. And so it commenced. I was sick like I had never been sick before; it kept coming and coming until there was nothing left to give...but still, my body continued to try. By later that evening I was lying in my parents downstairs bedroom because I couldn't have made it up the stairs; I was completely wiped out. The bug was horrendous and had taken hold; this was norovirus. Perhaps this was why I had felt so unable to eat over the last two weeks?

Mum was now worried on two fronts: how ill I was and the fact that I'd been in contact with Dad. For these reasons none of us had a settled night; the next day was no better on either front. Dad now lay on the operating table and we all were just clinging on, waiting, barely breathing. I couldn't lift myself off the bed, as much as I wanted to care for my mum I had to accept that right now she had to care for me. As the afternoon wore on, I heard mum say to John that she didn't know if they'd be able to go and see dad even if the hospital called because she was afraid to leave me given the state I was in. Hearing that as I hung over the side of their bed, sweating profusely, still retching, panicked me - if the hospital called mum needed to go, and she needed John to drive her there. I fell into an exhausted sleep again.

When the phone finally rang it woke me to find John sitting on the edge of the bed next to me. We both listened to mum's end of the call we'd been waiting for from the hospital. Dad had made it through the surgery and was in the recovery room - in the immediate term that was all that mattered. As mum put the phone down I heard her burst into tears; I mustered what little energy I had and shoved John to indicate that he needed to go and comfort her as there was no chance that I could.

48 hours later I'd been free of the vomiting long enough to go and see dad; he was by this stage already out of Intensive Care and in the High-Dependency Unit. It was distressing to see him wired up to various machines, but simultaneously a huge relief - he was weak, but conscious and, according to the medical staff, doing very well. In fact, in a moment when we were briefly alone, he managed to nag me about helping mum with lunch on Christmas Day! Not too poorly then. It made me smile, and feel hugely reassured that, despite being surrounded by all this equipment, my wonderful

dad was definitely still there.

Intermittently I'd been able to keep in touch with Brad and let him know how things were going. I longed to see him, not least because he felt like a light in all this darkness. I insisted to my family that I needed to show my face at work given that I was still new to the business and this was the first Christmas production run I'd been through. I could tell John wasn't happy, but that was not my greatest concern - I needed to escape the suffocation that I was starting to feel. So on the day before Christmas Eve, I drove back home. 'Sensible' me would have been resting, my body ached from all the retching and I felt weak from the lack of food my body had welcomed for the last few weeks. I couldn't afford to lose any more weight, my clothes already felt looser. Yet it's amazing how the mind and an unrelenting desire can bring us the extra strength we need. The journey was worth it just to gain a few surreptitious hours alone with Brad; he was the best medicine to give my spirits a much-needed lift. Just to be held by him and reminded how he felt about me.

As I drove back to my parents' house on Christmas Eve, however, the sinking feeling began to fall even lower. When I was with Brad I felt amazing, desirable, funny, vibrant - the opposite of how I now felt with John. He had been beyond amazing both before and throughout my dad's surgery - I had so much to be grateful to him for, but I just felt perpetually 'dialled down' in his presence. It was as though if I made myself invisible to him he wouldn't be able to see how culpable I was.

So what ensued was the most miserable Christmas on record for us all for a number reasons. Dad was still in the hospital, now back on the ward, but his absence at the table at lunch was like a gaping hole. For a slight, quiet man we were suddenly reminded what a huge space he occupied in our family. Mum had done her best to create the usual masterpiece that adorned our Christmas table every year, but without dad, it was missing that magical sparkle that my parents' hospitality normally provided. I was still recovering, so my shrunken stomach coupled with my guilt meant I had no appetite. None of us could face the meal without dad there; we pushed our food around our plates and counted down until some of us could climb in the car and drive to the hospital for visiting hours. My baby nephew had also become poorly and as he sat in his highchair looking desperately pale we spent the entire dinner talking about whether he too needed to go to a hospital. Added to that I didn't want to be anywhere near my husband; everything about him annoyed me. That sounds so wretched to say, but I couldn't help it.

Let's call it out: I was love-sick. I was pining for Brad and it was excruciating to not be with the person my heart desired. Yet mixed with this was the torture that I was torn between wanting to be with the man I now loved and the man I had loved my entire life, who lay alone in his hospital bed. All I could think was that both were out there somewhere, but neither was with me. And everywhere else, everyone else was happily enjoying their Christmas, or so it seemed. Meanwhile, John knew that my malaise was not norovirus, but uttered nothing.

Initially, at least, time apart at Christmas had done nothing to dampen our ardour, and what the New Year bought was greater urgency, depth and increased risk-taking. Brad spoke about leaving his wife, marrying me, of our life together, and I fell further into the dream of this relationship as the pull between us remained undeniable. As the weeks and months of the year progressed, however, the pressures of the job started to show and it reflected in his behaviour towards me. He started to become volatile on all fronts. It was hard for his team to judge what he wanted or what mood they'd find him in - firstly from day to day, but over just a matter of weeks, it became changeable from hour to hour. I experienced this too. One moment he would be kissing me in his office with an intensity I had never known - totally in my thrall, swept into the vortex of an attraction to me that he was helpless to contain. Just hours later he would be aggressively barking orders and humiliating me in front of my peers, placing pressure on me to enact things on others in the organisation that professionally I disagreed with. Don't misunderstand me, I did not unquestioningly acquiesce - it's not my style! It was as though nothing positive had ever happened between us. It was a crashing come-down from the high of the last few months. He behaved like I was a drug from which he was battling to withdraw - oscillating within each 24-hour period between breathing me in and going cold turkey. I was being punished for how he felt about me and his inability to effectively control it. It was a lightning turnaround that left me reeling and exhausted; my nerves were in shreds from the growing gap between elation and fear.

When it came to turnarounds, the changes he'd promised in the organisation also didn't begin to materialise. Quite the contrary, it was losing money every month as more issues were uncovered and he started to struggle to get his arms around the business far more than he struggled to get them around me. Troops were drafted in - permanent appointments and interim support - as he continued to speak to his more senior leaders about the need for a cavalry to resolve the issues at the site.

To start with, I sympathised with the need to sort it out - just from a people perspective alone there was much to do - but as time went on, it became clear that he was out of his depth. It started to look like he'd blagged it this far, but now that the rubber had hit the road and his honeymoon period was over, it wasn't working. The extent of his capabilities was being questioned by his team, even if those to whom he reported were still backing their decision to appoint him. Worse still, he began to behave like it was all a game, like it didn't matter to him; he displayed an arrogance in the blame and manipulation he exercised on those around him - there was always someone onto whom the fault could be deflected.

One after another, members of our board team came and went - each one hailed as a 'white knight' to help us, only a matter of months later to be ousted from the business for not bringing about the improvement he needed; they were frequently broken and always ridiculed. We were all stunned, no-one more so than me, at how we'd been duped; he was not at all who we'd experienced in those first 6 months. He was out of control as his behaviours hit new extremes - either excessively charming to everyone (to the point of being a Joker-esque caricature) or ruthlessly cruel (in my role I spent a lot of time handling the removal of countless people to whom he'd taken a dislike). What started to become apparent was that he seldom did any of his own dirty work.

The swiftness of the 180-degree about-turn in his attitude towards me was devastating. Yet it wasn't like the light had been switched off, rather that the wiring was faulty and it flickered eerily; I never knew how brightly it would shine on me each time I walked into his room. What had, it now seemed, started as a bit of fun for him (could he get the girl?), had got out of hand in his emotions, and certainly had with mine. Me never knowing where I stood with him and being deliberately played like a pawn on a chessboard; it was a boost, feeding his extravagant ego whilst he had me at his mercy. He was attracted to me, but would he be able to charm and manipulate me for his own ends? Could he get what he wanted out of me, and then just discard me when he was done? The answer was - almost. What he hadn't counted on, was that he would start to 'feel'.

My friendship with Jen had deepened significantly

in the adversity of our work situation, and we now knew we could say anything to each other without judgement. He knew that she knew about us, which was a knowledge that meant she got punished even harder than the rest of the team; I felt desperate guilt for her. He intended to pull us apart from one another, to drive a wedge so that the fact of his infidelity - to his wife and to the position of responsibility he held at the company - could not be proven. Yet he failed at every turn; he couldn't get a cigarette paper between us and this infuriated him even further.

The whole thing was a total head-fuck. I struggle to find a more articulate, non-sweary way to describe it. I agonised at length with Jen about his behaviour - hating myself for my idiocy of getting caught up in this rouse and then completely confused by the tenderness of some of the sentiments he expressed. I spent so many hours crying in Jen's office that it was a wonder we managed to work so hard. My pain hit an all-time high when he said, "It's such a shame you cannot have children because in you I have finally found someone with whom I could imagine myself having a family". Having been consistently derisory about his wife's desire to have children with him, he now intended that I would melt at the wonder of his words. Instead, the knife wound it inflicted in my gut made me want to fold in two and collapse onto his office floor. How could he say something so cruel?

I guess it seems easy to say, "of course he loved me" like it justifies what either of us was doing - let's be clear, it doesn't. But if you were there, if you saw how he behaved towards me, you could see how impossible it was for him to let me go. He unravelled too.

And boy, had I unravelled. Not knowing what nightmare I might be faced with every day - a business that was haemorrhaging money, where morale was at an all-time low, where the atmosphere was either euphoric or suicidal, I was hated one minute and adored the next, where I was having to stand over my team like a lioness to protect them from the craziness because they were sticking with me despite the constant demands...you get the picture.

One morning, when I had to get changed three times before I could find an outfit that vaguely looked like it fitted me, I knew that things had got really bad. My emotional agony had translated into physical suffering; I wasn't eating properly and it was showing. The fashion transformation that I had undergone in the flourishing few months of rediscovering the sexy woman within me, was now coming back to bite me. Gone was my subscription to the 'navy suit' attire favoured by many professional women at the time, and in its place were more overt expressions of my personality through fitted dresses, pencil skirts and heels. Yet now, nothing fitted. I was a fraction of my former, already slight, self. My broken heart was showing up via my broken body. Guilt was everywhere. At home, John knew something was going on and was devastated, but he remained dutifully quiet. His characteristic kindness, silent suffering and the unmentionable truth that sat between us, was killing me. We'd talk about anything apart from what needed to be talked about; continuing our lives side by side, but without any connection for fear of what that would mean. At work, I was determined to maintain my professionalism in what I delivered for the business, but the guilt I felt for the extra burden his attitude towards me was placing on Jen and my team was almost unbearable.

In the space of a few eternal months, the whole sorry thing spiralled to collapse; it had been a complete whirlwind and now the shattered pieces lay strewn far and wide: me, my life, my marriage, my family, my friends, my team, my job, the people we were trying to serve, Brad, the site, the employees, his marriage, the wider business, our customer…

Finally, by June, it was totally over between him and I. I was desolate, barely holding it together, and having to think consciously about breathing in and out just to survive for the next 60 seconds. I wasn't sure I wanted to survive; my humiliation and heartbreak felt so all-consuming that I wanted the ground to swallow me up. My daily calls with Brad on my way to work had been replaced by concerned calls from Jen. Throughout that period she rang me each morning to check that I had got up and out of the house to face the day; she saved me during that time. Her love for and belief in me never wavered; she held my hand physically and metaphorically every day for weeks, and, once she discovered the truth, so did my amazing friend Anna who worked in my team at the time. They held me together, getting me from one end of the day to another, and building my belief that I could keep doing this until it got better. I could not see that it ever would. Seeing Brad at work every day was torture; seeing John at home every night was excruciating. I had no respite anywhere from the shame of what I had done. My spell with myself had been broken for good - I once again was not the woman I thought I was, but this time it was all my fault.

He had been nice thought the little girl. The husband. Kinder than the others. Safe. She'd thought he'd be someone who would stay. She thought she could make him stay. She'd tried very hard. But she couldn't get it right. She'd been naughty.

Wrong.

Again.

She'd hurt him. She really must not be nice. She didn't deserve someone who would be that kind to her. She wasn't good enough.

She looked at her reflection in the mirror. Pale skin. Boyish looks. Ugly. Now inside as well as out.

She was unhappy. She deserved to be. She must push down her sadness. No-one would want to hear about it. Not when it was her fault. Her own, silly fault. Silly little girl.

TWELVE:

THE BOOBY PRIZE

I t was self-hatred that led me to make that first enquiry phone call, although I'd already made up my mind what I was going to do. I wasn't doing it to make myself feel better, quite the opposite. I was doing it to inflict physical pain on myself to try and assuage the emotional pain I was feeling every waking moment. Of course, I didn't tell anyone that - I just told them that I couldn't have children and getting a boob job was the obvious thing to do, right? That would make everything better.

Once I climbed aboard that run-away train in my head, however, there was no disembarking. I'd made my mind up, and away I went. Bizarrely, from his work in the medical arena, John knew a good surgeon. So I did what every woman does when she's going for an appointment about cosmetic surgery - I got a spray tan! Now, let me explain. I am very pale; translucent. The only thing that horrified me more about my appearance back then than my small chest, was the colour of my skin. I stayed covered up in Summer no matter how hot it got, not just because I have the 'ginger gene' and need to stay out of the sun, but because of my mortification at my milk-bottle-white legs! So, the thought of going to a consultation with a surgeon where not only would I need to show him my small chest, but also a very pale small chest, was horrifying. He was (hopefully) going to fix my chest issue, so I went to the salon to remedy, albeit temporarily, my skin issue. Even though my discussion with John had led me to believe that the surgeon was a more mature man, I decided that I would feel better about the situation if I had at least attempted to eliminate one of my two hang-ups from the situation. How wrong I was.

My consultation was held at an office in the private hospital where the surgery would take place. It was tastefully decorated, not overly done so that you wondered how much of your fee was helping fund an interior designer, but good enough to know you were not at an NHS facility. I grew increasingly nervous as I waited to be called into the surgeon's office, and when I was this was by an exceptionally tall, blonde nurse who ushered me discreetly into an expansive room with a desk at one end by a large window that flooded the room with light. To my left was an examination area with a large couch and a pristine white curtain pulled back around it; it was a million miles away from that terrible episode at the hospital where I'd had my internal scan. As I took in my surroundings on my way to the chair to which I had been guided, what I saw behind the desk made me hold my breath for a moment. Far from the old black dude that I had somehow conjured up in my head from John's scant description, holding out his hand to greet me was a handsome guy of about my age; he had the most perfect milky-coffee coloured complexion and a beautiful smile. "You're going to have to get your tits out in front of him", said my head. Oh shit. He was not at all what I had been anticipating, but the name on the desk plaque was that of the person I was expecting to see. Suddenly the fact that I was sure that he would recognise the sight and smell of fake tan (and which had turned me only a couple of shades darker than a ghost) made me mortified.

He went to great lengths to describe the process involved if I were to opt for the surgery, but bluntly very little of it hit home. I was aware that the only part of me that now had any colour was my face, and my brain just kept repeating the same sentence it had when I'd first laid eyes on him. He was, in fact, as lovely as his face conveyed and as competent as his pre-billing recommendation. He was happy to proceed, as was I, and so I was booked in within a couple of weeks. I was delighted that, as had happened with an old colleague who had gone through the same procedure, I was going to get weeks of agony to take my mind off my heart-wrenching misery.

First, however, I had to determine what 'weight' of implant I wanted. As with any quality surgeon, the final cup size is not guaranteed, but instead, I had to tell him the look I wanted by trialling various weights. He instructed me to buy a larger sized bra, a bag of rice and some small plastic food bags; I was to weigh out 2 portions of the rice at three different weight increments, place the rice (uncooked!) into the plastic bags, then put each of the weights of rice into the bra to see what size looked and felt right. It was like Pamela Anderson plays goldilocks! I decided it was a task that only a girl's best friend could help with, so off I went to Jen's the following weekend armed with my 'ingredients'. When I unpacked them upon my arrival, her husband took one look at them, looked at the both of us slightly warily and said, "I think I'll go out and mow the lawn". God love him, he didn't even flinch when, my task over, he got served up the rice for his tea.

The surgery didn't go as planned. Oh, I got the result I wanted and then some - my new boobs were better than I could have possibly imagined - but a quality surgeon does a very skilled job; he put in extra anaesthetic to manage the discomfort. I'd had the surgery with John posted faithfully by my bedside, who then drove me to my parent's house so that I could stay there for the initial two weeks I'd taken off work to recover. I thought that the physical care of my parents, in particular, would help, as well as some time away from the tensions at home and work to let me get some proper restful sleep. What hadn't worked, however, was the pain. There was none. A bit of pulling discomfort as my skin was stretched tight over the implants. A little awkwardness in getting washed and dried - you know you've reached a new milestone in your relationship when your mum helps you, as instructed by the surgeon I might add, to dry your bandaged breasts with a hairdryer on low heat. What I loved particularly was my dad asking about how I felt post-operatively in a bid to compare notes between his recent surgery and mine; there wasn't any comparison in what we'd gone through, but bless him for trying!

I'd had the operation on a Thursday, was discharged on Friday and by the Tuesday I was out shopping with my mum in town. This was going well, but well wasn't what I'd planned for, hoped for even. There was nothing for it, I had to accept that the pain I'd longed for wasn't going to come. I'd stopped taking the painkillers I'd been prescribed because they weren't required. I'd had some rest. So I decided to go home and back to work a week early; there was satisfaction in the element of surprise.

The site was, by now, in serious decline, it had never picked up despite Brad's big talk; the buck stopped at his door and you could see the pressure wearing him down as he tried desperately to claw back his power. He'd run it almost into the ground, helped along by some poor innovation decisions and massive product recall. Head Office finally started to send in senior management to have a poke around. One of the Group Directors came to site on the pretext of doing some research for a project he was working on. When he came to speak to me, I decided to be professional, but candid, for the good of the site, it's employees and my team. I owed it to them all to take the opportunity to tell things how they really were for those working there.

In the weeks that followed, I could sense that there

were some mood changes higher up in the business, until one evening I received a call from one Group Director. He told me, in confidence, that Brad was going to be leaving the business. Essentially, he was going due to his poor performance, but they were allowing the pretext to be that of redundancy. Brad himself would be announcing it to the team the following day. Even better.

I barely slept that night, but the next morning I was filled with an energy that I'd not experienced in a while. Once I got in the car to work I immediately called Jen; with only a matter of hours to go until the news was revealed, I knew that I could trust her with this information. I owed it to her to tell her so that she too could have the composure in the moment like I had been gifted.

At the office, we were the picture of calm, even though between us we were like a couple of kids on Christmas Eve waiting for the moment when the senior team were asked to assemble in the Boardroom. As Brad stood there centre stage, I allowed a slight smile to alight on my lips just so that he'd know that I knew before he even began to speak of the farce that was about to play out. With a typically grandiose manner, he began relaying all the reasons why he was being made redundant. Jen and I exchanged a furtive glance with a knowing look. A self-absorbed show-off right to the bitter end!

Jen and I left early that afternoon. Unusually we went

to the local pub. We needed to celebrate. It had been the best of times and the worst of times.

৵

THIRTEEN:

PERFECTLY TIMED PROFITS

I was devastated by what had happened with Brad. My heart had been broken in several different ways: I'd thought I was in love with him and him with me, but mostly I felt like an idiot and deeply ashamed at what I had done; it seemed so out of character. I'd actually broken my own heart, which hurt the most.

Between John and I there was so much that was unspoken. He'd worked out what had been going on and I'd reached a point of desperation in the end where I didn't even have the strength to hide it. One night we lay in bed after his drive back South and I asked if he was okay, to which he answered that he would never be again. He said the day that I'd met my new boss it was like the light in me went out. Despite all that had happened and the carnage it had caused in our lives, I still maintained meeting Brad was when the light went on. I remained confused as to why.

The months that followed were horrible as we tried separately to pick up the pieces of what I had blown apart. I took full responsibility that what had happened had been my fault. Once again I was the 'troublemaker', the one in the wrong; I'd also let my family down spectacularly - again. They were shocked and appalled that I could do such a thing; they adored John. Mum told me that dad was disappointed in me. I was cut to my core by that; I adored my dad, he was my hero, what he thought of me probably mattered more than the opinion of anyone else. The fact that I had done something to make him think less of me, floored me. And so the slide into deeper self-loathing continued. I was empty inside, struggling to summon much of any kind of emotion other than hate for myself. I was numbed by the intensity of the pain and I couldn't even begin to fathom what I felt for John other than remorse. What about what he felt about me? I couldn't contemplate that he might love me, 'like' me even - how could I ask that of him when I didn't even like myself?

Throughout this desperately dark time, the one bit of gleaming light was that the company started to pick up and eventually, with a strong new leadership team in place, turned a corner. Jen and Anna patiently walked alongside me as I tried to heal; I hated myself a little less as time passed, but it never healed. The wound remained infected even though the desire to lie down and stop breathing that had consumed my entire being after my ruinous dalliance with Brad had ended, abated a little. I spent much of my non-work time with Jen and her family; they accepted me as I was, in whatever emotional or physical state I presented myself. They were a temporary respite from the crushing guilt at home, where John's permanently despondent expression was akin to being escorted continuously to the gallows.

Nearly 9 months on from when Brad had left my life and to celebrate my birthday, Jen decided that we needed a night out. These occasions were notorious. Jen had a charisma that attracted 'characters' so we often ended up joining others' conversations and celebrations. On this occasion, we found ourselves observing a stag party where the betrothed gentleman was dancing wearing what looked like his grandmother's dress and hat, and a pair of gentlemen's brogues. We were commenting on the natty outfit when a member of the party approached Jen; he'd been watching us, watching them. He was nice looking with a broad, open smile and a soft Irish accent. At a time when I felt extremely rubbish about myself, he made me feel good that evening. He was pleasing, chatty, funny, he twirled me around the dance floor in a way that made me feel 'lovely' for a change. I'd buried what it felt like to bask positively in the spotlight of a man's attention, so when that was ignited I was a captive audience. A moth to the flame. Jen sat back and encouraged me to enjoy the moment.

Two days later as I sat on a train, the Irish guy, Connor, texted me. He decided to come clean. He had a girlfriend. They lived together. He wanted to see me again. I threw caution to the wind. If he was attached that was his problem, not mine. Besides, stuck in the black hole of my conscience I deserved a little fun, right? I had no emotions and he seemed harmless, so there was no risk of me getting involved in something that might cause me further pain; he was a welcome distraction.

A frivolity. A bit a light relief wouldn't hurt anybody; it would do me good, I was sure.

We began to see each other as and when we could; he was a bit 'goofy', not particularly smart, but he was easy on the eye and made me laugh. The no-strings sex was good and his constant attention I enjoyed. I started to believe that I felt more positive about myself. Connor left his girlfriend in fairly short order and soon we were regularly stealing opportunities in hotels when I travelled for my work, which I was doing more often at that time.

On one such occasion we'd arranged to meet at a hotel near my company's offices; it was an expansive 5-star establishment with a large reception area at its centre. I walked in with my overnight bag and straight up to the desk to check-in. Whilst the gentleman processed my booking, I turned back round to survey the glamour of the voluminous setting. As I did so I spotted a man, some way off across the room, but who was walking most definitely towards me. His gait, his puffed out chest, was unmistakable: Brad. My breath caught for a moment, I'd not seen or heard from him since that final day. I quickly gathered my composure, after all, I reminded myself, the tables had turned in our dynamic; there was no longer any need for me to be fearful of him - he'd been held to account for his performance and mine had flourished in the aftermath.

He slowly sucked his breath in over his teeth before he spoke my name like a villain from a James Bond movie. Then, "How are you?".

"I'm really good, thank you", I said with a smile, which widened as the realisation swept through me that I wasn't having to put on a front.

I'd regained some of the weight I'd lost during the time he'd been playing his mind games with me; the happier version of myself I felt on the inside was starting to show up on the outside. And, let's get to the nuts and bolts of it, I'd had my hair done, so my roots were fresh and the colour was glossy! Shallow? Yes, but it's the little things that matter sometimes.

By contrast, he looked older, more stressed, I observed. What couldn't have been more perfectly timed, however, was that our monthly financial results had been published that morning; the site had cemented the turnaround path we'd been aggressively pursuing and we'd broken through to make a profit for the first time since the previous year. I slipped that fact into our exchange - it would not have been lost on him that it was the first month of profitability since he'd left.

I politely asked him what he was up to (although I already knew - the world in which we operated was pretty small at the time) and he blustered his way through an explanation that was designed to convince me why the interim role he was doing was the epitome of success. He was in the hotel to have dinner with clients.

The receptionist had handed me my room key by this time, so I indicated that I ought to go.
"You look well", he commented.

"Thank you", I smiled graciously. I knew I did.

We both turned and walked away...my confident strides took me around a corner that presented me with the entrance to the underground car park. I peeked my head back around the corner, checking he had gone. The guy behind reception chuckled and silently pointed me towards the right route to the lifts. I grinned, knowing I was giddy from adrenalin; I couldn't believe what had just happened.

As I got into the lift I pulled out my phone and brought up Jen's number - I was bursting to tell her the news. From the background noise, I could tell she was in her car when she answered. "Guess who I have just bumped into at my hotel", I said very deliberately. There was a pause. It was then that the screaming started: "NOOOOOOO?! OH MY FUCKING GOD! NO WAY!!". She knew there was only one person whose significance would cause me to call her with such excitement.

I'd reached my room just as she was squealing and shouting profanities. I grappled my way in whilst keeping my phone to my ear, as we allowed ourselves to take it all in. I recounted events several times over at Jen's request; by this stage, she had pulled her car over and got out to avoid swerving off the road. She was the only person who would truly understand the importance of that moment, professionally and personally, but not least to my recovery. I'd faced him. I'd confronted a fear of running into him that I hadn't realised I'd been carrying with me. I'd always imagined the next time I saw him would be near where we both lived and somewhere in my tortured thoughts he'd always been holding hands with his wife, that worst-case hadn't materialised. Instead, it was so much better. It was just me and him, face to face, like that first night he kissed me, but this time I stood there as his equal - maybe even more than that. I was composed, articulate and unafraid.

When Connor joined me later, we went downstairs for some food. "I fancy a glass of Champagne", I declared. He looked a little surprised but agreed to join me. As I sat there with my younger, good looking companion, sipping my drink, Brad walked past; undoubtedly he saw us, but neither of us acknowledged the other.

Fate. Karma. Closure. Call it whatever you will. It drew a line.

FOURTEEN:

HOTLINE TO HIM

Whilst I tried to escape from my true emotions by falling into yet another secret relationship, this time with a younger man, and topping that pretence of 'happy' up with buying sports cars and drinking Champagne, my world further diverged from that of John. He'd moved on in a different way by joining the local church. He'd always held religious beliefs that didn't resonate with me, but he'd not been a churchgoer thus far during our relationship.

Suddenly he'd found religion again and, more concerning, the church had found him. Far from what he seemed to think was comfort and solace, I saw it as desperation - both on his part and that of the church. He was young (relative to the rest of the dwindling congregation) and, in my derisory view, 'fresh meat'. Soon he was their treasurer, attending every event, and began taking the necessary steps to become a lay preacher. It quickly took over his life and I'm not saying that the people weren't being genuinely welcoming, but he had no respite from it. Neither did I. He talked incessantly about all things religion, to the point it was rammed down my throat every time I saw him. We couldn't even watch the TV without him proudly telling me about how which presenters were practising Christians - like that somehow made them better people. It tapped directly into my persistent self-perception that I was the scarlet woman. Fallen. Shamed. Juxtaposed against his 'holier than thou' victim persona, I felt wretched by contrast. I wanted to scream. I wanted to tell him to shut the fuck up! For an extremely long time, I pushed that down; I understood how hurt he was, how that was all my fault, how we no longer had a marriage in the proper sense and that was because of me. He was a genuine, lovely guy, who was kind; he'd loved me and was dealing with his grief his way.

When he started to regularly mention a young woman from the church, however, my ears pricked up; now I was curious. It had been sporadic at first, but her name was coming up with increasing frequency. She was training in accountancy and he began going to her house to help with her studies. He shared she was from Asia and married with a small child.

After a couple of months, I asked him how her husband felt about all the time John was spending with his wife, at which point he casually revealed that they'd split up and she was now living alone with her son, whom John was also spending time with. He showed me a picture of the child on his phone that she'd sent him. Now that was interesting. Alarm bells started to sound. Unfettered by what I felt were months of silent

152

chastisement, I was blunt with him: he was a meal ticket - a vulnerable, kind guy who was being sold a ready-made family idyll. Irritably, he told me not to be silly.

I'd been spending every possible weekend with Connor; making excuses that I was staying with Jen, my parents or my sister in order to be out of the house and away from the interminable sermon that seemed to be the soundtrack of my home-life. I came home unexpectedly, however, one a Saturday evening and the house was empty. Unusual. John never stayed out late and I began to get worried; for anything else we'd been through, his car crash remained imprinted on my memory. I messaged him to check his safety and whereabouts. I was concerned. And curious.

Following some time spent posted next to his bedroom window, the phone rang. He was okay. Safe. After a little skirting around it, he admitted he was at her house and would be staying the night. A seething set in. Now I appreciate that may seem hypocritical, but all I could think was that for years in our marriage he'd been unable to have sex with me, never made a move on me - I'd been like his little sister. Even after my boob job, of the several guys who had hinted, or outright asked, if they could take a look (or more!), he'd never been one of them! What was wrong with me? Why was I so repugnant? What did this woman have that I lacked? The hurt stung so badly in a quagmire of mixed emotions. After all, what right had I to feel any pain? Was this jealousy? Or just dented pride at the rejection? Was I relieved he was moving on? Did it assuage my guilt? Or was I annoyed? What did any of this say about my feelings for him? Whatever it was, it stirred emotions in me that I had long buried: I wasn't entitled to love him anymore.

The next morning after he'd done the 'walk of shame' into our home having, of course, attended church, a more composed version of myself told a sheepish John to be careful as she was (obviously I thought) using him. He disagreed. I laid the situation out to him as I saw it: a young, single mother in a foreign country meets a hurt, lonely more mature man with a good life and income whose wife has been unfaithful and cannot give him children. I know it might seem cruel because he is a wonderful guy and in no way should that be diminished, but I couldn't help thinking it was not borne out of love for him that she was offering him a vision of a perfect life. A life I'd failed to offer.

"Did you use contraception?"

He looked grossly uncomfortable.

"I have no right for it to make any difference to me, but please be careful - I have an awful feeling that you getting her pregnant might just be part of a plan to secure a life for her and her son. Just be clear about what you want. Don't fall into a trap you can't get out of".

He understood what I was saying, but he didn't think it was like that, she wasn't like that, that she was lovely. He offered to show me a photograph of her. Like somewhat that would prove it. Really?!

"I don't think so, John. That's a little bit like bringing home the used condom as a trophy! I'll give it a miss, thanks".

The confused paradox I felt of both caring about his welfare, yet hating what it was doing to me, remained. When he'd admitted that he'd slept with her and said that she made him feel wanted and needed, it was a knife straight through my heart. Not least because I recognised the desire for that feeling; it was exactly what I'd thought I'd got from Brad and what I was now indulging with Connor. She could give John everything that I could not - apparently that I couldn't from way back in our relationship, long before Brad arrived in our lives and blew them apart.

What she did do, to her credit, was instigate some deeper conversations between John and I. I shared with him some of the irrationality and hurt that the situation was causing me - the confusion about how he could do things with her that he obviously was unable to do with me. This honesty was a long-overdue conversation between us; issues and feelings we should ideally have discussed, but we'd both been doing our best to avoid like the plague. I said that I couldn't understand why he'd never initiate sex, didn't want to see my (new) body, never appreciated the gorgeous underwear that I now had the figure to wear. I deliberately omitted that this was exactly what Connor was enjoying in spades. John told me that underwear had never really done it for him, on anyone, that he'd preferred me naked. He'd never said before.

Whilst it was not my experience of the handful of other guys I'd been in relationships with, I guessed it made me realise that we are all different in subtle ways. I questioned him about what did turn him on, what he'd liked when we had sex, what he liked that this new woman did to him. I didn't get many answers, but what it shone a light on was how difficult he found it to discuss sex openly. For all the years we'd known each other, it was the first time we'd said this stuff - and the fact was he said very little at all. He just said that he felt that some of what I was describing sexually seemed potentially disrespectful for him to ask for. It provoked a sadness in me that he needed to repress this side of him. What I saw was how the tragic mix of a broken childhood home, staunch religious beliefs and familial abuse had left such a mark on him.

We seemed to have made some progress in crossing the divide between us. In fact, Jen said she thought that this was the beginning of us sorting things out and getting back together. I wasn't sure what to think. He clearly still loved me on some level, of that I wasn't in any doubt, but I felt unworthy of him, undeserving of his love or anyone else's. I was damaged goods both physically and emotionally - why would anyone want me? So we continued to do this dance with each other; we'd made progress in terms of opening up a little, easing some of the tension between us, but nothing about our relationship progressed in any other sense. I kept seeing Connor in secret, trying to enjoy it, even though he was getting more serious than I could cope with and I had to keep batting that away. Keeping it 'fun'. I wasn't up for falling in love or getting hurt; I liked the control I had over my emotions and him. It was different. It was what I deserved.

John's relationship with the woman from church meanwhile began to unravel. She became quite intense - I'd say 'obsessed', but John continued to disagree. With his inability to express how he felt for fear of hurting anyone, he led her on in my opinion. That aside, as he began to ease off, she was starting to make my assessment of her intentions look highly likely. By now she knew where he (we) lived. Yes, I know, John and I were still living in the same house together; I never claimed that anything about this was 'normal'. It was when I arrived home one day to homemade cakes hanging from the door handle that I decided I'd had enough. It was a desperate attempt to win him over and another gesture of her wifely credentials (and, of course, the way to a man's heart...), but I was seriously unimpressed. I'd been pretty patient up until that point, but this was too far; I asked him to show me some consideration as this was my home too. It was clear from his response that this wasn't the first time she'd shown up. I told him that if he wanted to be with her to that extent then he'd have to move in with her because conducting their relationship in my home was not going to happen. He seemed distinctly uneasy at that idea; evidently things for him were cooling down.

It was one Sunday evening when the situation escalated. The phone started to ring in the lounge, cutting across the sound from the TV. I turned down the volume on the telly as John answered the phone; it was highly unlikely that anyone would be calling me at home as my family and friends knew that these days my mobile was the safest bet. As soon as he answered it I could tell from his face that it was her - the slightly panicked, sinking expression said it all. So now she had our home number and thought it was acceptable to call that too?! I raised an eyebrow at him as he walked through to the kitchen; he ensured the call was respectfully quiet and brief. When he came back in he sat down with a sigh and confessed that it had got out of hand; he didn't want to see her any more as he didn't feel the way about her that she did about him, but in his efforts to be kind he was struggling to get her to understand and accept that.

About 10 minutes had passed before the phone sprung into life again. We exchanged a look - his was of fear, mine probably said what was in my head, which was: "What the fuck?!". His face swiftly rearranged into a look that could only be described as 'pleading'. "What? You want me to answer it?", I asked. Christ! I rolled my eyes, but a smile threatened on my face at this bizarre situation. Picture it: the wife, speaking to the mistress as across the room the husband sits looking like a frightened rabbit caught in the headlights.

Just as he'd dreaded, it was her. Her English was broken, although I was sure from what John had told me that she understood more than she claimed to speak. She asked to talk to him. I told her as clearly and as kindly as I could that he didn't want to speak to her. I had nothing to gain from being cruel to her. Rather, I felt sorry for her; she was just trying to do the best for her and her son. John had strung her along. Now he was being spineless and not facing into the consequences. I listened to the fragmented words as she declared her love for him. That was a little odd to hear. It looked like I was going to have to sort this out. I tried to let her down gently, but, in reality, she needed to understand that he didn't want a relationship with her. I tried to convey compassion in my tone, even though my words must have felt like daggers; I was acutely aware that it must have been so much harder for her to hear this from me. She was crying and I understood about heartbreak. There was nothing more I could do than to tell her I was very sorry and hoped she would be ok. I said goodbye. As I put down the phone I appealed to the God they shared in common to make sure she was safe. John looked suitably sheepish. I tutted, then laughed.

Shortly afterwards she moved away.

Meanwhile, I kept seeing Connor. He was, in some respects, good for my confidence. A good match physically, we made a handsome couple. On the other hand, however, he was emotionally needy, requiring constant reassurance and clarification about how I felt. The truth was, I felt very little. So much had happened to me physically and emotionally, I was kind of 'numb'. Although irritated. I felt that. Mostly when he cried. Goodness me did he cry! Sorry, that probably sounds unnecessarily harsh, but the waterworks came so often and so profusely that it was hard for my patience not to wear thin; it was so draining! "I love you". "Do you love me?". "What do you want from this?". "Where do you see this going?". "Why won't you tell me you love me?". Then would come the threats that it was over, followed quickly by the remorse (and more tears). When he got into one of those cycles, it drove me insane! This was meant to be fun, surely?! To the contrary, however, it became more like a game. A classic cat and mouse situation. The more he tried to pressure me, the more unruly I became; I'd been controlled and it wasn't happening again. He wasn't going to get the better of me. I knew he was being made to suffer for what others' had done.

Meanwhile, another relationship seemed to be blossoming for John.

෴

FIFTEEN:

TO ABSENT FRIENDS

A s one storm settled, another seemed to brew. It was all change at work. Jen had left after the endlessly difficult relationship with her functional boss had become untenable. I was desperately sad after so much had improved once Brad had left. The situation was particularly tough because by this stage Jen's husband was working for us too; he'd remained dignified throughout the difficulties she'd faced.

Not long after, another body-blow. Our new leader, who had transformed both the feel and performance of the site, had to leave very suddenly for personal reasons. I was gutted. They drafted in his replacement immediately from elsewhere in the business; unfortunately for me, this meant the return of one of my former foes. I was anxious as to what this would mean, but to give him his due, he cleared the air with me at the outset and I received reassurance that they didn't want me to leave. I decided to try and keep the positive trajectory I'd been on.

The next significant conversation with my new boss, however, was less positive. They had decided to remove Jen's husband from his role as they didn't feel he was performing. I'd never seen that. I was suspicious that this was linked to what had transpired between Jen and her line manager, who remained with the business, but I had nothing other than my intuition to back up my theory. My manager was abundantly clear that the decision had been made; there was nothing I could do to change it or persuade them into an alternative. I was devastated. In all that I had been through, Jen and her family had been there; they had supported me, laughed with me, seen the best and worst of me, and loved me regardless. I couldn't believe that this was going to be inflicted on them. My boss knew the history I held with them, so he at least asked me how I wanted to handle the situation. In doing so, he made it very obvious that if my loyalty to the friendship overrode my work, then my professional integrity would be shot to pieces. He didn't state it explicitly, but we both knew I'd lose my job. There were no misunderstandings. No room for compromise. It was a horrible situation; they gave me 24 hours to consider. It was an agonisingly impossible choice, but I had to put emotion aside and deal in facts first: I couldn't save him, no matter what I did. That was a certainty. So if I forewarned him, all that would happen was that we would both lose our jobs. I would likely be fired for gross misconduct and leave with nothing other than an irretrievable black mark against my career.

I returned to my boss and said I knew the decision they'd made was unalterable, so they had my assurance that I wouldn't tell anyone in advance and I wouldn't advise Jen or her husband in the aftermath. In return, I asked not to be involved in the situation in any way; it would need to be handled by HR from elsewhere in the business. He agreed. I felt sick as it played on my mind constantly; waiting helplessly for it to happen. By the end of the weekend, I was finding it unbearable, knowing I could say nothing. I had to settle for texting Jen to say I wanted her to know how much I loved her. It was the best I could do; my eyes filled with tears as I hit the 'send' button.

When it happened, my worst fears were realised; Jen was furious. I had expected her to be upset, of course, I had, but she blamed me, even after I explained the situation; she felt deceived and couldn't forgive me. The venom took me by surprise, but I understood how they must feel betrayed and had to accept how she felt, even though I believed that she wasn't seeing the impossibility of the situation I had been placed in. I simply had to give it time and not keep trying to explain myself. What had to matter above all else was that I was able to look at myself in the mirror and say if I had to make the decision again I'd stand by it. I could. If keeping my integrity meant that I had to lose their friendship it would be devastating, but I had to do what I believed to be right in the circumstances. It was a dark time. To lose them from my life left an enormous void - that special person to talk to, the one who got me like no-one else ever had. I couldn't believe after all we'd been through that it had come to this. For all of his malicious attempts, Brad had never been able to come between us, but now this had. I was so sad.

I continued to see Connor. Yes, his neediness annoyed me at times, but as long as I kept him on the emotional straight and narrow (which sometimes felt like a second job!), it got me out of the house and we went some nice places together. By saying I was seeing my family, I kept it from John. I think he didn't ask questions because he didn't want to know the answers. Ignorance was bliss. Any thoughts of us getting back together seemed to have evaporated. Besides, he was starting to form a close relationship with a woman he worked with; he spoke of her often and they seemed to have a genuine bond. She came to the house and I thought she was lovely. I wanted him to be happy and I hoped that she would be the person to succeed where I had failed. If he had found someone else it would lessen my guilt, which continued to take me to dark places I never knew existed inside of me. I carried the responsibility for what I had done with me everywhere; there was never a day off from it. I was an adulterer. I was a failure as a wife and as a woman. I was a liar and a fraud in my own life. A disappointment to my family, who, as much as they loved me, still couldn't understand how I'd destroyed my marriage. Neither could I. I didn't know how to resolve it all or to let it go, so the weight of it dragged my self-worth into the gutter. I was cried out. No more tears could be produced, I existed inside a shell that had once been me; it was like a prison. So I turned to my usual distraction - work - and piled more of that pressure on myself by starting to study for a Masters degree. If I couldn't excel in my personal life, then I would pull out all the stops to achieve at work.

After I began the course, things were all set to change yet again at work as the company was sold. It seemed there was no time for anything to ever be settled. The changes the new owners were making both to the culture and the expectation of how we'd work, which included removing members of my well-functioning team, I knew from before the transaction was finalised was not going to suit me. Fortunately, I had been head-hunted about a position whilst all this was taking place; it was a larger role and taking me back into an international remit, which would be good for my CV.

One of the distinct advantages of leaving my employer was that it brought to the end that chapter of my life with regards to Jen. The absence of her in my life had been immense, and had undoubtedly been what had pushed me further into the relationship with Connor. I took solace with him to take my mind off what I had lost: John's love, my family's respect, and Jen's friendship. I used him to hide from them all, and he seemed like the one person who was happy to have me and couldn't get enough of my presence. I was comfortable with why I'd lost Jen. I stood by the decision I'd made that led to this circumstance, and the passage of time had cemented that further in my mind even though the cost had been so high. That didn't mean the pain wasn't indescribable. So when, after many months had passed and she got back in touch, I was so relieved. Space and time were what she'd needed, we'd both needed after the things that had been said. We agreed to meet - on neutral territory - just before Christmas.

I was nervous about how it would go, but first and foremost I'd missed her terribly. Every day.

She just 'got' me and I yearned to share my world with her again - the good and the bad, and all the nonsense bits in between that made us both laugh. No-one made me laugh like her.

It wasn't the easiest of meetings, but it was a start. We had to talk about what had happened. We both spoke about how we felt; it was measured and reasonable though. I said I was sorry for how hurt they'd been, but I wasn't going to apologise for the decision I'd made. In an almost impossible situation, it had been the only real choice I'd had. Whether she liked it or not, Jen accepted that. We both knew that it would take more time for the hurt to subside, but seeing each other reminded us both of the friendship we'd had; it seemed like an awful lot to throw away on a company that had already put us both through so much. It turned out that she felt my absence as keenly as I did hers. The path back could have been slow and incremental, but neither of us was inclined to make it any harder than it had been; we were strong and loved each other enough to just move forward. I was so grateful to have her back.

∾

SIXTEEN:

SOMEWHERE OVER THE RAINBOW

As my 40th birthday loomed on the horizon there was, as ever, a lot going on in my world - keeping multiple plates spinning had long since become my way of coping with how I felt about myself; being busy helped me ignore the pain.

I was deeply into my Masters degree again. Work in my new job was also unrelenting. Oh, and by this stage, I had taken up learning to dance to the extent that I was now co-teaching it to a room of up to 150 people every Tuesday evening! As much as that overlaid extra time-pressure, I loved it, it was my happy place - it was the one place I showed up as me, not someone's boss, daughter, sister, lover, wife, friend. Just me.

Therefore, planning a birthday party to celebrate this milestone might not seem like the wisest thing to do, but doing what was sensible had long since gone out of the window. A black-tie, 3-course dinner for 80 guests with dancers and singers...yeah, let's do that! My family were clear from the outset that they wouldn't know where to start, so the arrangements were all on me. So just to make it easy on myself, I decided to perform a dance for the assembled crowd of my nearest and dearest with the guy who I taught with.

What this all meant, however, was the one thing I'd been putting off was going to have to be faced into several months prior: I would have to tell John about Connor. As my 'partner', I would be inviting him and his family - even though they hated me for the separated, used goods that I was. I secretly hoped if they saw me amongst my family and friends they might see something in the way I was cared for that might make them think better of me. Despite this scenario, it was unthinkable not to invite John, even though Connor was less than impressed at the idea. "It's my fortieth", I reasoned, "he's been a huge part of my life. He's my friend". I knew I could at least say that much about my relationship with John. "I can't 'not' invite him". I didn't want to upset Connor, or his family (ok, I was a bit less bothered about whether I upset them), but my night would lose something if John was not in the room. I had to tell him about Connor. I had to tell him that I still wanted him to come to the party.

It was awful telling John. I felt like I was betraying him once again. He was hurt. Sad. Yet in his typical way, he responded with limited emotion and a huge dose of pragmatism. In many ways, it made it worse. I wanted him to be angry, make a fuss...truth be told, I wanted him to fight for me. It didn't happen. He just seemed a bit resigned. But more than that, he still cared about me. He was characteristically gentlemanly about the party; he was prepared not to go if it was going to cause trouble, but I insisted. For him to have some moral support, I'd invited his aunt and uncle with whom we'd always been close when our marriage had been something more than a piece of paper and suggested he also bring a 'plus one'. He chose the lady from work, which I was pleased about; he deserved someone kind, who made him happy. As most of the guests were staying at the hotel where the party was to be held, I asked him whether they would be sharing a room. He was embarrassed (a good sign!), but declined that they would. What I sensed in the weeks before the party was that there was something new on the horizon for him, something had shifted, which I guessed was what the news about my relationship with Connor had freed him to pursue. This was good, I wanted him to find someone good for him, opposite to the way that I had been so bad.

With the party successfully out of the way, and my latest Masters assignment handed in just a matter of days before, it meant a couple of major items were ticked off my eternal 'to do' list and my head cleared a little. This meant that I could come up through the surface of the water, catch my breath and look around me. This was always a scary place for me to be... space to breathe meant time to think, but something was telling me that I needed to open my eyes.

John's behaviour had changed - there was a frisson about him that had not been there for a long time; I wasn't sure if it was positive or negative. Nerves about the impending party or something else...? Now I was able to observe it in a way I'd not allowed headspace for. We got into a discussion late one evening in the week following the party. As we talked he seemed agitated, distracted. When I once again watched him leap for his phone as it lit up, I was filled with a familiar sensation. I knew how that felt - the early excitement of something new. I asked him if he was ok and he said that he wasn't sure, that he was behaving in ways that were "out of character". I asked him what he meant, but he didn't seem to be able to articulate it; he couldn't find the right words. Something stopped him, but then he'd always struggled to talk about sex and relationships, so I understood that it might take time for him to be able to tell me how he felt.

It's hard to pinpoint exactly when all the pieces of the jigsaw fell into place; it happened so rapidly it seemed, once I allowed myself to think about it. To stand back and look with a clear head. And there it was.

The weekend after my party was beautifully sunny. I had a few chores to do, so I asked John if he fancied a trip into our nearest town; we'd often go out together for a bit of shopping or some lunch, such was where we were now at with each other. Aside from anything else he had always been great company (when he wasn't talking about the church!): funny, smart, interesting. It had gradually become easier to hang out with him.

As we walked down the main street, I remembered something I'd learnt about how standing side-by-side with someone was a better way to approach a difficult conversation - less confrontational than face-to-face. I'm not sure why it came to me at that moment, but it did and I began to speak:

"Who's Gary?", I asked.

"Ummm. He's a friend. "

"Oh, you've not mentioned him. How did you meet?"

"Errr...through work."

"Oh? What does he do?"

"He's in recruitment. I met him at a conference."

"Ok, right. That wasn't what I was expecting you'd say."

"Oh. What did you think I was going to say?"

"Well, he's popping up on your phone quite a lot. I thought you were going to tell me that you're in a relationship with him."

Silence.

We kept walking.

"And what if I said that I was?"

"I'd say that would make a whole load of things make a whole lot of sense."

"Ah."

"Would you like to go and get a cup of tea and tell me all about it?"

"Yes," he said. "I think I'd like that".

We sat tucked in a quiet corner of our favourite teashop; today it was as if we were the only two people there. We were face-to-face now as he told me everything, the relief in him was palpable as he spilt his secret into the small space between us. He'd been holding onto this for a very long time. Not his fledgeling relationship with Gary, but that he'd known since the age of 14 that he was homosexual; he'd realised that his feelings for a boy at school were more than just friendship, although he said nothing had ever transpired between them.

I listened as he told me how he'd never been able to consider voicing how he felt or admitting to who he was. Separating our relationship from it, I was desperately sad for him. To hide those feelings, to have to lie to everyone, especially to those you love the most, must have been an unbelievable burden. He'd told me much over the years about his abusive stepfather - a malicious, manipulative paedophile who, John now shared, had often called him a "poof". How could he possibly have come out and proved that evil bastard right? I had to think too to a time when being a homosexual was illegal - back in the 1960s when John had been born. The law does not change attitudes, I knew that from my work - attitudes take much more time. In a family where one half was deeply entwined with the church, and the other involved a philandering father, it was not hard to imagine how in these tightly woven communities concealing who you were had seemed like the easier choice.

I asked him why he'd not come out when a friend had at University, but he said he'd been horrified when that had happened; he'd seen it as the wrong thing to do. He said that his friend had "gone off the rails" a bit when it happened; that wasn't what John wanted. He wanted to be 'straight'.

He'd had another key opportunity, as I saw it, when

his first marriage ended. He was by himself, and the world had changed with regards to its acceptance. Yet, he needed to accept it to do that, and that was clearly where the barrier lay. To be honest about who you are requires an inner confidence and self-trust that was notably absent in John. For all his success and likability, he suffered from an Imposter Syndrome greater than anyone I knew outside of myself. It now all made sense - if one of the most fundamental parts of who you are is so carefully hidden from view, then the fear of being found out in every aspect of your life must be huge. To be constantly standing vigil, guarding against being caught out; I'd known for a while just a little of that feeling as I'd hidden my relationship with Connor, and I'd known how wearing that had been. At least I'd been able to share that relationship with other people - my family, a few of my friends - and it was, ostensibly, just a relationship, no great shakes there. To conceal, effectively, your identity - that was another level of anxiety. Only one person had known because they had shared John's secret. That person had died, so he was left alone to handle his emotions.

As I sat there listening, taking all of this new information on board, hearing all kinds of truths, I felt strangely calm with it all. If anything, my overriding feeling was of deep sadness for John; compassion for how this lovely man had felt compelled to lie about who he was. There was a relief too. Relief for me. Suddenly, so much started to make sense. I had never been able to reconcile what had been 'wrong' in my marriage that had drawn me to Brad. None of that had made sense, it had seemed so at odds with where I thought I was at in my life at the time, but now I could see in glorious technicolour what had been absent, what the void had been that I was trying to fill. Emotionally I mean. Not in the literal sense that you're imagining. Filthy! It wasn't that John wasn't doing it for me in the bedroom - to be fair at the start of our relationship the sex had been good - it was more holistically that our relationship was just comfortable, like a really good friendship.

When the menopause news had hit, I'd needed someone to make me feel like a woman; that, now for really obvious reasons, was never going to be my husband. He'd looked after me the only way he'd had at his disposal: he'd fed and watered me, cared for me, been kind, but failed spectacularly with what I needed. Now, I don't want to give the impression that I felt exonerated - I took full responsibility for the decisions I'd made that led me to have an affair, to hurt and deceive people I loved - but what I now had was understanding; an appreciation as to why that had happened. I had been searching for answers for the last 6 years.

I wanted John to be happy. He was worthy of that. It had eluded him all his life, at least for the last 40 years. If he had found that with Gary, then I was delighted for him. Genuinely. So I embraced that; we talked about their relationship and Gary came to stay twice at our house. We went out for dinner together. I liked him. He, too, was stepping into who he truly was for the first time, so it felt like we were all learning together and there was a strange kind of comfort in that; an honesty to it.

If only it was that simple. For John and Gary, it didn't work out. In many ways that wasn't a surprise; it was their first proper gay relationship, and for Gary, who was a similar age to me, it was his first real relationship ever. That was a lot for them to overcome. The end of the relationship left John hurt and panicked; he was vulnerable to what I think he saw as yet more failure and rejection. As much as I had been grappling with learning about his sexuality and dealing with the, often uncomfortable, answers to the many questions I'd had, I'd felt like I had some kind of stability in myself about it. I was handling it calmly and with maturity. That changed in the immediate aftermath of the end of their relationship.

In his panic, John began to overshare with me. He was instantly on a dating app, and within a couple of days of it finishing with Gary, he was set to meet a guy for a first date near where he worked. I counselled caution; it seemed very soon I said to him, and perhaps he should give himself some time to let this new 'him' settle in before bringing yet someone else into the mix. I could tell as I spoke to him that my reasoning was having no impact - he was gone, lost to this new freedom; he was running across the uninterrupted landscape of what he saw as the real him. I recognised this feeling, which was why I also knew it was dangerous territory; it was false security to think that the shift could be made so easily. When he returned from their first date completely giddy, I knew there was trouble brewing; his head was gone and any logic was redundant.

By this stage, I was in the throes of writing my dissertation for my Masters. It was a lonely process under any circumstances, but having to take 6 months out of my course near the start when I'd changed jobs, I was now not undertaking this alongside my course peers; they had all finished and, understandably, were not in the mood to extend the support network beyond the allotted time they'd recently had to endure it. Coupled with that, my job was relentless - the demands on my time were extensive. The only good thing was that my role had changed, and they had agreed that I could be based from home, which meant that apart from when I travelled to Ireland (which was once or twice a week to be fair to me) then I could not waste time in the car every day making the nightmarish journey from home to the office. So I got myself into a routine of getting up and starting work on my dissertation at 5am, working until 7am when I would shower and have breakfast, and then working from 8am through to about 6 or 7pm when I would start my studies again and collapse into bed sometime between 11pm and midnight. Get up the next day and repeat. Weekends now would often be 8-12 hours study on each day (and spent at Connor's house trying to pay him attention and pacify him).

In this regime, the last thing I needed was any trouble from John, and as his relationship with this new guy, Andy, took off rapidly, I did try to tell him that and appeal to his better nature. I was wasting my breath. Within days Andy had our home phone number and called one evening after less than a week of them meeting.

I sat in the study trying to concentrate, but unable to avoid hearing John's end of the conversation; he was giggling like a pubescent schoolgirl and it was making my stomach turn. This wasn't about whether the person on the other end of the phone was male or female, this was about respect and dignity. Perhaps I had no right to demand that of him, but for whatever else I might have done, I had always tried to be discreet. I was stressed, and furious - mostly because this guy, who we knew nothing about, had our home number and, when I asked John whether he knew where we lived, I could tell by his body language that he probably did. My safety was everything. I was livid. John tried to tell me that it was all fine, that Andy was lovely. The more he tried to reassure me, the more alarmed I became. Now, don't get me wrong, bad stuff can happen to good people, as I knew only too well. It was just that as John described him, he was the kind of person that ordinarily would have been repellent to him: bankrupt, poorly educated, no ambition, tattooed, a smoker, and even John expressed a bit of a worry about how much he drank.

"Can you hear yourself when you say those things about him?", I snapped at him. "If I came home and said I'd met a guy and described him like that you'd be locking me indoors and saying I mustn't ever see him again!".

John stammered a bit; he knew I was right, but he desperately didn't want to admit it to either of us.

"You're in lust, John; it's clouding your judgement!".
There was no telling him.

The following week, my anger still simmering as he started to come in and out of the house at all hours so that I never knew whether he was coming home at night or not. In itself, that shouldn't have mattered, but in a remote countryside location where my current life was making sleep a precious commodity, it did matter. I was at home at the end of the week when the post arrived at lunchtime. There was quite a thud as it came through the door, so I went downstairs to see what had arrived. Amongst the usual junk nonsense was a large white envelope weighed down with documents. It was addressed to John with a postmark from the city where I knew Andy lived. I was immediately suspicious. I opened it even though it wasn't for me. What I pulled out I was not prepared for. It was a set of tenancy agreement documents for a property - in John and Andy's names. It was less than 2 weeks since he had first met this guy! This was not the only shocker. The reference address that John had used and which appeared also on the formal contracts, was my home address. I say it was 'mine' because a couple of years before John and I had purchased the house next door to our cottage as an investment to renovate. To do this we'd had to get a mortgage in his name on that property and put the existing mortgage on the cottage we lived solely into my name.

I appreciate these facts are probably really boring, but it's so that I can explain that the address he'd given as a contact point for this contract he was setting up with his bankrupt lover was the one for which I was solely accountable - as far as my bank and the law was concerned. To say I was seething was an understatement. He was lucky that I barely knew my way around our kitchen, let alone to the knife drawer. I was so angry, I was possessed. I called him at work and screamed down the phone. I was apoplectic that he would risk the security of my home for someone he didn't know. How could he?! I felt so betrayed. It lifted the lid on all the betrayal I felt.

All my grief began to pour out. These hours and days became the darkest. I cried until there was nothing left to give. Huge, heaving sobs that consumed me… screaming sobs that left me on the floor with no energy. I thought it was going to kill me; I felt like I was dying from the inside out. It was the loss of everything; it all rolled in on me like storm clouds. The only analogy that I had for it, was that it was akin to waking up on your 18th birthday to be told by your parents that you were adopted. It had all been one enormous lie, and everything that I'd known for the prior fifteen years with John was shattered. How could I rely on any of it? Had he ever loved me? Had it all been a facade? All that time we'd spent with my family, how much they had taken him in and given him stability when he'd had precious little in his life - all thrown back in our faces. Had he ever wanted to be there in the first place? Our wedding. Each anniversary. The heartfelt cards, the letters, and words. I went and found them, poured over them and looked for clues - were there signs that I should have seen? Every conversation, every significant occasion...it all rattled around in my head, robbing me of sleep and stealing my sanity. I looked at the photographs round our house and hated myself even more - how could I have been such an idiot?! The shame I felt about my menopause and my own body's failures came back a thousand-fold; I was so embarrassed that I wanted to curl up and never leave the house again.

Yet it was more than that. It was where it had led me to from there that I couldn't forgive him for. The affair, the destruction of my view about myself and how I had thought I behaved; that had all been torn apart when I got swept up by a man who made me feel like a woman again because I had an unmet need that my husband had failed to fulfil. Then there was the heartache that had come with the dawning realisation that Brad was never going to come good on his promises of marriage and a life together; that I'd been played for the fool and had to turn up at work every day and stare that humiliation quite literally in the face. What that had put me through, Jen through and my family through. And there was the thing. My family had all believed that it was my fault, that I was wrong, bad, trouble...they, my father, in particular, had said they were disappointed in me.

All the grief of these emotions was overwhelming - because John had stood at close quarters and watched what that had done to me. It had crucified me, but he'd stood there and stayed silent, knowing that it wasn't because there was something wrong with me, that I was ugly or unattractive or a bad person or incapable of being loved - all the things that I'd been telling myself for the last 6 years. I'd taken every ounce of blame and he'd let me. I'd pushed the self-destruct button and he'd just watched the show for years as I'd got into one harmful encounter after another - with family, with 'friends', with men - but mostly with myself. He couldn't possibly have loved me; no-one could do that to someone they loved.

When I looked back I felt like he'd stolen my life for his selfish means. Fifteen years of my life. The best fifteen years of my life. Gone. Everything that was contained within it tainted forever with his lie. I was, as the internet advised me, a 'beard'. Oh, the shame of it. It had a name, it was a 'thing': women who are used as a cover for a man's homosexuality. I suddenly belonged to this elite gang with whom I desperately didn't want to be associated. I hated it. I was so furious that this even existed and that John had made me a fully paid-up member of this group.

All the details that he'd excitedly shared with me about his new sexual encounters - they stuck in my brain like sores now and I felt sick. Throughout our relationship, he'd been toe-curlingly coy about discussing sex, but here he was showering me with details like they were confetti. He even told me that any time I'd commented about a guy I believed to be good looking on the TV that he'd had to stop himself from joining in with appreciation. It was both morbidly fascinating, yet very damaging. I wanted to open the closet door, shove him back in it and lock it. Not, I must be clear, because I had a problem with anyone being gay (before everyone gets excited and starts gathering outside my home with torches and pitchforks), but because he was a gay man who had chosen to marry heterosexual women. Twice. It wasn't even that... it was at a much more local level - it was the fact that he'd done it to me. I felt used in a way far worse than any man had ever subjected me to. I felt utterly worthless.

The shouting match that ensued at home about the tenancy agreements must have been heard across the whole village. I pushed him so hard with my words that he squared up to me at one point; momentarily I was terrified. I screamed like a banshee, pure fear fuelling me. "Don't you fucking dare!", I yelled; it passed as quickly as it came, but in that split second my body had responded instinctively to what it had perceived as a genuine physical threat.

The point of contention was that I believed that the tenancy agreement and how that bound Andy and John together, put our shared assets at risk. If they fell short on the rent or things turned ugly between them and they'd been living together, then I imagined it could get messy if Andy was to stake a claim to a certain standard of living. As I stood in front of John I found myself in a take on the famous Mrs Merton interview with Debbie Magee. I yelled, "What do you think first attracted the bankrupt Andy to the six-figure-salary-earning John?!". He told me I was being ridiculous, that I knew nothing and was an idiot to think that there was any risk. I felt humiliated and chided like a small child. He'd always managed our finances and legal affairs; he knew much more than I did.

Something still wasn't sitting right with me a couple of days later when I had cause to respond to a call from our solicitors regarding the signing off of our wills; with three properties between us and a marriage that neither of us was minded to dissolve, we'd known for a while that we needed to ensure that things were taken care of. I mentioned to the solicitor on the phone about the situation with John and Andy, and their plan for the rental property. My emotions were conflicting when the solicitor said I was right to raise it; that I was correct in thinking that Andy could stake a claim on our shared estate once they were living together. On the one hand, I was vindicated for having my concerns and cross that John had tried to dismiss that there was even an issue. On the other hand, I was scared that this may already be getting out of control because John had been clear when we'd argued that the flat arrangement with Andy was going ahead regardless of my ridiculous ideas. Time was not on our side and I was determined not to end up at the mercy of this interloper.

I'd be lying if I wasn't slightly self-satisfied when I called John and gave him the news: "the solicitor is going to also get a property expert, as well as a family lawyer, involved because we need to discuss the entire situation", I informed him. "Oh. Right", was all he managed on the other end of the line.

The enormity of it all, however, was taking its toll on me. Lawyers, grappling with legal complexities, as well as emotional ones, was yet another burden. I called Jen and for the first several minutes she couldn't understand what the problem was as I was sobbing so hard. I couldn't get my words out in any kind of coherent sentence to help her understand what had now transpired. Eventually, I managed to tell her about the tenancy documents, of John's plan to live between the property with Andy and our home, and about what the solicitor had intimated about the legalities of this. She was, as ever, the light in my darkness.

With an incredible knack of getting to the heart of an issue, even when that was tricky, and delivering the news with kindness, she told me exactly what I knew to be true.

"You cannot remain in this situation; it's doing you so much harm", she said gently. "It's been making you ill for a long time; I don't know how you've coped really", she continued. "You need to bring it to an end. I think you know what you need to do, Lovely".
"I need to ask him to leave", I choked out through my tears.
"I'm sorry, but you do".

I started to cry again.

"Why don't you write it down? Tell him how you feel rather than have to face him".

It was the best advice; I couldn't face another showdown with him and I certainly wouldn't have got my feelings out in any kind of lucid manner. I spent the day writing that letter; it was the only thing I managed to do. It was the hardest thing I had ever had to do up until that point in my life: I was sending away the person I had committed that I would love until the day I died. Whatever else had gone on between us, when I married John I had meant those vows; that I would love him forever. Yet here I was, turning my back on that and him, but I had to for my own sake. As I wrote in the letter, I could no longer be a spectator at this car crash and instead, because of my love of him, I was having to hold his feet to the flames.

૭

SEVENTEEN:

THREE'S A CROWD

I left the letter to John on the kitchen table at the cottage one Friday morning. Next to it was the CD of the song that we'd chosen for our first dance at our wedding; I wanted it to have some significance to him. I knew that he was coming back that evening and I wasn't going to be there.

I was meeting mum and Emma for our annual Christmas shopping trip; it was late November and I'd still not told them about John's sexuality since I'd found out at the end of May. They loved him, and I knew that this would break their hearts. Somehow me being the fall-guy for the breakdown of our marriage had gone on so long that I wondered if it might be easier for me to keep taking the blame rather than throw this grenade into the mix. Whilst I did eventually confide in Connor, I'd not relished it; he'd never liked John and saw him as a threat in his perceived battle for my affections. I think he thought that I would fall in love with him if I stopped loving John, so understandably he was having to fight hard not to look like the cat that got the cream when I told him.

The preceding weeks had been tough with John, and leaving him the letter as I set off for this shopping expedition had left me drained; I was on edge wondering when he'd see it. I was anxious as I entered the café where we always met; mum and Em were already there and had got me the obligatory Earl Grey tea. I thought I was fine, but as I sat there I could feel myself teetering on the edge of tears. It was when, amongst the chitchat, that mum said they'd bought presents for John for the last six years, but she was struggling to know this year whether she should buy him a present or not... she'd not even fully finished her sentence when I exploded in an almighty sob. I couldn't contain it any longer. There I was crying my eyes out in the bustling café, with customers staring, whilst mum and Em looked confused about what was the matter with me. Once I got the crying under control I told them everything – about John's sexuality, Gary, Andy, the flat, the lawyers - it all poured out in a continual purge of words punctuated with sobs.

They waited patiently until I'd finished, each one cuddling me. Mum said that she'd known deep down that something wasn't right; she said that when our marriage ended she'd just not been able to square the circle as to why I seemed to have just given up on it. They weren't so much shocked as cross, with mum acknowledging that she and dad had always blamed me for the break-up, but saying they had always loved me. I started to cry again, "but you said that dad was disappointed in me". "Oh, Darling", she said, "he was disappointed that your marriage was over, we both were, we loved John, but we're not disappointed in you".

The relief I felt at finally sharing the news with them left me completely drained, but it was a weight lifted from my shoulders - now they could see the situation for what it was and not how it had appeared for the last six years. I knew it would take time for them to process the change in perspective, just as it had done me, and that there would be more discussion and questions to come. They would no doubt go through a range of emotions as I had, so I was glad that I was at least a little way ahead of them to help them through it.

Having read my letter, John acknowledged it by text; he requested a couple of weeks to get himself sorted and move out. On one of the days that he was taking another car-load of his personal belongings, we both went to get the legal advice we'd argued about. In the room with us round the table sat three lawyers: the Will expert, the Property lawyer and a Family specialist. It would have been funny, like sitting there with the three wise monkeys, had it not been so tragic.

As we talked through the situation I felt unbelievably calm. Upset, but calm. I wasn't going to make it easy for him though: I made him explain to the assembled panel the situation we found ourselves in and why. It was time he started facing into who he was, not because he had anything to be ashamed of as a gay man, but because he needed to understand the consequences his lying had on others. I was no longer prepared to cover for him. What we needed, the lawyers advised, was a cohabitation agreement - a bit like a prenuptial agreement; it would mean that Andy would sign away any claim to our assets. Who was the idiot now, huh? Time was of the essence, they said, and it would rely on John now persuading Andy that he should sign it; the tenancy agreement was already in place and they had moved in. John assured everyone that getting a signature would not be a problem.

After the meeting, we walked back through town to the carpark; it was the same route we'd walked six months earlier in the sunshine. How much can change in such a short space of time, I thought. I began to cry, the pressure of trying to hold my tears back in the lawyers' office had just become too much. I still couldn't believe that I was having to ask him to leave; that I'd been driven to it because of his stupidity with Andy, and that despite all his protestations that this was the guy to truly make him happy. Pride would prevent him from admitting that for some time I suspected, but I knew him, as a person at least, and I knew that stimulating his loins and not his brain would only satisfy him for so long.

We said an awkward goodbye, but as I drove along the motorway on my way to see Connor my phone rang. John said that he felt completely wretched.

"In that room, all I could think was here is this beautiful, intelligent woman sitting in a lawyer's office, being completely reasonable, mature and dignified, and these lawyers must be looking at me thinking what an absolute bastard I am. They must have been thinking how on earth could he be leaving her to run off with another man".

"That you'd only known for a fortnight", I added. My dignified composure had started to crack.
"Well, yes", he said awkwardly. "Andy isn't a bad person. He's a good person".

My silence was all the response he needed.
He started to cry.

"I'm so sorry that I've hurt you. I never wanted to do that, you don't deserve it. I sometimes think it would have been so much better if I'd died in that car accident, then you would have been spared this."

"I agree. It would have been so much better. Then I never would have known and I'd have got my life back. You stole my life. You stole it for your benefit. I could have met someone else, had a proper marriage, a life with someone else who would have loved me as I should have been loved!"

"But I do love you. I've always loved you. I've been the happiest I've ever been with you and I don't regret a single moment of the time we've been together. The reason I never told you before now was that I was terrified of this - terrified I'd lose you. You're my soulmate."

We were both sobbing now.

"Well, you're not mine. You cannot love someone when you're prepared to do this to them."

I hung up.

He left the following weekend for the last time. I was away overnight at my work Christmas Party, which we agreed was a good opportunity for him to come to the house and get the last of his things. When I arrived home late morning on Sunday he'd done as we agreed: as I pushed open the front door I saw his key lying inside on the mat. I picked it up as I brought my bag into the hall. With the key still in my hand, I walked into the kitchen and sat down on the sofa. Alone and able to just let it all go I sobbed. It was over. He was gone.

I'd lost my soulmate. And my heart was officially broken.

&

EIGHTEEN:

YOU CAN RUN, BUT...

As much as hiding under my duvet for the rest of my life might have been preferable at this point, I still had reasons to get up and out of bed. Sometimes those even extended to going out of the house.

I was still in my gruelling dissertation-writing/study regime, which now entailed going out first thing in the morning whilst it was still dark to fill up the bird-feeders in my garden. Living in the countryside I was lucky enough to get the most amazing array of wildlife and it had, I'll admit, become a bit of an obsession. I'd officially morphed into crazy bird lady! There I would be with my coat on over my pyjamas and my wellies on, striding around the garden at the front of the house with seeds, peanuts and mealworms. Well, what the hell, no-one was going to want this 40-something wife of a gay guy were they?! So fuck the lot of you, I'll look how I like! Thank goodness that I loved the wild birds so much, otherwise I was at risk of getting cats and then the situation might really have deteriorated. To be fair, the dishevelled bedtime look only extended as far as the early morning feeding routine and I was still managing to pull myself together when I actually had to go somewhere.

Suffice it to say John and I continued to share some very difficult conversations; I was desperate for answers to try and make sense of this madness. Some awful things were said on both sides - vindictive words that reopened wounds, but at that point, I felt entitled to use him as a punchbag. In reality, it just made me feel worse, but for a while, I couldn't help myself because I wanted him to understand how much I hurt; I wanted him to feel the same.

What was happening was that so much of what I had failed to deal with was rearing its head - the pain around the menopause, the childlessness, the affair - I sometimes wondered how many tears a person can cry in their lifetime. If there are too many, do they eventually dry up? Despite it all, however, some force kept me going as I never missed work or my studying. I was running purely on adrenaline, as my deepest fear was that if I should stop, as every part of my body was screaming at me to do, I would not be able to pick myself back up again. I paid no attention to my needs. I was not sleeping, barely eating, not taking care of myself, but just continuing to push when the effort to do so was peaking at its most difficult.

Maybe it was a stubborn streak, but I grabbed hold of this invisible force. My dissertation was giving me some purpose and without that to focus on I wasn't sure where I would be. I let my anger propel me every day; he wasn't going to ruin this for me and undermine all the hard work and great grades I'd achieved so far. Which is why, when John offered to help proofread my dissertation, all 40,000 words of it, I took him up on the offer and made sure he stayed true to his word to help me.

A matter of days after I handed in the dissertation, John's Grandmother died; she was in her nineties and had been the matriarchal figure in his life. I knew that he would be pragmatic, but devastated. He called to tell me and I meant it when I said I was sorry for his loss. For him, I was sorry. Yet when he asked if I was ok, however, my heart felt like a stone.

"Why wouldn't I be ok?", I asked.
"Because you'd known her for a very long time," he said.
"The reality is that I'd not seen her for seven years because of what happened between us. She thought I broke your heart. I was the one in the wrong."
"She never thought badly of you," he said gently; always the diplomat.
"You were the golden child, your family know that. Yet she's died never actually knowing you, hasn't she? You were too afraid to tell her the truth about who you were because you were worried it would change what she thought of you."

It was cruel. I knew it was, but I couldn't help myself. The woman it had been impossible to win over, who had never deemed anyone was good enough as far as John was concerned, had died without hearing the truth. He'd put off telling her, despite my previous challenges to him to do so, and now it was too late.

John insisted that she would have been fine about him being gay. I was far from convinced. Even my mum said, "His Gran loved to boast about him, but I bet she won't be running out into the street to tell the neighbours about this!".

So when he called to tell me about the date and time for the funeral, I was horrified to learn that he intended to take Andy with him.

"What the fuck, John?!", I said to him, "She'll be spinning in her grave before she's even in it! You're using the opportunity of your Grandmother's funeral to introduce your gay lover to your family?!".

Yet the decision was made.

I strode into the church looking like the mistress in a TV drama - the full-on 'other woman' (or 'person' in this case!). All high heels, red lipstick and oversized shades. I was ready for whatever they had to throw at me. John's dad, whose relationship with his erstwhile mother-in-law had been fractious, to say the least, was already waiting in the crematorium's 'holding pen' with John's younger sister. "Have you come to make sure she's actually gone too?", I said. I always knew how to raise a laugh out of my beloved father-in-law.

As the room started to fill eventually the funeral cortège pulled up outside. Shortly after a guy joined the room who was talking in a loud whisper and saying that John was "walking in with Gran". Andy. My blood started to simmer; how dare he talk with such familiarity about a woman he'd never met. It was all in such poor taste. I started to wonder if this was such a good idea when my Mum's words came back to me from the previous day. Not one to usually encourage confrontation, she'd instructed: "If you go, don't you dare hide at the back! You go and sit at the front and take your rightful place amongst John's family!". So I held my nerve as I slid into one of the front pews, smiling to myself as John and Andy were relegated to the row behind. I could see the gesticulating in my peripheral vision and knew that John was informing Andy who I was.

Afterwards, I stood outside on my own, glad for some fresh air, and to see the sunshine again, not least because it justified my sunglasses and allowed me to hide how hard I was having to work to hold it all together in the face of John's family. I didn't want to upset them, but my indignation that for so long I had been considered the one at fault was just so all-consuming. This day wasn't about me, but 'me' was all I felt I had now. I wanted some acknowledgement. Recognition. I wanted them to tell me that they knew it wasn't me who'd been wrong. This wasn't the time or the place, I knew that, but I wanted my presence to tacitly communicate that I no longer had anything to be ashamed of. Out of respect for everyone, and for the sake of my sanity, I gave the wake a miss; I needed to go home. I'd no longer hidden in the background and that was good enough.

All my efforts with my dissertation paid off. A couple

of days after my birthday I heard that I had gained a 'distinction' grade for it and had gained the highest score on the course across all my assignments combined.

At work meanwhile, they had announced that they were moving all of their research and development work, as well as the majority of their support functions, over to a purpose-build facility in Ireland. It became inevitable that unless I wanted to move as well there wouldn't be a role for me in the long term. Whilst I had always fancied a stint working 'abroad', Ireland wasn't it.

For a while, however, it left me in the scary position of no job and the knowledge that I had my half of the mortgage payments to maintain on two properties. I was determined not to have to go to John and tell him I couldn't pay my way. There were opportunities out there, one in particular that I was keen on, but as ever with senior-level recruitment, nothing was happening quickly. I'd already resigned myself to the fact that it was unlikely that my next role would still allow me to be based where I was, so I'd opened myself up to opportunities across the UK. I was getting some good interest in my CV, so despite the immediate work situation, the sense of opportunity that these new beginnings brought were giving me reasons to be cheerful.

That was until Emma found a lump in her breast.

෴

NINETEEN:

MOVING NORTH. HEADING SOUTH.

The recruitment process for the job I wanted was dragging on interminably, such that I began losing hope that it would ever come good. Perhaps it was a sign? Maybe I wasn't meant to get the job based back in the North because I was going to be needed here; staying local, because Emma was going to need me. There were several lumps in her breast and she had been back and forth for tests. She'd always been 'lumpy', she'd had her first needle biopsy at the age of sixteen and several in the intervening years. It was a waiting game on that news too; combined they were driving me insane.

Then dad called: "Em has pre-cancerous cells in the lumps. They're going to have to operate and then there will be radiotherapy. They've also talked about whether a double mastectomy might be an idea, though, just to be on the safe side for the future; she said she'd do it if it meant she would live for the kids' sake".

He stopped speaking for a moment, I wasn't sure whether it was to allow the news to sink in with me, or to give him the chance to pull himself together. When he spoke again, it was to tell me that mum had been too upset to call me. I was worried that he too might start to cry. I sat down. I was only an hour and a half away from them, it was the closest I'd ever lived since leaving home at 19, but I now felt like there was a gulf between us as I couldn't put my arms around them to make the news feel even just a little bit better. Instead, my role at this point was to be practical and pragmatic. Matching my mum's upset wouldn't be helpful to my dad.

"Look, we have to see the positives", I said, trying to think of some whilst I said it, because right now the whooshing sound in my head meant I was finding it hard to conceive that there were any. "The cells are pre-cancerous", I managed to say as an opener, "which means that the news could have been worse", I continued. Dad agreed. "I know it seems bad at the moment, but if it was required they would be giving her chemotherapy; they wouldn't risk not doing that, I'm sure".

I wasn't entirely sure, but it seemed to make sense even though my brain was travelling at a thousand miles an hour. Dad again agreed. I felt desperate for him, he was trying to be strong for us all, when I couldn't help thinking that he shouldn't have to be. I tried to step into that space. "You're always good in a crisis", my Gran had said to me many, many years prior and as I reflected I thought that perhaps she was right. So I tried to step up now. "We have to just deal with the facts we have in front of us", I said, "and try not to think forward to a future scenario that we're not sure of. Don't let your imagination run away with you".

"I know, Lovie," he said, "it's just that Em is so upset and Rich said she cannot stop crying because of the kids. I don't think he knows what to do".

I waited until I'd put down the phone before I cried. It all seemed so fucking unfair! Em had everything to live for, aside from who she was as a person - smart, quick-witted, beautiful, kind - she had a husband and two amazing children. I would have done anything to swap places with her. It would have mattered so much less if it was me; the consequences would have been less catastrophic. I only had me to think about. No-one would end up without a wife or mother. I felt so guilty.

What if Em needed me to help look after her and the kids (and Rich, he was never shy in asking anyone to do stuff for him!)? Christ, I hoped for their sakes they didn't need me to cook meals! I'd started to wonder whether taking a role that was less demanding of me might be required for a while - take something local that allowed me to be more on hand. Whilst they were amazing, it was too much to ask my parents to step in and fill the massive void that Em being ill might create in the kids' life.

It was the day after Em's news that I got the call about the role I'd wanted: "We're delighted to tell you that the company want us to extend an offer to you for the job", the recruiter's voice was full of excitement. It certainly had felt like a long couple of months to get to this point. I couldn't believe it. It was wonderful and awful all at once. My mind was now blown - I'd prepared myself that I wasn't going to get this job, this wasn't how this was meant to turn out! My silence on the other end of the phone gave her cause to check I was still there.

"Yes, yes, sorry. I'm just really surprised", I said. I paused, and then, "and yesterday my sister got told that she is at risk of breast cancer - she has pre-cancerous cells". I couldn't help but tell her the truth. She'd been so great throughout this process and I now felt awful that her anticipation of a delighted me on the other end of the call had fallen suspiciously flat. She was wonderfully compassionate, "It's happened in my family, I completely understand. Take the day to get your head around it, and then call me tomorrow". I was unbelievably grateful for her kindness.

I called her back the following morning with a clearer head as I drove up to see my parents. As good timing would have it I'd arranged this visit a few weeks' prior. I welcomed the opportunity to see them - big hugs were in order. As I stood in my parent's hallway, we talked about the top priority for all of us: Emma. They seemed in a more positive mood now that the news had settled a bit and whilst Em remained understandably upset, they said that she was thinking a bit more pragmatically. They even managed to joke that Rich had already decided that if Emma died then I could just step in - in all departments of their marriage apparently! It was a long-standing family joke that he often offered to have sex with me if I needed it, which led to much eye-rolling from Em and giggling by my dad at his brazenness. So much for my father defending my honour!

"Anyway," said mum, "how are you?"

I winced a little as I said, "they've offered me the job". I waited for their reaction.

"The one you really wanted?", dad asked. I nodded slightly. "Then you should take it. Well done".

I could have cried as he hugged me.

"We're proud of you", mum said as she too put her arms around me.

"Thank you". I couldn't say any more as I was so choked up; all I'd ever wanted was to make them proud, to justify the chaotic place I felt I occupied in their lives. I wanted to not be 'trouble' now more than ever.

It was a huge relief to know I'd get some security back in my life again, and once I had that, maybe, just maybe, I could start getting my life back on track.

Due to the need to relocate and as we were heading towards Christmas, my new employer agreed to a January start. Then there was the matter of Connor, who had, I suspected, been hoping beyond hope that I didn't land the job; he didn't understand my passion for my work, why I tried so hard at it, or what drove my ambition. I knew that this would be make-or-break for us. In the first instance in respect of whether I was moving North by myself and then, when he decided to come with me, whether our relationship would stand the test of living together for the first time. We had plodded along.

As I reflect, the fact that there was so little of note to

write about him sort of summed us up really. We did 'nice' stuff. He was 'nice'. It was for that reason that I tried hard to love him. I told myself that this dialled-down emotion that I felt for him was perhaps what real love felt like; the passion I'd experienced in the past hadn't served me well, so it was a good thing to accept this more muted feeling. Whilst he remained needy and I felt like his parent rather than his partner at times, it was, in essence, uncomplicated. And the sex was good. I liked that; it was fun and was an element of our relationship that had endured from the outset. I pushed aside that it was the glue that had held us together, but if you'd put a gun to my head and told me to tell you what I truly thought - it was that we wouldn't survive our new life together. Despite his Irish roots, Connor had lived most of his life on the mainland and even then only within a small radius of where he'd grown up and his parents still lived; taking him away was going to be a big deal and I knew we'd both have to dig deep.

With John's consent, our cottage was put on the market; we agreed to keep the one next door and keep going with the renovation because it made better financial sense. In the meantime I found a house to rent in a town near my job; I'd lived there before so it seemed like the least hassle option. My well-honed house-moving skills kicked in. As the one that wasn't working and, let's face it, knew what they were doing, I took the lion's share of the responsibility for making it all happen. We were packing up two houses before taking their combined contents 250 miles North. What the hell, it would be an adventure!

January was freezing, not the most idyllic time of year to be relocating, but I was excited to have a fresh start all the same and be properly moving forwards. New year, new job, new home, new life! I'd told Connor that if he wanted to retrain to do something else then I would support him with that, so I tried to set him about thinking about what he might want to do career-wise and enthuse him about a whole new set of possibilities opening up before him. His current job certainly didn't seem to float his boat and he wasn't able to settle down to study for the exams that were required for him to progress any further. He didn't view the opportunity with quite the same enthusiasm, however, and I fast discovered he seemed unable to cope with the change as he proceeded to unravel.

I was loving my new job, but it was challenging to navigate my way through an unfamiliar company, a different role and getting to grips with a different team of people. Yet I was doing a day at work and then repeatedly going home to find that Connor had done nothing. Nada. Not around the house, not about finding a job, not sorting a meal for us. Nothing. Well, apart from lying on the sofa and watching TV or on his laptop. To begin with, I was extremely understanding - genuinely - I appreciated how hard it was that he had moved away from his job, his family and the few friends he seemed to sometimes hang about with.

As the days rolled into weeks and the 'Connor-shaped' dent in the sofa seemed to get deeper, I started to lose a bit of patience. I tried everything to motivate him: I help him with his CV, I looked at training courses, found him local recruitment companies, spoke to him endlessly about what he liked to do, what jobs might pique his interest…but nothing created a spark. I tried kindness. I tried tough love. I even suggested that he go to the doctors for some help with his lethargy in the end because I was all out of ideas and definitely out of energy. He was, as my sister would say, "a mood hoover". Having enjoyed my job all day, it was draining me to come home each evening to start again on another full-time 'job'. I was trying to hold together the house, our finances and my sanity as I felt myself slipping into the 'nagging wife' role. The latter certainly wasn't giving me any satisfaction as it just wasn't 'me'.

The further he regressed, and the more I felt like I was turning into his mother, the less attractive he became until I realised that our sex life had, as I'd suspected, been the only thing that had held us together all this time. Now that I found myself in a state of permanent irritation at his sloth-like self-pity, I was struggling to find things I liked about him. As someone once said, "it's the things that make you fall for someone at the start that are the things that make you want to leave them in the end". So true. His financial frugality, that I had gently teased him about, was now causing me significant stress. He'd rented out his house so he was financially neutral, whereas I was still paying my half of the mortgage for two houses. I'd even taken the company car option so that I could give him my nearly-new car instead of the knackered old heap he'd been driving for the last six years I'd known him. We were no longer going out anywhere as a couple as he constantly said he couldn't afford it, and as much as I could most of the time I was starting to resent having to get my purse out all of the time when I knew that he could contribute.

Things hit a low when I came home to find that he'd scratched the alloy wheels on my car. Now these things happen, goodness knows I've done it plenty of times myself! But when I asked him how it happened he denied it was him. He was a compulsive liar, even about the smallest things where there was absolutely nothing to be gained from lying; it baffled me. "You're the only person driving this car, how can it not be you?". He shrugged. I hated going on about money, it wasn't the most important thing, but right now in our current situation, it had increased in significance between us. I had to ask: "and who is going to pay for that?". "I thought you would", he said. My jaw dropped. I was speechless.

So when I got home a few days later to find there was no food left and I was up to my overdraft limit, I asked him if he could go to the supermarket and get some supplies. It was met with a refusal - again. So out I went, tired and cross, to sort yet something else. By the time I got to the shops, I was in 'sod it' mode. I stocked up on the non-food items we needed and went home. When I got back he started going through the bags and protested that there was nothing to eat. "You want to eat? You go and buy food", I said. Food and money were each of his Achilles heels - that would make him think. I felt horrible, but something had to snap him out of his stupor.

I knew it was over well before I went to America with work at the end of May. Before I left I'd found somewhere new to rent that was nicer, warmer and more spacious. I'd taken a week off work after the US trip because I'd been warned it was going to be tiring (it was, but also worthy of its own chapter: it was the most awesome, uplifting experience!). The week was designed to give me a few days to get over the jet lag and to get on with packing up the house - yet again.

Having travelled home for over 24 hours I was greeted by a miserable Connor who, I assessed as I walked through the front door, had managed only to mop the hall floor and put on a load of washing just before I arrived back. The rest of the house was dirty and messy. I checked the fridge: empty. The perspective granted by being away had done me the world of good; there had to be a better life than this. Connor wasn't good for me, and I wasn't good for Connor; our view on life was just so fundamentally different. I thought it was for living; he thought it was a means of saving up for your retirement. As I packed boxes I surreptitiously sorted my stuff from his; I needed to tell him it was over.

I sat him down and explained how this situation was making neither of us happy; he didn't seem to respond much, but he certainly didn't argue. I told him that he had 3 weeks before I moved to the new house to get himself sorted with somewhere else to live - either here, or by going back to his home. As the days and weeks ticked on, however, true to form, nothing happened. His apathy extended to all areas of his life. Eventually, he asked if could move with me to the new house for a couple of weeks because he wasn't sorted. I longed for a fresh start by myself, but I didn't want to be unduly harsh; I said he could come for two weeks and have the bedroom on the top floor of the townhouse. I told him he'd have to pay rent - no more free ride. He'd landed a temporary role (doing the same job as he'd had before we relocated) - so at least he was starting to earn money.

In stark contrast to the move North, this day was a scorcher. Connor disappeared off to work having helped only to pack his immediate belongings and lift a couple of heavier items into my car. I had moved a lot already, having cleaned every inch of the kitchen at the new place and filled most of its cupboards to make life easier on moving day; I had worked incredibly hard in the evenings and the previous weekend. The removal firm guys came up trumps. I explained I was by myself to which they said, "Don't you worry, Love, we'll look after you". All I needed to provide was copious sweet tea and the occasional bit of direction for various pieces of furniture; they took care of the rest. They were true to their word. In intense heat, they got the whole house sorted, making sure all the large pieces of furniture were assembled and exactly where I wanted them. When it came to Connor's belongings I told them to put all the boxes of his stuff in the garage. "Good for you – good riddance to bad rubbish," said one of them. I chuckled.

I adored the new place and, with the extra space, I barely noticed Connor hidden away on the top floor in those first few days. Very soon though, I began to feel like a visitor in my own home. One Sunday, around the two-week mark, he hid in his room all day; I found myself concerned that he was ok, so I went up a couple of times to check. By now I knew what an unravelling Connor looked like and this version seemed fine, perky in fact, which turned my concern into suspicion. When he finally appeared downstairs, later on, I told him his behaviour was making me feel uncomfortable; he claimed he was upset over us splitting up and was struggling to get it together. I didn't buy into that for a second; I knew what 'upset' looked like for him and this wasn't it.

When he next went out for a run I took my chances to take a peek in his room - it was my home after all - I looked at his phone and laptop; the most likely places I'd find evidence of what was going on. Sure enough – he'd spent the 'upset-because-we're-splitting-up' Sunday signing up to dating websites. Then he'd set about looking at cars to buy (after damaging my Mini and not 'fessing up, I'd traded it in). As I browsed his search history, he'd done absolutely nothing about finding somewhere to live!

I decided to have a bit of fun. Via his phone, I could get straight into his online dating account. I changed all his settings so that far from seeking women aged 29 - 39 years old as he'd specified (hang on a minute, he was nearly 40... 29 year olds??!!), he was now looking for the over 60s. Next, I re-specified his interests to include roller-skating, cheerleading and needlework. None of that would really 'bite' though and now I was on a roll. Money. That's what would hurt him. So I switched away from the 'free' dating service and signed him up for any paying option that it presented me with. I clicked 'Yes' to everything. I waited for the purchase confirmation email to come through... and deleted it. He was so atrocious with his personal admin it would take a while to clock that one.

It was with a sense of indignation later that evening that I thought, "what's good for the goose is good for the gander" and signed up to a dating site myself. I picked one geared to professional people, avoiding the sites that Connor was on. It was the first time I'd ever used one and I found the whole experience cringe-worthy and rather degrading, but I'd talked to numerous friends and understood that it was now how people seemed to meet, so I pushed on. I was in a good place now. I liked my new job and home, had lovely neighbours, and I had started to make some female friends. I was ready to meet someone else. I decided that being transparent on my profile was the best way forward. I wrote that I wasn't able to have children, but that being close my niece and nephew meant I was happy to meet someone with or without kids.

It wasn't long before I got chatting to a guy.

આ

TWENTY:

A DATING APP & A DIFFERENT CHAP

Online dating was more depressing than cringe-making. Now, don't get me wrong, I've not got tickets on myself with regards to how I look, but guys really do fancy their chances don't they? Having opted for a more 'exclusive' experience, I was disappointed. Sure, there were professional guys on there, but what I discovered was that whether they had a good job or a not-so-good one, many of them just wanted to know if they could bag a younger woman (my word, do they lie about their age!) and, basically, whether you would shag them. It all seemed like a 'dance' just to find out your answer to that. I thought there were specific Apps just for that?? I got plenty of 'likes' and comments/messages early on - their algorithm was designed to get you excited and keep paying the exorbitant monthly fee for the promise of a deep and meaningful relationship. I quickly got a bit despondent: is this the best I can hope for? I started wondering whether I should get a cat...

I couldn't bring myself to engage with those that had contacted me in the first few days; I decided to be discerning whilst I gauged whether those early shows were a benchmark of what I could expect longer-term. Then I received a 'smile' from a guy who looked much more promising. A genuinely similar age to me (finally) and one of his profile pics was decent; his bio sounded a bit more 'normal', down to earth. We started messaging and he seemed lovely. Funny, not taking himself too seriously. A father of three, he'd lived a life and that suited me. We exchanged numbers and, after a few more days texting, we arranged to speak on the phone.

One of the things I wasn't prepared for as I answered his call was such a strong accent. I was used to Irish thanks to my previous work environment and Connor's family, and also the earthiness of the accent in the North where I'd lived and worked, but this was much stronger and, as such, charming. It made the funny stuff he said even funnier because of the way he said it, the intonation amused me in its own right. As I sat on a patch of grass in the sunshine, we chatted easily. He seemed open, self-deprecating; at one point I laughed so hard that some passers-by looked around and smiled. I was filled with a positivity that reminded me that 'happy' was my default setting; he made me feel engaging too. He asked to meet for dinner, despite his stories about previous disastrous dates, saying with a smile in his voice, "I think I'll take the risk". We arranged the following Friday evening.

I thought carefully about what I was going to wear - trying to strike the balance between looking smart, not too overdressed, and a sprinkling of sex-appeal. It was a very long time since I had gone on any kind of 'date', so I tried to go with something that just made me feel good and a bit of 'fierce' for courage. As I drove to the restaurant in a local hotel, my main concern was that I wouldn't find him physically attractive in person. I don't want to sound shallow, but let's be honest, that stuff matters to some extent or another to all of us! I gave myself a talking to: "even if you don't find him good looking, you find his personality attractive and so you'll have a good night. Take it from there".

He got out of his car as I walked across the car park and I knew instantly that I needn't have worried. As he went to order some drinks I texted Jen - I'd told her about the date so that if I got abducted someone had known where I was. I wrote, "I like". I tried to relax into it, especially as he seemed nervous. The conversation flowed, however, and we both shared quite a lot about our lives. Unlike Connor, who had led a sheltered life and sometimes made me feel that I ought to wear my past like badges of shame, this guy, Simon, seemed to just accept that I too had a history. He took the 'gay husband' news with a bit of surprise and a good dose of pragmatism; he even laughed at my jokes about it given that by now it was the source of some of my best comedy material. He even took in his stride that Connor was currently still living in the top floor bedroom: "a bit like the madwoman in the attic from Jane Eyre," I said. "Life is complicated," he said, as I went on to explain that Connor had (finally) sorted out somewhere to live and was moving imminently. I hadn't anticipated ending up on a date quite so soon and certainly not before that was all resolved.

I was pleased that he'd felt relaxed enough to order the very sumptuous-looking burger and proceeded to tuck into it, slightly inelegantly. I liked the fact that he was just being himself. Once we'd eaten, the waitress asked if we wanted coffee and we seemed to agree automatically that we wanted to stay longer. "I'd like an Earl Grey Tea though, please", I said. As the waitress nodded acknowledgement, Simon said, "make that for two please". I was a little surprised and wondered whether he was doing that to fit in with me. If he was, he was about to get a shock - as much as I loved it, I knew my choice of tea wasn't for everyone.

We said our goodbyes that evening with just a peck on the cheek, but from what had passed between us I felt as sure that we would see each other again. A little bizarrely, I went home and cried; it was relief that I had spent time with someone who didn't judge me, for my past or my present. Having lived a long time under the weight of Connor's (and, let's face it, my own) condemnation, it was like it suddenly lifted. We just accepted each other's history; it had a maturity that felt befitting of the kind of relationship I wanted. It was always going to be likely that at this stage I was going to meet someone who had been married, had children, had relationships that were less than what they would have liked. I'd accepted that and it was great to find someone who understood that too.

It had gone as well for him as it had for me - he messaged the next morning to ask me if I fancied meeting up with him that afternoon. I was sorely tempted, it would have been lovely to see him again, but I already had plans that day. He was undeterred, asking if I would be free for Sunday lunch instead. I couldn't refuse that offer and set off into my day with a spring in my step.

In the car the following morning we fell into the same easy conversation of our first meeting. He was charismatic; attempting to be smooth, but falling short in an endearing way. We went for lunch in a beautiful pub - all quirky interiors and good home-cooked food. The landlord, who knew him, came over and put a lit candle on the table between us in a very obvious way. Simon looked embarrassed.

After lunch, he drove me along the clifftops to a small carpark so that we could walk along the beach. It was stunning - rugged coastline and hardly anyone else around. He told how he'd visited the area as a child and I could see why he'd bought a holiday home here - somewhere to make family memories. A romantic idyll maybe, but when he described it I could see his vision too. We walked back along the beach - he was animated telling me about the area's history. In his enthusiasm, he tripped over a rock in the sand, but I decided to pretend I'd not noticed. I didn't want to embarrass him, but I smiled inwardly at his charm.

We sat down side-by-side on the beach, looking out at the crashing waves, feeling the breeze across our faces. As we chatted intermittently, I thought he might kiss me. I realised that I hoped he would kiss me. He didn't. The moment passed. It got a bit cooler so we headed back up to the car.

What I'd discovered about Simon was that he was something of a local success story. He'd built a business, made a sizeable chunk of money when he sold it, and had invested that in properties. He was a smart guy with his head screwed on right and someone for whom my career wouldn't be seen as a threat. I was struck by how similar our view of the world was. As looked back out at the view from the clifftops I felt a calmness that had eluded me for a long time. So when he dropped me back at my car and still didn't kiss me - apart from a rather ill-placed peck on my cheek - I was a bit deflated. It had been a great day, but I wondered if I'd been friend-zoned. My geeky comedy turn could sometimes have that impact... well done me!

We continued to text extensively in the following days, however and arranged to meet for dinner mid-week. I decided to give it one last shot - he either fancied me or he didn't. I needed to know. I picked a dress that showed off my figure to its best advantage and coupled it with some heels; if this didn't decide it, nothing would. I stood up from the restaurant table to greet him as he arrived so that he could take me in. As our meal had come to an end and we sat there each with a cup of Earl Grey tea, he began to tell me that he liked me; the dress had worked. Like the fall over the rock, his words were a bit clumsy so I let him talk for a while to be sure of what he was trying to tell me. I liked him, so despite my calm exterior, I was holding my breath in the hope that my ears were not deceiving me.

As we sorted the bill the heavens opened - a heavy, late-Summer storm after a good spell of dry weather. "Let's make a run for it to your car," he said. We dashed across the gravel car park - me in my heels - and leapt in, laughing as we looked at how drenched we each were. He turned to look at me. "I want to kiss you, would that be ok?". I smiled and nodded. He licked his lips, which must have gone dry with the nerves, as he leant towards me. It wasn't the best kiss I'd ever had, but how I felt about him from the quick connection we'd built, it created electricity in me.

Things between us accelerated. He started to lay himself bare in terms of his past: what had and hadn't worked in his previous relationships, how hurt he'd been, and how he felt about his children; they were a huge part of his life, which I respected him for. He took his responsibilities and share of their care very seriously; he was obviously a very involved father.

He soon said he was coming off the dating app and deleting his profile completely; he asked me if I was up for doing the same. I was. He sent me screenshot proof that he had; it felt like a very definite, positive statement from him. I felt fantastic. He seemed to be able to anticipate my every move, want and needs; he listened intently and what mattered to me mattered to him. It was the small things he did - the attention to detail that took me by surprise. It was all so romantic that I was walking on air: I felt special, important. I felt seen. Heard. 'Chosen' almost. I was enjoying our little bubble of happiness, finding out about each other, lost in the whirlwind of it before the 'real world' would inevitably have to kick in. He was keen to see me again and asked me for dinner a week later at a restaurant near where he lived.

When I arrived at his house we both knew it was inevitable that we would sleep together that night. Neither of us mentioned it, but the tacit excitement of that knowledge spilt over into dinner, where we laughed and chatted non-stop. What I learnt that night was that as charming, confident and alpha-male as Simon appeared, his ability in the bedroom didn't match who he was outside of it. It came as a bit of a surprise that first time; quite contrary to everything else his self-assuredness had led me to believe. That he didn't seem to know what he was doing was, I have to say, a disappointment. The chemistry and my anticipation fell notably flat. I told myself, however, that in the early stages nerves can get in the way; there had been quite a build-up, which I knew may not have helped. I just needed to give it time to allow him to settle into it - and perhaps provide a bit more 'direction'. That was fine, I could do that. I liked him, so the investment would be worth it. The good thing was he was enthusiastic - he fancied me, he wanted to have sex with me, "every day". I could work with that I was sure.

Things were certainly pushing forward, we were spending as much time together as we could around Simon's commitment to look after his children. Only a month into our relationship he asked if I'd join him in meeting some of his family. This felt like quite a big step, a vote of confidence that I was deemed to be 'presentable'. I would admit to being quite nervous. "You'll be fine", he assured me, "my brother loves a redhead". He gave me a wink. He'd talked about them all so warmly that it would be good to put faces to names. Indeed, they were as lovely and welcoming as he'd described. As we sat outside enjoying the late Summer sunshine, it felt remarkably easy and relaxed. In fact, his brother questioned us about how long we'd known each other; he couldn't believe that it had been such a short time given how we were in each other's company. "Well I think you're lovely; we all think you're lovely!", his brother declared. "He's done well for himself", he nodded towards his sibling.

To be so accepted was fabulous, it felt so perfect. We went back to his home and ended up in bed. It was an unsuccessful encounter. I began to doubt that he found me attractive; the demons from how I felt after my marriage started to creep in. They were demons I'd carried with me much of the time throughout my relationships: not being right, not being good enough, that I should be more. It left a bit of a shadow across us as we snuggled up back on the sofa. I had to get ready for work the next morning so I went to gather my things. He came into the bedroom, wetted his lips and began to kiss me. He took me to bed, clearly with a point to prove.

I left later - we'd fallen asleep and woke up to darkness

outside. I drove home a bit confused about it all. I liked how we got on, the intellectual chemistry and the laughter - I just wasn't sure that I did it for him sexually. I was caught examining what it was that I was, or wasn't, doing to have caused this situation; it was the antithesis of my relationship with Connor, which was (almost) all I had known for the last seven years. I was so afraid of not getting this right; this guy was great and I felt so lucky that he had found me. He was the first and only person I had properly spoken to on the dating app; it was so romantic.

He called me at work the following day; it was bothering him too. I paced around outside my office as we talked. I expressed my concern over whether he found me physically attractive. I'd decided to be completely honest with him, it was the only way forward as I saw it if I wanted this to work, or to find out now if it wasn't going to. I stopped dead in my tracks when he said, "I could meet a million women, but I'll never find another you". He said it with such vulnerability, I was overwhelmed. I tried to keep it together on my end of the phone, all the while the tears welled up in my eyes. I was so relieved that he felt as I did. He admitted that he'd lost his confidence in the bedroom whilst with his last partner. "She used sex as a weapon against me", he confessed, "she'd lead me on and then deny me. She'd tell me what to do and snap at me, and it took away any self-esteem I had. Then I'd decided it was over, but she told me she was pregnant. I had to do the right thing". My heart went out to him. I certainly understood what it was like to be shamed and belittled. "It's fine, I understand", I said choking back my emotion, "we just need to communicate more about it. We'll get there if we want to".

"I really want to," he said.

That conversation took us to another level. There were an intensity and inevitability about the future that continued to propel us. He began talking about me meeting his children. I wanted to make sure we did this correctly, and I shared that with him. After some of what had gone on with his ex's and the children, and how that had unravelled, I knew it was important that we managed the emotions and dynamics of everyone involved carefully. My top priority already was the welfare of the children, but alongside that was the respect it was important for me to show to their mothers, who I was sure would be understandably concerned about a new woman being introduced into their children's lives. I wanted to get it right.

It was only a few weeks further on when Simon called me out of the blue at work. Once again I went outside for some privacy. The weather had turned and it was windy outside; I found myself shouting above it to be heard. He was upset, not the happy, positive guy I had been getting to know. He told me about a conversation he'd had with his ex and how she had wounded him with things she'd said about his family - historically they'd never got on with them and it had caused a significant rift. He was devastated - his voice and tone were different from what I'd known, but I was struggling to understand a little why it was such a big deal. Her comments were unpleasant, I grant you, but, as I challenged, if he felt nothing for her why let it matter so much? From the way he'd described their relationship, he didn't have much respect for her outside of her being the mother to one of his children. I advised him to not to let it bother him. "It just makes sense," I reasoned, "that if she doesn't have any hold over you emotionally that you don't let this get to you". It seemed sensible to me.

He came over to see me that evening as arranged. From the moment he walked in there was an atmosphere surrounding him that took me by surprise. I asked him what was wrong. What I got back completely floored me. Far from what his ex had said to him earlier, it was my reaction that he was upset by. He was "really, really hurt" by my behaviour. I was shocked. I thought I'd just been logical, empathetic and reassuring, in a 'don't let it get to you and ruin your day' kind of way befitting of the incident as he had described it.

"I was so hurt by you. I've been so hurt in my life. I can't be hurt anymore." He kept repeating those words, kept on declaring how deeply injured he felt by me.

I replayed our conversation, trying to think if I had said something really bad - been thoughtless. I must have misread it completely as I didn't see or recall the phone conversation the way he was describing it; it was as though we were talking about different conversations. I was incredulous, not least at how I could have misjudged it so badly. The happy, gregarious guy had completely disappeared. He was replaced by this teary, hurt and sulky individual instead. I felt thrown off balance; it was such a dramatic shift. Our conversation should have been about how upset he was with his ex, not about how upset he was with me. I apologised, profusely, genuinely shocked. I said I'd been conscious that I'd had to shout a little to be heard because of the windy conditions. I accepted that I had underestimated how distressed he'd been when he called.

I should learn from this. I certainly knew that I didn't want a repeat of this scene. It niggled me how I could have got it so badly wrong. How he had got so dramatically upset over something that I thought to be so trivial. I felt uneasy, but I pushed the feeling down; it was a temporary blip. It was our first 'tiff'. Nothing more.

꙰

TWENTY-ONE:

HEARTS & HOUSES

In the following days, I got the original Simon back; it had been a blip. I was so relieved. I loved what we had together - his charm, his attentiveness, his humour, his desire to be with me whenever he could. Since selling his business he didn't have a 'job' as we would conventionally understand it. He did a bit of consultancy work, but other than that his time was spent looking after his children and doing work on his properties.

What it meant in those early days was that he spent the rest of his time reading, walking a bit, and researching. He was a very smart, well-read guy, especially about history (although I used to joke that he could have made it all up and I'd have been none the wiser!). The time he had meant that whenever I mentioned something I liked or wanted to do, he'd come back full of knowledge, or having arranged it; I laughed that I was like a project.

As my working hours were at odds with his life, he had a key to my house by this stage; it made sense that he could come and go as he pleased rather than managing around my working hours - not least because I quickly learned that he wasn't a 'morning' person! We just fitted together so well and, whilst we didn't share the same passions for absolutely everything, I was amazed at how many similarities there were. We wanted the same things in life: stability, love, happiness and a sense of belonging. These shared values meant that things were accelerating quickly; he continued to be keen for me to meet his children. It made sense given where we were heading, and he talked about them so much I was fascinated to meet them; I felt that I couldn't know him unless I did. True to my desire though, we arranged for me to meet one of the children's mothers first. His relationship with his ex-wife was the better of the two, so it would be the easier meeting.

I suggested we met her at her house - I figured that she would be more at ease on her turf. I was a little nervous at first, it was always daunting to meet an ex, but there was a lot riding on this with regards our future - if she didn't like me and wouldn't entertain me being around her children then there was no future.

To be fair she made it easy, which allowed me to be open about not having kids; I shared how I had a very close relationship with my niece and nephew. I wanted her to know that I'd always aim to consider her feelings when it came to the children and asked her to tell me if I did anything that upset her. I was sure there would be things that I would trip up over, but I wanted her to be reassured that my intentions would always be good. We spoke about Simon's more recent ex (clearly not much love was lost between the two women), but contrary to his presentation of the situation, she firmly believed that the relationship had been a product of an affair that started before their marriage was over. I was a little surprised, but I knew myself that life was not always straightforward; it was who he was with me that mattered. She warned Simon "was very difficult to live with", which I took to mirror what he'd said about her fiery temper. He cared about her I was certain, but said she could be "a bit of a maniac, a nutcase".

We'd got on so well that I mused that had the circumstances been different she might have been the kind of woman I could be friends with. She seemed a decent, straightforward person, so some of what she said about Simon left me feeling a bit destabilised rather than reassured. But then, she was the ex-wife. Their split had been pretty acrimonious as Simon had outlined it, even though they were on better terms now, and no doubt things were said and done on all sides that this far down the line they may have been a little sheepish about. I'd understood from him that when he'd split from his ex, this lady may have harboured hopes of reconciliation; I was conscious that my appearance may have dashed those.

When I arrived back home after the meeting, Simon messaged me to ask how it had gone. For some reason, I needed space to think about what had been said. I was tired and not up for a lengthy text exchange (we couldn't speak by phone when he had the kids). I said it had gone well, but that we would talk properly the following day. He didn't seem particularly pleased by that, but I wanted time on my own.

The next day I came down with a virus that forced me to come home from work, which was unheard of for me as usually, I would soldier on; this was wiping me out and forcing me to do the only thing I felt was possible - lie on my sofa. I reasoned that this was probably why the previous night I had felt a bit out of sorts. Characteristically, he turned up at my house armed with food and drinks to make me feel better. This was when I discovered he was excellent at dealing practically with illness, but fell short with the bedside manner. Sometimes you just want a cuddle rather than a thermometer shoved under your tongue and your glands felt!

As he tended to my needs he was like a cat on a hot tin roof - desperate to discuss how my meeting had gone. I asked him about her claim that he'd had an affair with his ex. I said that what had gone on was not my concern, it was all in his past as mine was with me, but that it was about trust and honesty. I just wanted him to tell me what had gone on so that I wasn't left with questions. He confessed he had been unfaithful in his marriage, but he insisted that what had happened with regards to meeting his ex-partner had been exactly how he had described it to me.

"You have to understand that she was really upset at the time. She can be a bit off her head, a bit mad, at times. She said and did all sorts of things when we were splitting up, some of which were very hurtful to me, and so it's to be expected that she'll tell the story in a way that makes her look good and me not".

His words about her seemed a bit harsh, the woman I met didn't seem 'mad', but then I did recall how he'd described the encounter between her and his ex-partner (which she had corroborated) where she'd nearly launched herself across the table. It was, after all, the first time I had met this woman, whereas he had known her since their school days. I was exhausted by this virus and tired of the discussion. Any wobble I had felt, I was sure, was just because I wanted this to be right. The ends of relationships were fraught with issues, I knew that better than most.

In the meantime, the term of my rental tenancy would be coming to an end; what I wanted was to find a more permanent place to put down some roots. I liked where I was, but I didn't want to keep spending money on rent. As a signal of how I had softened to the situation over the gap of time, John and I had agreed that he and Andy would move into our cottage, which still hadn't sold, which meant they were no longer paying rent themselves and could continue to oversee the renovation of the property next door. This meant I had a little financial relief to buy a place of my own. I'd found a house I liked; it needed work but had potential, and when I arranged a second viewing Simon offered to come with me. One of the things we shared was a passion for property, so I welcomed his opinion.

On the morning of the viewing as we were getting ready to leave he said, "I don't think you should buy this house". I was a bit crestfallen. I'd spent ages looking on property sites and had finally found something that was within budget with the opportunity to improve over time. He led me to the sofa and we both sat down. "I don't think you should buy it because I don't want you to get somewhere on your own; I want to live with you. I want us to buy a house together". For a moment I was speechless. I was not expecting that! I was blown away. He wanted to buy a permanent home with me. I was overwhelmed with happiness, as though my heart would burst. My biggest dream was coming true, what I'd yearned for, for such a long time. I had so much love to give and what I craved was a lasting relationship to share that love - could it be possible that it was finally coming true? It had been just over 3 months since we'd first met - we'd had a fantastic time together and whilst it had moved quickly, Simon made me feel incredible. He understood me, he knew what I wanted almost without my saying it and treated me so well; we were remarkably alike. Sure, I'd seen a couple of isolated moments where I saw a very sensitive side to him, but we all had history and I accepted this knowing how much he had been hurt in the past. Now this wonderful man wanted to cement our relationship further, which meant the world to me. I basked in the moment of feeling so wanted by someone so special and different to anyone else I'd ever met. Being a huge romantic at heart I couldn't quite believe that after all my searching I had found my desires reciprocated by this amazing man, who was prepared to make himself vulnerable to tell me he felt this way.

We honoured the viewing, but we wandered round hand in hand, giddy at what had just been agreed between us and itching to get back to my house to start our search - the search for our home, a family home. It was madness, a dizzying madness, but he made me feel safe, like anything was possible, like I was all he wanted, that our life would be perfect and happy, that I was all he was looking for.

We looked online together to establish the kind of thing we'd like and where - there was my job to consider and his care of the children with the need to get them to what was, at the moment, three different school locations. As Simon had more free time, we agreed he'd narrow down our choices, both through further online searching and by driving out to look at options. Often he would send me links to possibilities whilst I was at work; it was all very exciting as we started to build a picture of a fabulous future together. We would find a dream home to establish that wonderful life in.

After intense searching, we found THE ONE. We came across a stunning village; houses rarely came up for sale here, but due to the death of an elderly gentleman, one had come on the market. It needed extensive work, completely gutting, but it had extensive outbuildings with potential to turn it into a wonderful home, complete with guest accommodation; it had a lovely garden with a view of the countryside. We spoke excitedly about how we would configure it, ensuring an area suitable for each of the children and us; it had so much character we could see the end vision of how it could look and of us settled there. We instantly fell in love with it and put in an offer just as I went off on a long-planned holiday for a week with Jen in the run-up to Christmas.

Just before I went away I'd had my first meeting with his children. We planned that I would go to his house where they would be comfortable and that I would just stay for a couple of hours to not overwhelm them. Truth be told, I think Simon was more concerned about me meeting them than them meeting me; by his accounts, they were a bit of a handful. With it being their first Christmas in a different home after his split from the youngest's mother, and being on his own with them, I suggested that I brought along a Christmas tree and decorations; it would be something for us to 'do' and focus on that wasn't about them or me.

The eldest, and only girl, I found to be very sweet; she was keen to be liked. She had taken the brunt of the fall-out from her parents' marriage breakdown from what I could tell and existed a little in a world of her own; if you joined her there she was very engaging. Simon told me that the eldest of his two sons would be my greatest challenge. Of any of the three children, he was the most protective of his dad. He'd been described as all heart and no brain; mischievous, and a bit of a clown. Yet I 'got' him as soon as I met him; within 10 minutes we were thick as thieves. As for the youngest, I knew that for a pre-schooler the enormous box that contained the artificial Christmas tree would be a hit, and I wasn't mistaken. To be fair, however, he was the one that stuck with me for the entire time we decorated the tree - the other two dipped in and out (his elder brother, in particular, had the attention span of a puppy) - but that little chap helped with every bauble until it was done. Once finished, Simon was impressed, "Oh my God, it looks like something from a John Lewis advert! It's the most beautiful tree I've ever had!". The afternoon was a success. Simon discussed with them after I left what they thought. The feedback was all positive. It was a huge relief and the green light to keep moving forward.

و

TWENTY-TWO:

THE CLAP

It was with great excitement that I shared with Jen whilst on holiday that Simon had called to say that the offer we'd made on the house had been accepted. "I feel a bit numb", he'd said on the other end of the line when I asked him how he felt; we were both surprised that our offer had been enough. It was the start of a whole new chapter though and our vision for this place was amazing. It wasn't going to be easy, but it would become a beautiful, long-term home. "A forever home", Simon said. "I want us all to just belong somewhere. I want you to feel like you belong; you so deserve to finally feel like you belong somewhere and I want it to be with us". It was possibly the most romantic thing he could have said. I felt so special.

Mum expressed her concern about the size of the project; I appreciated what she was getting at and why she was worried. When John and I had done this kind of stuff it had, as it transpired, been all about avoidance. Each time we moved, displaced ourselves, were distracted by a project, it just stopped him addressing what was really going on. Diversionary tactics, although I didn't think he'd realised that himself; it wasn't done consciously. Then there I'd been running away from myself after the menopause diagnosis. I'd not wanted to confront who that might mean I was; it seemed too horrific to contemplate as a woman in her early thirties. Now, however, I was 10 years on and much had changed in my life and my mind. It had still surprised me though when mum apologised about how they had responded when I was diagnosed. I think Em's illness had caused them to reflect:

"We failed you", she said, "We all just stood back and watched you pick yourself up and just get on with it. Had you been diagnosed with cancer we'd all have been there and have been running around looking after you. We should have stepped in, as the diagnosis you had was devastating and just as life-changing".

I couldn't argue with her because she was right - they'd not been there. Not in the way I needed them to be. What I had needed was for them to put their foot on the ball and say, "you need to talk about this". That would have hurt. It would have forced me to confront how I felt. I'd have had to grieve my losses and not bury them. But I'd needed that to push me through the grief stages, whereas instead, I'd stood still for years. It's not that they didn't talk to me, but we all avoided getting under the skin of what it meant and how I felt.

Whilst I appreciated her words immensely and they did move me on emotionally, I'd deemed the apology unnecessary. I knew that I was also responsible for how they'd responded; they had taken their lead from me in my 'push down the emotions and keep going' approach. As I'd seen it, my diagnosis was not immediately life-threatening as much as it was life-changing. For me and the 'condition' I had there wasn't any hope; there was no cure available and my best response was to try to stave off the worst of it. My reaction to it was more than that though. I'd wanted to spare my family more worry. I'd wanted to protect them from the terrible emotions it stirred in me that I hadn't even been able to articulate. I didn't want to be trouble. I just wanted them to like me. I was trying to be nice.

So the house purchase was underway, but even so, it was January before Simon, the children and I all went out together for the first time. We had a birthday to celebrate and a noisy American-style dinner had been selected by the middle one as his eating place of choice. Being a Saturday evening it was extremely busy, but luckily we got seated in a circular booth, complete with celebratory birthday balloons, so we were all in high spirits.

Simon, I'd learnt, liked to make an 'occasion' of things, so he'd made quite a point about this being our inaugural outing together; it was important to him that it went well because I think he wanted to show me his good parenting skills in a 'this-is-a-family-you'll-want-to-be-part-of' kind of way.

Our evening was going well, the usual mix of junk food, fizzy drinks, balloon games and laughing loudly above the sound of other diners and background music. We were mid-conversation when Simon looked at me slightly quizzically and wrinkled up his nose before turning back to his youngest on his right, who had been hitting a balloon back and forth with me across the table for a little while. I carried on talking to the elder two whilst out of the corner of my eye I could see Simon lean towards the littlest one and then back towards me as he stood up to leave the table. I turned towards him, but before I could speak he said in my ear, "He's fucking shit himself and it's on my hand". With that, he left the table.

"Where's Dad going?", said the eldest.
"He's just gone to the toilet", I said quickly.
"What's happened?", asked the middle one.
"Nothing, he just needed to go to the toilet", I said.

I already knew my audience. The moment I told them what had really happened there would be uproar. I was conscious that Simon might want to deal with this his way with his children, and that sitting looking at me was a small boy who knew that something wasn't right, but wasn't sure what he'd done. I knew that look and how quickly it could dissolve into tears: "It's ok. Daddy has just gone to the toilet", I smiled at him. The blue eyes stayed wide and continued to look back at me, although he seemed a little reassured when I picked a balloon back up to resume our game.

Simon came back to the table after what felt like a lifetime, not least because I had a desperate urge to laugh. He was mortified, not least because he confessed in my ear that somehow, by the time he'd reached the gents, the faeces that had been on his hand had 'disappeared'; he feared that somewhere in the throng of people around the bar someone was now wearing it. This was so funny I thought I was going to stop breathing. His confidence in his few days of toilet-training his son had been a little misplaced. He'd bought him out without a nappy on, and with no back-up supplies in the car when I enquired. I had to ask again just to make sure I'd got it right: "so you don't have a nappy or any change of clothes in the car?". "No", he looked a bit confused as to why he would have. If the evidence had not been sitting next to me slurping fizzy drinks, I'd not have believed this wasn't the first time he'd been through this phase. He'd failed to recognise that with the excitement of the situation, different surroundings, distractions, me as a relative stranger in the mix...it would be unlikely that at this early stage the littlest one would volunteer his need to go to the toilet. "Well, we're going to have to go home", I said with a smile, "we don't have any other choice". Fortunately, we'd had our main courses, but now it was time to tell the elder two that the birthday celebrations were going to have to be cut short.

The hilarity that I'd predicted was exactly what we got when I told them what had happened and why we were going to have to get the bill and leave. I lost count of the times I had to "Sssh" them, whilst trying not to laugh myself, which made the elder boy especially worse as, like his father, he loved to play to the crowd.

Having calmed that situation down and placated their

protestations about the lack of dessert with promises of treats when we got home, the kids started to don their jackets as we made moves for a hasty exit. This was contrary to what the restaurant staff had in mind. Just as we were about to get up from our seats a crowd of them appeared, the one in the centre holding a slice of cake with a lit candle and copious amounts of squirty cream. They proceeded to sing their special 'Birthday Song' (I didn't know there was such a thing until that moment!) that seemed to include lots of vigorous clapping by the assembled waiters. We sat back down in our seats, conscious of the disaster in our midst and the creeping stench that was emanating from the smallest member of our group. "Can we take that with us?", I asked as soon as the singing had finished, "we need to go".

Simon was gathering up the children having hastily paid the bill, as I took the packaged up dessert from the hand of the slightly stunned waiter - he was concerned about his tip. As we got the raucous children into the car I suddenly asked, "Have we got tiger?" - the youngest's current favourite toy. Panic then ensued as we looked in and around the car; we were in unison in our understanding of how important it was to find this piece of plastic. With no joy, I ran back inside and to the table we had vacated.

Our waiter was standing there surveying the carnage we had left behind us - I vowed then that I never wanted to be one of those families that just walk away from a scene of devastation they've created in a restaurant, but needs must in these circumstances. We looked at each other across the mess and I smiled my apology at him before saying, "I'm looking for a miniature tiger. We think we left it behind". He looked at me a bit blank, so I took matters into my own hands and started to search through the debris. In a frenzied 60 seconds, I finally found the invaluable object on the floor, snatched it up and ran back out into the car park.

I was declared a hero as I handed over the toy. Simon quickly started the engine and we set off, with the eldest pair moaning about the smell and hanging out the open windows despite the cold air. Their father was mortified; he was apologising profusely and lamenting that I wouldn't ever want to go out with them again. I thought the whole incident was hysterical.

Back home, I put the kettle on to make tea for Simon as he sorted out the (literal) fall-out from the incident in the restaurant; he was noisily protesting about this up in the bathroom. The elder two danced around the kitchen, enjoying every moment of his anguish as Simon stood their youngest sibling in a plastic bag so that he could pull off the soiled clothing and dispose of it; the sounds of his shenanigans conveyed that wasn't going very well. Having showered him down and settling him into bed, Simon eventually came downstairs and sat with his head in his hands. He at least started to laugh, albeit from a place of 'trauma' as he saw it. I reassured him: "it's what kids do; they shit and they vomit". I was prepared for this.

Thereafter, on the weekends when Simon had the children, we spent most of them all of us together. On the alternate weekends, he and I built a life based on laughter and adventures - staying away and going out. I was loving what he brought to life. It gathered momentum when he spent one journey home telling me how he wanted to get married again and then explained, in detail, what he'd want the wedding itself to be like: the music, the venue, the speeches, what the bride would wear. It was all so romantic. It had become a running joke between us about a colleague at my work who had a large diamond engagement ring - he used to laugh about how he wanted to buy a diamond that, "would make her eyes bleed" with envy. What he was describing was clearly about me, even down to how he wanted us to learn that "one special dance" together. I was starting to believe that I was going to get the marriage I deserved. It came with a ready-made family.

In the week preceding Valentine's Day, Simon's ex-partner asked to meet him; this was cause for concern. When they met she informed him that she intended to move abroad, back to her family; she was, of course, taking their son with her. He was devastated. He adored that little boy. It was obvious from the outset that there was a clear ranking in Simon's affections with regards his children. He loved and connected with his youngest in a way he didn't the other two; sadly that was blatant. The elder two seemed to accept it. After all, their younger brother was cute and smart - what wasn't to love? He liked to think that his youngest was the most like him, whereas that was his daughter who was, also clearly, his least favourite; somehow they just couldn't seem to find any common ground. It led to her constantly seeking Simon's attention through her littlest brother, "Dad look at what he's doing". I felt for her, it was a long shadow that her sibling cast and often when she was allowed to step into the limelight it was for all the wrong reasons; she wasn't naturally academic and it frustrated her father.

The news of this possible departure sent Simon into an understandable tailspin; he'd unravelled at speed and by the time he arrived at my house that evening he was in bits. I was upset too - for Simon and the enormous change this would signal in their relationship, for his son given how much he adored his dad, and for myself as he was the kind of child that you loved instantly; the thought of him not being with us for long periods was already really hard to grasp. I tried to approach it by being practical. In my opinion, being upset was a necessary part of the process of grieving the change, but in the end, the best way to get back some semblance of control was to look at what could be done about it.

Simon's forte was research, so I used that to encourage him to start understanding his rights - what could/couldn't his son's mother do with regards to taking him away? What access was Simon entitled to? What would it mean regarding their financial agreement? All questions that I felt he needed to focus on, not least because the departure had been muted as being imminent - the boy's mother had mentioned she was well into a selection process for a job and, if this went ahead, they could be gone by the Spring.

As hard as it was, Simon was going to need to come to terms with the situation quickly and find a sense of direction. He began to do this, but it remained against a backdrop of complete emotional devastation. I appreciated the hurt of the situation, but I did start to feel that his constant emotional out-pouring was beginning to get a bit out of hand. I felt terrible for thinking such thoughts; I didn't have children and probably couldn't understand how this must feel. Yet, I was also an emotionally intelligent individual who easily empathised with people...or was I if I thought he was being a bit over-dramatic? Perhaps was I a bit cold-hearted? I started to doubt myself as I grappled with these two sides of myself. It just seemed that he was constantly projecting forward to worse-case scenarios that he had no idea would happen - we didn't even know if his ex would get the job or that they'd even leave - she'd only said it was a possibility; I couldn't see the benefit of getting so over-wrought by this many 'maybes'. There seemed to be a level of 'wallowing' that made me feel a bit confused and uncomfortable; it was almost as if he were enjoying the drama. I wouldn't have dreamt of saying it to him as I knew from experience how hurt he could get, and it felt disloyal to mention it to anyone else.

As the next weekend approached he didn't have the children; it had become our 'normal' to be together. However, he ceased to communicate with me, falling off the radar in an out-of-character way. I went to the hairdressers on Saturday as planned, but feeling rather on edge. As I left the hairdressers I checked my phone: still nothing.

Eventually, late afternoon, I received a text saying he'd gone to his holiday cottage to clear his head. Then silence. It was odd and I had a disturbing sense of foreboding. I got that this was an unprecedented situation, but after all the support I had given him I felt insulted to just be cut off. I started to get cross - he knew I'd not have made plans without him. I got more and more wound up - I'd done everything to console him as he'd endlessly cried, but now was cast aside. Finally, mid-evening he messaged to say he was getting some food before going home; cold and factual - nothing about us or enquiries about me. Whilst he'd spent the day feeling massively sorry for himself, I'd been left furious stewing in my juices. I was annoyed that I suddenly ceased to matter.

He wouldn't speak to me by phone, so I drove to his house. Reluctantly, he answered the door. He was completely cold with me. Unemotional. It was like dealing with a different person, which only increased my anxieties. His distance and indifference made matters worse; I couldn't help but give him a piece of my mind. I reminded him that we were planning a future together: I'd met his kids, we were buying a house together and if something bad happens I'd be upset for him, upset for the kids and, instead of cutting me out, that the kids and I should be considered too. He flatly informed me that his eldest two had already been 'considered'; he'd been and told them earlier that their youngest sibling was going to be taken away to live in another country. They were, as you would imagine, and taking their cue from their father, completely gutted.

"Why would you tell them that at this stage?", I asked.

"Because they ought to know", he replied coldly.

"Yes", I agreed, "but surely only when you know for certain that it is happening?".

I was astounded that he had put them through this upset so soon when there were so many questions about how it would work and whether it would happen at all. Added to which his emotions were still so raw and ill-equipped to deal with the added layer of those of his older children. "You've taken adult matters and laid them at the door of your children", I reasoned. I couldn't get my head around his logic. What exactly had telling them at this stage achieved? They had already endured two relationship splits and the associated upheavals. It didn't feel like he was acting in anyone's interests other than his own. I reasoned that it was the upset of it all that was preventing him from thinking straight; he was seeking sympathy wherever he thought he could find it. He stared blankly at me whilst I told him straight that it was time for him to stop wading through this alone and that it should be something we faced as a couple. He listened to me getting it all off of my chest with little response. So I went home, still fuming at how he could treat me as though I was nobody.

The following day brought a texted apology and asking if I wanted to talk. I responded that I was going for a walk at my favourite country spot as I needed a boost; I said he could join me if he wished. He did. The tension was palpable as we drove there, but he was sorry for the way he had behaved and how that had made me feel, so as we walked and talked things started to ease. As we sat by a beautiful lake, however, he declared that he'd made the decision that we couldn't buy our dream home; he couldn't build a life without his youngest being there. I was gobsmacked. I reminded him that he didn't yet know that this was definitely going to happen as there were so many uncertainties and that, even so, we'd still all need a home. He insisted that he needed stability, which meant staying where he was.

I was shocked and distraught. I was stunned that he'd just made that decision on my behalf, without discussion or consideration of my opinion. It was a fait accompli. I began got to sob. I couldn't help myself. In a single moment, everything that we'd dreamed about had been taken away, and worse still, it had been settled upon as though my feelings on the matter were irrelevant. I couldn't stop crying, and I couldn't even really explain why. Even he seemed unsure what to do; he'd never seen me in that state before. My usual 'we'll sort it' approach had evaporated. My only explanation was the frustration I felt at being ineffectual in what was also, although it had seemed to have been forgotten, my life! It was not, I gathered, the response he had been anticipating, although I am not sure how he thought I might take the news that the rug was being unceremoniously pulled out from beneath me. He escorted me back out through the park as we went back to my place and away from the curious gazes of passers-by. It was a tough afternoon. Every so often he'd dramatically declare: "maybe I should leave, just go", whilst I was needing to hold him to account for his decision. We got to a place of relative calm, probably out of exhaustion.

I went to work on Monday morning, still shell-shocked about what this change of plan now meant, but putting a brave face on it. We were both unusually quiet via text that day, but it suited me; I was drained from the previous day's emotional outburst and time with my thoughts was welcome. I was still bruised by the choices he had made on my behalf. I returned home to a note he'd left next to one of the silk rose petals he'd bought me for Valentine's Day laid next to it. The note said I was the last person he'd ever wanted to hurt and asked me to forgive him. Whilst it all felt so horrible and our blissfully happy days now sullied, it was a note and an action that thawed my heart. I loved him. He loved me. It was just a house. I needed to accept that. It didn't matter. Right now my role was to help him through this difficult time. Without further debate he took care of unravelling us from the house purchase and absorbed the fees we'd incurred; we didn't speak about it further. I accepted there was no point dwelling on it.

In the following weeks, we got back to normal. He took advice about (and some control of) the situation with his ex and we started to look forwards again. A bit of stability, which I welcomed. We'd arranged to go out for dinner on a Saturday evening to a restaurant he wanted to try. He arrived at my house a couple of hours beforehand and we ended up in bed before going out. The sex had not improved much, but I was beginning to adapt.

As I started to get ready for dinner he suddenly said that with everything going on in his life, he wasn't sure if it was right to have this relationship at the moment. I stopped dead in my tracks. I was completely confused. Was he breaking up with me? "You've just had sex with me. What are you now saying?!". He spoke a lot of words, but none of them seemed to indicate an answer. I was breathless with shock, but I called the restaurant and cancelled; there was no way we were going for the special dinner we'd planned. I couldn't comprehend what I was hearing!

Without a clear answer, he still insisted that he needed to eat, so we set out into town. I was shaking inside so as we walked I tried to get clarity about what it was he wanted; it wasn't easy as he seemed unusually incoherent, but also was behaving like what he'd said meant 'nothing'. I told him I appreciated his hurt and uncertainty about the situation with his son, but that with the advice he was getting he now understood his rights and as such I'd thought we'd started to move into a different place with it. Not least because his ex had gone quiet about the move and it certainly seemed less imminent.

As we sat having a pre-dinner drink, I just wanted to know where I stood - the uncertainty of a relationship that he'd described with so much certainty only weeks before, was bending my brain. I tentatively suggested that recently I'd been thinking about a possible solution to our housing situation, which, from what little I could gather, was maybe what was bothering him about 'us'. He said he was keen to hear what I had to say. My idea was for him to keep the continuity he wanted for his children, so I proffered the option of him keeping his home with them (which was about an hour away from where I lived) for all the times when he had them. They would have the familiarity of their current surroundings and no upheaval and I would, as I had been doing thus far, join them as often as I could and definitely on the weekends when they were with him. Then, as stability for me and us, and to keep my commute to a manageable daily distance, I suggested we buy an apartment just for us in the town where I lived. He was a changed man. He loved the idea. Suddenly he was explaining that he loved the time we spent together as just a couple and that it was the life that he wanted; he found being a single dad hard to cope with and it gave him some respite in a more 'adult' world. This idea would solve our problems and give us all what we needed. "Genius!", he declared as he licked his lips and leant in to kiss me.

The search began immediately in the restaurant; he was animated with excitement once more. It was that night that we saw the beautiful Victorian apartment we finally settled upon - high ceilings and spacious rooms, but with room for some improvements that lent themselves, over time, to our shared passion for property development.

We started the purchasing process and plans began for setting up 'our' home; building a life together. Not quite how we'd originally envisioned, but for now it was a solution that worked for us. We were heading towards moving day and I'd sold the majority of my belongings in preparation.

But it was April 2016 and the chancellor had plans in his budget.

&

TWENTY-THREE:

CREEPY COTTAGE

We'd been in the apartment measuring for furniture and carpets when it had been announced in the government's budget that they were putting in place with immediate effect additional stamp duty land tax (SDLT) to be paid by people purchasing second homes. As Simon owned a private residence already, and my cottage down South still hadn't sold, our SDLT went increased by £12,000 overnight. Between us, we could have afforded the additional money (as painful as it would have been to hand over money for nothing), but Simon decided that we couldn't go ahead with the purchase. From the demeanour he'd displayed when we were in our future apartment, I had a niggling feeling that this had suddenly provided him with a convenient 'out'. I'm not sure why I felt that - he'd been totally on board as I'd sold the majority of my furniture and got rid of the relics of my relationship with John. It had been stressful to part with items that had been familiarity in my life when so much had changed, yet Simon had been right when he'd said it was time to leave that past behind and start afresh with things that were 'ours'.

I went temporarily into free-fall as the decision was communicated to the vendor that we'd no longer be buying the apartment. I had given notice to vacate my rental home. My landlord had found a new tenant. I had to remove the remainder of my belongings in less than two weeks and had nowhere to go. I would be homeless.

I understood the decision, but at the same time I didn't; his lack of comprehension of what it meant to me (because, after all, nothing was changing for him) left me a little stunned. We had a tense exchange during which I informed him that I had only one choice and that was, temporarily, to move in with him. "Fine", he said very curtly. "Good", I said with equal irritation. We both knew it was far from fine, but as far as I was concerned he'd more than contributed to putting me in this position - for a second time. The remainder of my belongings were to be split between being stored in the garage at his holiday cottage and being taken to his home, which now constituted a nearly 3-hour daily round trip to my job. This wasn't going to be easy. Then there was the small matter of the children. "I know this is far from ideal, but you're going to have to tell them that it is just temporary whilst I sort myself out with something else", I said. I was full of worry that I was inflicting this on them. "I'll speak to them and explain", he said. A bit softer, "they'll understand".

Whilst he organised the items to go to his garages, we both then moved the remainder during numerous trips in our cars one Saturday. By the time we had finished, we were tired and generally tetchy with each other. Simon's poor mood oozed out of him and I sensed I was unwelcome; I walked on eggshells as we manoeuvred around my many boxes and bags to get ready to fall into bed.

The next morning, having benefitted from some sleep, I got up and assessed the situation. I suggested that he disappear to the coast for the day to give me time to unpack and sort as much as I could: "I'll make it better, I promise", I said as he got ready to leave. We agreed on some space in wardrobes and cupboards before he left and then I set to it - determined to create a transformation in his mood by the time he returned. He hated clutter as much as I did, so we needed this for the sake of both of our minds. Without his bad mood, but under the threat of it returning later, I worked harder that day than I had ever worked. I didn't stop. I didn't eat. I was relentless in my efforts to put right the 'mess' that I had abruptly brought into his life. I found clever ways to house my stuff and get it all stored, mostly out of sight. I organised what could be put for now in his spacious loft, placed things in the garden shed and even tidied up his cupboards a bit as I went along (he had a very 'man' way of organising that I knew I could make more efficient!). I did the washing and drying and general titivating that resulted later in his daughter saying "She's made your house a home, Dad".

After fresh air and a day doing satisfying 'man tasks', he returned in a much-improved mood. Yet he was genuinely impressed at how much I had achieved; the house was unrecognisable from the morning. Apart from some boxes I needed him to lift into the loft, it was all done. He smiled as he licked his lips and pulled me in for a kiss, "Let's go to the pub for dinner, I think we've earned it". As we sat there, we returned to a level of comfort between us that had been missing in the preceding couple of days. I told him I had worked hard so that he (and the children) didn't feel unduly disturbed by my presence and repeated that this was a temporary measure whilst I looked for somewhere else to buy. He smiled at me, and then said, "Well I hope you like it so much here with us that you don't ever want to leave". I knew the commute was going to be hard, but after the last few days of feeling like a huge inconvenience, I was overcome with relief that he wanted me to stay; somehow this arrangement might become something permanent in my life. His warmth had reappeared, and he reinforced the point just days later when we were out for a walk with the children: "She might leave us - we don't want that do we? We need to persuade her that she wants to stay with us!". Luckily for him, they agreed. Perhaps now we could get back to that loved-up state we'd enjoyed during our first 6 months together.

Things calmed down. There'd been no more mention of the youngest leaving and we got into a routine of normal life. Mind you, my 'normal' life now consisted of this ready-made family that we housed half of each week and alternate weekends. Alongside my full-time job, extra commute and maintaining my recreational interests (precious time for 'me'), I was now washing and ironing for five, changing beds (because the idea of that seemed alien to Simon) and helping keep the house clean. Simon hated the chores, they made him grumpy (especially being the taxi service to the children) and he made sure we all knew about it, so I took on as much as I could to maintain some semblance of calm in our very noisy household. I was conscious that my presence had been ousted on them, so I was keen to do what I could to ease that burden. The deal was that I didn't cook. It was a juggling act. If I got it wrong, all I'd get was complaints that I was always busy and without free time to spend with him. So I got up earlier to do what I could whilst he and the children were asleep. Whilst it was tough it at least meant I got a bit of time to myself and the chance to deal with the numerous heating and hot water issues that riddled the house and meant that, without careful planning, we could only manage one hot shower at a time. It was starting to take its toll on my well-being. I was forced to rise daily before 5.30am to a chilly house so that I could switch on the immersion heater before I needed it just to be able to have a hot shower and allow it to re-heat for his eldest to do the same - we shared in common a hatred for the cold.

Aside from this, much about our lives together was relatively good; I seemed to be able to keep him mostly on an even keel. My main issue continued to be his inability to take any direction with regards to our sex life; he took it personally when I tried to make suggestions from a positive perspective. Having previous confided how he'd lost confidence due to his ex being quite forthright in this department, I knew it was a delicate subject, but I was starting to have some sympathy with her. When I talked to Emma about it, the only way I could describe it was that it was like having sex with a fifteen-year-old boy. Not that it was over quickly, but that there was no thought about my needs or pleasure, but rather that he just pumped away relentlessly until he was satisfied. When push came to shove (excuse the pun), he was clueless. Jen laughed when I said, "I'm worried that he might be deskilling me!". I meant it, I was finding it less worthwhile to put in any effort.

What his technique (or lack of it) meant for me, besides some significant unmet needs, was a dogged determination on his part that resulted in me developing chronic cystitis. I believed I could pinpoint the incident with Simon that had triggered my pain. Persistent visits to the doctor and rounds of antibiotics to try and stem the flow of blood in my urine as well as manage the constant pain that nagged at me 24 hours a day. When the GP concluded that antibiotics were not going to sort it because it wasn't a bacterial infection, they offered no options as to what to do next. I prompted that perhaps they might refer me to a specialist, had I not, I got the distinct impression that I'd have been left to just cope with it.

The referral allowed them to find that I had developed a cyst near my bladder, which was causing all the issues. The answer, the consultant told me, was to leave it for six months.

"If it turns hard during that time it will indicate that it might be cancer. We will need to consider surgery to remove it, but we would want to avoid that if we can because the consequences on your bladder could be life-changing".

So basically I would end up incontinent. I was 43. I was scared. Another 6 months of this pain and how constantly unwell I felt, and a waiting game. Simon gave me an awkward cuddle when I told him, but it's fair to say that in the months that followed he expected normal 'service' most days. I obliged even when the pain was at its worst; sex seemed to help keep him happy. I didn't want a deterioration in our sex life in the same way I'd experienced with John and for that to be a reason Simon didn't want me anymore. I was in deep by this time in my love for him and his children; I wanted us to keep the kind of happy that we'd had at the outset and, whilst there had been some bumps in the road, he said he loved me too. That's all that mattered. All the while we kept this equilibrium, he seemed able to cope with the pressures of being a 'single parent' whenever we had the children. So I soldiered on, coping and keeping this daily routine.

In June we did manage a much-needed break away, just a week for the two of us; it was all that we could manage without significant changes to the children's routine and, more to the point, without what seemed to be protracted and stressful negotiations with two mothers, neither of whom seemed minded to do the other, or him, any favours. At times there seemed to be little goodwill around. Yet a week away was a luxury, so he organised it all, as was his usual desire, and after much research. We hopped over to the Italian countryside to stay on the edge of a small village; it looked and sounded idyllic. We hired a car so that we could explore.

Simon had found us an old cottage, which looked rather romantic, set in its own grounds with a pool. I knew how thoroughly he liked to look into such things, so I'd happily left him to it. The reality when we got there, however, was that it was a bit dirty and had a strange smell we couldn't fathom, especially on the bedsheets. None of this was great, although I was trying to make the best of it because I wanted a lovely break away with him so badly.

Yet soon Simon was brooding ominously; it was making me increasingly uneasy as the hours ticked by. I began to ruminate as to the possible causes. I concluded that it was being away with me, imagining that it was as people said - that going on holiday with someone was one of those things on the list of most stressful things to do, along with getting divorced or married. His attitude towards me, the limited communication, perfunctory conversations...in the end they turned out to be hiding something far greater than I could have anticipated: fear. Now, I knew he wasn't good with insects, he tended to get himself in a bit of a tizzy anytime that something flew or crawled near him, but I had not appreciated just how bad his phobia was.

Whilst I was quite enjoying the bees and butterflies that gathered on the wildflowers outside the cottage door, Simon was crawling out of his skin having discovered in the information folder that our holiday home was also housed an ant colony. The ants weren't the only issue. Inside the cottage flies and moths constantly accumulated. When an unusually large, dead insect he'd found on the bedroom windowsill disappeared overnight - clearly disposed of by the army of ants that seemed to be continuously on the march - Simon, I realised, was barely sleeping.

On the evening of day three, he broke the silence of his sullen mood and confessed that he couldn't stand it any longer. He was very apologetic for selecting the place. I was filled with relief that it was just the insects. "Can we please get out of here?", he pleaded, "Just leave tomorrow and go somewhere else? I want somewhere clean, with white sheets and no insects!". I laughed, I didn't care where we went so long as he was happy again. He jumped online, taking advantage of some rare internet connectivity, to search for alternatives. We found an amazing hotel to stay for the other four nights just a half-hour from where we were.

We drove there expectantly having done an early morning flit. Nothing could have prepared us for the beauty that welcomed us; from the moment we drove across the bridge over the river that ran alongside the hotel, we felt that we were in heaven. It was when we walked into the reception that we finally felt able to breathe; it was gorgeous, sophisticated, with a view to die for and, as we soon discovered, bedrooms awash with crisp white linen and oozing Italian class. What a contrast! Having dropped our bags, we threw ourselves back on the sumptuous bed and started to laugh. THIS was what it was meant to be like.

Those four days were perfect. We explored, we giggled, we ate, and we talked about our future together. Dinners on the terrace overlooking the beautiful garden were a culinary extravaganza that just added to the romance that sparkled between us each evening. By the time we got home, we were once again in a great place, all the burgeoning romance was back just in time to mark the first anniversary of when we went on our initial date.

To celebrate, we returned for the night to the hotel where we had that date. We dined in the restaurant, sitting at the same table (thanks to Simon's intervention with the waiter) as that first meeting, reminiscing about everything that had transpired over the year in between. I was overjoyed that we'd got back to our happy place; when it was good it was really, really good. The next day we had breakfast in our room before we got dressed up for lunch; Simon was making the whole stay one of his 'occasions'. With an hour to kill before lunch, we went for a stroll around the grounds; he steering us into the oldest part of the hotel, where they held their special events. That day they were setting up for a wedding. As we stood in the main hallway in front of the sweeping staircase, Simon enquired of a member of staff whether this was where the bride would walk down on her wedding day. As he did so he turned to me with a smile and a wink - there was no doubting what was on his mind. It was all coming from him, he had it all mapped out - I was just waiting for his wedding ideas book to come out with every last detail planned like Monica from 'Friends'! I was reminded of our conversation on the train several months before. He had definite plans for our future together.

It was around this time that he began looking at houses again; he was relentless. I laughed as I refused to look, saying that we'd been here before - more than once. I told him straight that I wasn't doing it again because I didn't believe that he'd go through with it. He turned on the charm offensive, reminding me how we'd just shared such a wonderful holiday, knowing that I couldn't dispute that. He was describing plans again for the long-term, the rest of our lives, and painting a fairy-tale as he did so. He would sit looking at houses on what he termed 'Rightporn', and "Ooo" and "Aah" in the hope of piquing my interest whilst I busied doing chores. I would just smile and shake my head. "Come and look at this one. It has [original features/a wood burner/dressing room/flagstone floors]!", he would insert whichever one of my house-hunting buttons he'd been able to find in a property - obviously the more the better. I couldn't help but get sucked into it again as he didn't give up; he knew I loved property with a passion, so would always be tempted to take a look. He was adept at convincing me how fantastic it could be; based on the good times we'd had and our wonderful trip away, I could visualise it myself. Deep down, not even that deep really, I desperately wanted to believe it with all of my might.

It wasn't long before he found us another "dream house". I reluctantly agreed to view it. The estate agent left us along to do a second lap around the Victorian manor house. Simon immediately asked what I thought of it. I couldn't deny that I absolutely loved it. It had vast potential with beautiful original features that needed releasing from their magnolia prison. The location was much better for me as it was nearer to my work, (still nearly an hours commute, but that was a win) and it would be great for the kids - loads of room for each of them, a fabulous walled garden and less than 30 minutes for Simon to get them to school. That situation was about to improve given that the eldest two would soon be at the same secondary school, which was just minutes away from the youngest's nursery. Everybody would be happy - Simon's face told me that. He grabbed me with excitement in what would become our bedroom, and span me around. This was my dream home. This was my dream. He licked his lips and planted a kiss on mine.

That was it then. We secured the house, got the seal of approval from the kids ("oh my God it's like a mansion!") and the torrent of videos from Simon began. While I was at work he'd walk around the outside of our empty dream home, filming it as he talked to me on and off camera. He was so giddy and I allowed myself to believe that this time it was going to happen. He knew I meant what I said - this time there was no pulling out.

❧

TWENTY-FOUR:

GRAPHING IT

I'd still not met the youngest's mother, but as she began to understand I was a permanent fixture due to our future plans, she asked to meet me as she wasn't going anywhere either: after all the heartache the emigration had never amounted to anything. Mutual territory was agreed in a café near her home for the forthcoming Saturday morning.

The day before I was due to meet her I received a distressed phone call from Simon whilst I was at work; he was in tears. I could make out through his sobs that he had his youngest in the car. My heart lurched wondering what was wrong. He managed to say that he was on his way to fetch the eldest from school. Just after he'd set off, her mum (who was away on business) had called him to say that the school had asked if she could come to collect her daughter. She'd advised them that her dad was collecting her as usual. They'd then asked her not to get in touch with Simon but told her that their daughter had gone into the school that morning claiming that he'd attacked her. She'd spent several hours in the school's welfare unit, who had contacted social services, and that they would await Simon's arrival so that they could interview him. Simon's ex ignored the school's request and called to tell him what was going on.

So as we spoke he was on his way to the school knowing that he was going to be met by a member of staff and taken to speak to social services. He was understandably distressed, with a small child in the car and driving into this nightmare. As parents, they were furious that this had been unfolding all day and neither of them had been contacted. I asked him why he thought his eldest had said that. He admitted that he'd shouted at her that morning; he was stressed trying to get them all out the door because, until the end of term, he still had three different drop-offs to contend with. The eldest was running late (a perpetual problem) and, in his words, had given him "some proper bloody attitude". I knew how that morning routine was for him and how much he hated it. That things got heated was not a surprise; he was prone to raise his voice at them in the mornings as he herded them out the front door. He described that he'd got hold of her blazer lapel as he told her off; then they'd got into the car to leave. He said that once in the car he'd put things right with her - he'd explained why he'd got cross. When he dropped her off at school he'd understood she was fine. I couldn't comprehend how it had now got to this. I put on my practical head and asked him what he needed me to do.

Shortly after the call ended, I left work and was on my way to collect his eldest son from school; given the distance I still had to travel, Simon called ahead to let them know that I might be a little late but was on my way. At least he was safe and his school knew to expect me. Back at his daughter's school, Simon had been made to wait in a side room; they'd provided some toys to occupy the youngest, but the staff had refused to let him see his daughter. They had liaised with social services and were being guided by their protocol. He called again whilst I was in my car, explaining further that he had intended to scare her a little given the way she was behaving so that she understood her attitude towards him was completely unacceptable. It appeared that her version of events painted a different picture entirely: her dad had grabbed her around the throat and pinned her up against the wall whilst shouting at her. Despite his view that they had smoothed things over, once she'd got to school she burst into tears and told her friends, then the staff, what had happened - at least as far as she was concerned. I was in shock.

I collected his son, who was surprised to see me at his school gates, but happy nonetheless. I explained that his dad was at his sister's school as she had been a bit upset; I would be taking him home instead. I deliberately played the situation down until we knew more about what was happening; there was no point worrying him unnecessarily. He chatted away about his day as we made our way home. Whilst we were in the car, Simon rang again. I let him know that we were both there so that he was aware that he could be heard on the loudspeaker. It didn't, however, deter him from informing his son about everything that had happened and that his elder sibling was not being allowed to come home. Instead, some people from social services were coming to the house and would want to interview us all; he would be asked what he'd seen that morning between his dad and his sister. Under the circumstances I didn't feel it would be welcomed if I intervened - this was Simon's son so he would know what was best to do - but as with his decision to share the possibility of their little brother emigrating, I couldn't help feeling this was too much to dump onto a young boy. Simon was, I could tell, in self-protection mode; not knowing when social services would arrive at home he wanted to ensure that he had 'briefed' his son. My heart went out to this little boy whose colour had drained from his cheeks as he sat silently in my passenger seat.

As we got home and out the car, I put my arm around him to try and reassure him, telling him that he just needed to answer honestly the questions he was asked, that was all that he needed to do. There was nothing more I could do to protect him now. Simon arrived back shortly after, also looking pale and drained. I set about getting the children some dinner and conveying a sense of normality in what felt like a very surreal set of circumstances. 'Normal' was contrary to the feeling in my gut; none of this was sitting right with me, but I guessed that's how you felt when something like this occurs.

When the lady and gentleman arrived from social services they were very pleasant; they understood how upsetting this was for all concerned. I kept the littlest child occupied in the kitchen whilst they spoke to Simon, then to his eldest son. We stood tortured downstairs as he cried in front of these strangers in his bedroom, wanting to know if he was going to be allowed to still see his dad; it was breaking my heart. Finally, they spoke to Simon and me together. They were trying to establish a picture of both what had happened and who we were as a family. It all felt a bit bizarre, you don't give much thought to that dynamic from day-to-day, so trying to put it into words wasn't easy. I was conscious that I didn't want to throw anyone under a bus. Simon's eldest wasn't a straightforward child, but then she had been on the frontline of her parent's marriage break-up and it had undoubtedly had an impact. Simon similarly was a complex character - emotional and prone to lose his temper, particularly when parenting. He also wasn't immune, I'd discovered, to a bit of drama.

Social Services left and Simon sat on the sofa - crying and exhausted. One of his first thoughts was the need to inform the youngest's mother; it would be likely that social services would be contacting her. "She'll love this. She'll use it against me", was all he kept saying. I knew that the threat of the move abroad was now back at the top of his mind, and this would be her golden ticket to enact that in a way that was disadvantageous to him.

When he rang her to explain what had happened, he said she wasted no time in taking the moral high ground; at the same time, she wasn't entirely surprised.

I silently agreed that his daughter possessed the same over-dramatic trait that Simon regularly demonstrated. He always insisted that she was like her mother, but as I spent more time around them both I realised the similarities were actually with him. A bit emotionally cold, slightly out of touch with reality, and the ability to cut someone out of their life if required. Simon prided himself on that last trait and now was threatening to use it with his eldest child, who he felt had "utterly betrayed" him.

When they next spoke, Simon's ex-wife didn't think he was guilty of what their daughter claimed. I should have been relieved. Instead, I had a gnawing feeling in my stomach that there was more to this story; something didn't feel right. I desperately didn't want to think that of him, it was too awful and I felt completely disloyal, but the niggle churned away deep down; the whole thing was making me uneasy. Yes, what had happened was upsetting. Yes, it was shocking, especially if completely unfounded. Yet something about Simon's dramatic reaction felt a little overplayed. It reminded me of something he'd once said: "the best lies were the ones based on truth". He'd admitted to grabbing her and that he'd wanted to scare her, so just how far had it gone? The people around us knew him - and her - better than I did, so I told myself not to be silly and threw myself into supporting his story.

The following day I still met the youngest's mum as planned; it seemed like the appropriate thing to do despite all the upheaval of the previous day. With how

Simon had described this woman, it felt right to meet her exactly because of the previous evening's events. Keeping things calm. Playing it down. As it turned out, she looked tenser than I was when I spotted her across the café. My plan with her was the same as I had adopted with the children and with the mother of the eldest two: to be respectful and just be myself.

My relationship with this woman's child was going great, so I had nothing to be concerned about.

At the outset, we inevitably touched upon the events of the preceding day, but after a brief exchange, I made it clear that I didn't want to pick over the bones of it or speculate about what might happen. She remarked pointedly that Simon would be inclined to punish his eldest for what she'd done. In her opinion, I needed to ensure that he didn't do that. I found her statement interesting but left it at that.

I didn't dislike her, she was intelligent and pretty straightforward (despite Simon's opinion of her), but she was not the sort of person outside of this that I'd choose to be friends with. I found this mother a bit controlling, and some of her parenting decisions questionable, but there was no doubt that she loved and was fiercely protective of her son. I didn't want her to feel uncomfortable about my relationship with her child, especially since the eldest's mother had explained how it had been like a knife through her heart when she had to imagine the woman sitting in front me taking care of her children when she'd lived with

Simon. I imagined a similar emotion was now behind the sometimes very specific instructions we received from the youngest's mother, particularly about the roles she felt I should play in her son's care. I tried to reassure her that my interest was always in doing what was right for her child; responding first and foremost to those needs. In fairness she did speak well of her perception of my relationship with her son, saying that he relayed that I tickled him and made him laugh. I appreciated her sharing that with me and hoped it might make her feel that he was happy in my company.

Slightly more puzzling was that she'd not agreed to see me sooner because, as she described it, she had been unaware that I was moving in with Simon. She maintained she'd not been told and had only realised that this was our home set-up more recently. I apologised if there had been any confusion, and made her aware that it had been the situation for over 6 months. In the interests of complete disclosure, I told her I'd met the other children's mother before I'd met them a year prior. I knew it was a risk to raise this, but I felt it was best to avoid any misunderstanding or a sense of politics; for me there were none. In the same vein, when she enquired when Simon and I had met, I played it straight - I had no reason to do otherwise. It turned out that in her assessment too there had been an overlap between her relationship with Simon and the end of his marriage, just as his ex-wife had said; she was keen to find out if the same had applied between me and her.

It turns out that his relationship with her was definitely over before I came on the scene, although I couldn't comment on any dating he'd done beforehand - that was between him and her. What did niggle me a little was that she said he'd told her we'd met in the October rather than the reality of August the previous year; I set this straight and decided it would be for him to explain if questioned. Back at home, I let it lie; we currently had enough to contend with and no doubt I was being a bit oversensitive under the circumstances.

She wasn't wrong: Simon didn't want to see his daughter and spoke often in the days after the social services visit about cutting her out of his life. He certainly refused to contemplate any situation where he may be left alone with her. This went on for a couple of weeks until I persuaded him to hold a 'summit meeting' between them, with me and the girl's mother present as mediators. We tried to get back steadily to some kind of family 'normal'. Part of me understood Simon's ongoing concern, I'd reflected on what it would mean for me both personally and professionally if she was to make any such accusation towards me. The other part of me deeply felt for this young girl, she was the child in this after all, and I wasn't sure how far she'd now backed herself into a corner before realising the magnitude of the situation. There was no doubt for me that she had learnt some of her attention-seeking behaviour from her dad, a vital element that he so conveniently chose to ignore; I had firsthand experience of how Simon could change moods like a chameleon.

It was during the same Autumn period that his eldest son arrived home from school covered in mud. A typical boy he loved football; it looked as though he'd gathered a generous part of the school playing field on his uniform during his lunch break. With the kids living between their mum's and Simon's house, sometimes they would run short on uniform changes if the visits were disorganised or items were forgotten (which happened with a frequency that astounded me). I got him to change out of his dirty things so I could wash and dry his trousers ready for school the next day. I rose even earlier the next morning to ironing them and, imagining Simon's moans, to clean and polish the caked-up school shoes. Anything for a peaceful life.

Later that day Simon collected them all from school – he continually found this very stressful, despite it being pretty much his only job; there was something about family chores and the daily stuff that massively wound him up.

Unusually this day I was already at home when they got back, so I headed downstairs to greet them and hear about their days. Once all inside beneath the kitchen lights, we all saw that Simon's eldest son was as covered in mud as he'd been the previous day. Simon instantly exploded; he went berserk. His rage was off the scale. He went for the boy like a wild animal ravaging its prey, screaming at him for getting dirty again and for being thoughtless in doing so. He smacked the middle child round the legs and sent him crying up to his tiny room. An eerie hush descended on the rest of us as I helped the littlest one out of his coat before he followed his sister upstairs into her bedroom. I stayed downstairs and put on the kettle in a rather pathetic attempt to restore some equilibrium by making a cup of tea; I was 'busying' trying to evaporate the atmosphere that now pervaded the house.

Moments later and without saying a word, Simon strode out of the kitchen and ran up the stairs. I hesitated for a few seconds, wondering what his urgency was and listening out for whether one of the kids had called us. I walked to the bottom of the stairs. I got there in time to hear a door slam and then raised voices. Simon was in his eldest son's room, bellowing at him once again. For a split second, I was rooted to the spot in shock, trying to work out what had happened to cause another outburst. As I went up the stairs I heard the child begging him, "No dad, no! Get off me!". He sobbed as Simon yelled above the obvious sounds of a physical scuffle in the confined space; I imagined his 6ft frame and accompanying rage filling the room. As I got onto the landing Simon flew back out of the room slamming the door behind him and stormed into our bedroom. In a violent flash, it was over as quickly as it had begun - my heart pounding in horror at what I had just heard.

I could hear the boy crying on his bed, but I went instead next door; I was conscious that the smallest one, in particular, would have heard the entire encounter and might, like me, be terrified. I picked him up and cuddled him as we went back downstairs.

I gently told him that whilst daddy was very angry, it wasn't at him; he'd done nothing wrong. He seemed to understand as I put on the TV. I was relieved to find it still on the children's channel from when he'd sat there for breakfast. I quickly got out some toys before going back upstairs - the eldest had started to cry when I'd left her. I completely understood. Had it not been for the kids, I would have been sobbing myself. Instead, I sat on the bed and put my arm around her.

I was trying to offer some words of comfort when Simon burst into the room - his face hard and angry, distorted as he spat out words of contempt at his daughter: "What the fuck are you crying for? Why the fuck are you upset? You don't even like your brother!". When she tried to explain that she was upset because he had hurt her brother, he screamed over her, "This is the thing with you, isn't it? This isn't about you. Why are you getting involved? It's got fuck all to do with you, but you're just like your mother - creating a drama, crying and making it all about you!". Had the situation not been so volatile, I'd have laughed at him. Just like her mother? Really?! I found my hold around her tighten as I remained silent. At times like this, I knew that as the 'outsider' my input would not be welcomed; the proffering of my opinion would be tantamount to insubordination. Any hint of criticism would be crushed. 'Protect the children' my conscience kept repeating; I knew that was the priority and I was smart enough to know that silence to let the heat dissipate was my best chance of doing that. It went against every instinct to not stand up to him, but this was not about me: 'protect the children'. If I'd been unsure in any way before how much I loved them, I was in no doubt that night. It crucified me that I'd not realised he was going back in for a second go at his eldest son; that I'd not made it in time to stand between them. To prevent it. I wouldn't make that mistake again. I'd never witnessed a rage like it. I'd never seen Simon in a rage quite that bad.

I tried to keep my voice level and calm as I suggested that perhaps he should go downstairs and check on his youngest; he might not understand that the shouting was not about him. I held my breath as he looked at me for a couple of seconds with a clenched jaw before he left the room without speaking; I tried not to let the sigh of relief come out too audibly. I mopped up her tears before going to comfort the small child who was still crying in the room next door. I did so quietly so as not to reignite the situation. Treading on eggshells.

What stunned me most was Simon's ability to snap out of his fury, and the all-consuming aura that seemed to come with it, as soon as he was with his youngest child. Downstairs now he was talking to him cheerfully in his impressive array of funny voices as if nothing had happened. The ability to switch between Jekyll and Hyde so effortlessly was unnerving. There was a distinct pattern emerging in his behaviour: he'd shout at either of the eldest two, but never at the youngest one. It proved he could control his temper. What I was also learning, was that often it wouldn't be just the one time – he frequently went back for round two.

As he loved a good graph (it was something we laughed about), I used that as an analogy when I tried to discuss

274

it with him, deliberately catching him in a calmer mood a few days later. This graph, I tried to reason, meant the children thought they'd had their telling off and started to move forward from it, only for it to be repeated, but more severely the second time. I wanted him to understand how shocking and confusing that was to the person on the receiving end, and how it prevented him from getting his lesson across. He sat quietly as he took in my words. I could tell he didn't like it, but I had to tell him, for the children's sake. I noted that he didn't have an equitable counter-argument.

One thing was for certain, that evening was one of the most vivid memories that had been created in my life thus far; it crouched in my brain thereafter as a constant warning.

❧

The little girl was very tired.

She was trying really hard. Doing everything he wanted. Being nice, really well-behaved. Making him happy.

He'd given her everything she wanted. She was so grateful. Finally, she'd got it right. This was it! She needed to make sure he didn't leave. She must make him stay. Not do anything silly. Not get it wrong. Not lose him. No longer be alone.

Although she was very tired. She didn't want to have to put on a performance anymore. It would be so good to have a rest.

၁

TWENTY-FIVE:

BE CAREFUL WHAT YOU WISH FOR...

Towards the end of November, the house purchase completion was imminent. What I hoped was that, once we were all settled, Simon would settle too. Most days now he seemed stressed and moody; moments of warmth or positivity were few and far between. I rationalised that as soon as we were away from this cold, confined space it would all be very different. We'd no longer go through this ritual of incandescent rage or how he could completely change character at the click of a finger, and be back to oozing sweetness and light. It was confusing. Yet the flashes of light in the darkness kept me clinging onto hope that things would get better. He'd certainly been so excited about all the possibilities with the new house.

We'd decided to furnish our first home from scratch; a whole new chapter for us with items that we had chosen together and none of the relics of either of our pasts. Simon's house gradually began to resemble a cardboard city with boxes of new furnishings, cutlery and crockery stacking up in every room. We were fortunate that Simon didn't need to sell his house to purchase our new one, which made the transition easier and less disruptive for the children. As he was self-employed, and despite the money he had from his business, I was the one with the perceived security through the income of having a job. So we got a mortgage based on my employment and were able to fund the deposit from the fact that John and I had finally sold our cottage. Simon and I agreed that I'd pay the deposit and he would pay me back his half once his house sold. It made sense and gave us the luxury of being able to do some of the work we wanted to at the new house without having to live around it as we did so.

By mid-December the house sale completed. I could hardly believe it; once we had the keys in our hands I sighed with relief that we'd gone through with it this time. We were about to have a stable home - and a beautiful home at that; it was the most stunning house I'd ever owned. All the 'behind the scenes' basics had been tackled by the previous owners so we could concentrate on bringing the numerous original features back to life and breathing some colour back into the expansive rooms; my vision for it had been forming for months. We found a decorator who specialised in period properties for me to work with - finally someone that I could share my ideas and discuss colours with. It was a standing joke between me and the kids that Simon couldn't even identify or name colours accurately, so I was relieved that I had someone to shoulder the burden of bringing to life the metres of walls.

We focused on the kids' rooms first. We worked incredibly hard, relentlessly, to produce a dream bedroom for each child, forging something to fit each of their personalities, trying to enact the wish list each of them had given me and aiming to create the idyllic childhood vision I wanted them to experience. We kept their rooms a secret from them until we were finished and unveiled them to huge delight. I was so excited for them all.

After moving in, unpacking all the new things we'd bought was like Christmas. Then we set about decorating the rest of the rooms. We replaced floors, ripped out fireplaces, put in woodturners and beautifully carved bookcases - we each had an extensive book collection that had been kept in boxes at Simon's house and couldn't wait to get them unpacked. Simon had numerous keepsakes and ornaments about which he was particularly precious (much to my sister's private amusement: "What is it with him and his 'special things'?!") and that he was keen to get out on display so that he could feel more at home.

When we were finished, the carpenter brought in a professional photographer to capture our two amazing front rooms; they wanted to use the images for their website and in a magazine. They truly were stunning. Simon said, "When you described what you wanted them to look like I had no idea what you were on about, but these are great. I don't know how this came out of your head, but it's mega". I was quite emotional; it was beautiful. I allowed myself a moment to feel rather pleased with my efforts. I had a fantastic vision for transforming the huge kitchen/dining area, which was currently a rather clinical space, and I couldn't wait to get going with it.

The massive surge of excitement evoked by the house buying adventure that Simon had so vividly created for us soon came crashing down, however. Almost from the moment the contracts were exchanged, his animated energy plummeted; his enthusiasm became notably muted. For months he'd been the driving force of this project so I was perplexed by his morose attitude. I was deeply disappointed, not least because I was in my element and delighted to have somewhere that was 'mine' after such a long time of renting or living in someone else's home. I couldn't wait to have the place where I 'belonged' that Simon had been so keen for me to have. I must confess to being slightly irritated that now we'd got there he was spoiling it for me.

The histrionics I'd thought would abate, continued and so did a creeping feeling that he wasn't happy. We had done so much to engineer an easier lifestyle for everyone, the fresh start we both craved, but the burning issue now had transferred to how hard it was for Simon with the length he had to travel to get his children to school. Yet still, he had it the easiest. I had the longest daily commute and I spent ages in my car, but you'd never think so from listening to him. We'd also gone through the considerable gymnastics of getting the children's mothers to agree to adjust the cycle of how their time was split between the two halves of their families, which made things significantly easier for everyone, but still, he moaned.

"The house hasn't moved", I said to him with some exasperation one evening, "You knew exactly where it was when we bought it. You did the journey here many times yourself. I'm not sure why the distance is suddenly a surprise or an issue given that you said beforehand that it was perfectly fine".

I couldn't help but think this was not the real issue, but that was what he was presenting to me, so I decided to knock that one on the head with logic and see what came back at me; he needed to spit it out, whatever 'it' was. I had a suspicion that having got what he'd said for so long he wanted, he now felt trapped. I thought back to the previous two aborted attempts at buying somewhere together, and this same attitude resonated with both occasions. He chased after something shiny and then freaked when it was within his grasp. Somehow this time he'd not found a way out; I thought perhaps it was the draw of the 'flash' house. Now he was having to deal with the consequences and he didn't like that he'd let his ego put himself in this position. I asked him what exactly it was that he wanted. I didn't get a definitive answer. He had as strong a preference for negative attention-seeking as much as he did for the positive, so along with copious moaning, there was also a dislike for any logical solutions.

After numerous attempts to get to the bottom of what was bothering him, it seemed to come down to this: for me to take on the whole home and family responsibilities, to leave my job, do the school runs and the ferrying to various extra-curricular activities, to allow Simon to renovate his other properties and go for walks in the hills. Mostly the walking in the hills bit. That was the reality of the pressure he was trying to exert on me. I laughed. I made it known that I had no intention of giving up my career to fulfil his dream for his perfect life:

"I love your children. I love the bones of them. But you are always very clear that they are exactly that - YOUR children, not mine. If that's how you want to live your life then they have mothers that you need to speak to in order to make that happen".

Let's be clear: I'd be giving up my career and my life to look after someone else's children whilst their father lived the life of Riley?! Yeah. Right. He liked to claim that having children wasn't his choice or his desire; they were an accident. This was certainly something that the mother of the eldest two strongly contested, telling me that both of her children were discussed and were planned. Yet the fact that he was now, "effectively a single parent" was an accusation he levelled at me to let me know that everything I did to support him was worthless. It was as if he'd suffered some kind of incredible injustice.

"Did they rape you?", I once asked.
"What do you mean?!", he said, horrified.
"Did either of the mothers of your children force you to have sex with them, ever?", I clarified.

"No."

"Then you had some semblance of choice", I replied, "You willingly had unprotected sex with women of child-bearing age, so them getting pregnant was a gamble you chose".

I was walking a dangerous line, but the 'woe-is-me' victim mentality of his parental responsibilities sometimes wore extremely thin - especially as I would desperately have liked to have suffered this particular type of 'misfortune'. But, of course, that maternal need in me was exactly what he was trying to appeal to; he could give me exactly what I'd always wanted if only I'd willingly play along.

No matter what logic I tried to overlay on his 'troubles', the unhappiness continued to ooze out of him; he could see no further than himself and his, apparently unmet, needs. None of my stuff mattered. None of my needs. Not the fact that I was holding down a stressful job whilst doing all of this extra work for us to benefit from, still commuting, trying to do what I could to look after our home, his children, do pick-ups and drop-offs when I could (even when it put me under considerable pressure from around a very unforgiving boss). For all of that and how much I was bending myself out of shape to make all this work, no-one ever had such a bad time as him; he made damned sure we all knew it. He had everything that most people dreamt of: money, a family, freedom to do what he wanted and so many opportunities, yet all he focused on was moaning about not doing what he wanted to. I was shocked at how ungrateful he was, and how resistant he was to any suggestions to improve his (terrible) lot in life. It just showed that what we think we want is often not what we need.

He started to complain that the children were not happy either. I responded that it was up to us to encourage them to make new friends just as we had discussed before we chose to move. What he actually meant was that he didn't have any desire to meet new people and became determined not to support the children either. The only people he spoke to were the lovely retired couple in the cottage next door, but only because (as he openly said to me) he thought he could "manipulate" the lady into cooking for us and baby-sitting (i.e. someone else to palm his children off onto). What he didn't count on, though, was that she was wiley - nobody's fool.

It became increasingly clear that he'd been in love with the fantasy of this house, but now we were living the reality it wasn't cutting it for him; he wanted the next new thing in his endless pursuit of evasive happiness. After only a few months of being in our new home, he outright declared that we needed to move. He didn't care for one moment what that meant for me. When I'd been living in his house I'd ended up so poorly with the extra stress and strain that the long journeys placed on me, particularly in winter and when I was unwell. Despite his misery, I now felt much healthier having cut an hour a day off my commute; the last thing on my mind was to move again.

Yet he continued telling me how isolated he felt - even though he had family nearby in all directions, whereas mine was hours away. My reasoning was met with one of his almighty meltdowns, yelling that he couldn't see any of his friends because of how far away they were. I was puzzled as to which friends he meant, he didn't seem to have any. He'd make references to people he knew and would say hello to people we passed when we were out and about, but there were no actual friends that I'd ever met; these were acquaintances at the best. Apart from a few guys he played five-a-side with each week, who all went for a pint after the game, he never seemed to be contacted by anyone that I would have classed as a 'friend', certainly not in the sense that I had friends. I reminded him that my friends were much further away, but that I still managed to spend time with them. I even offered to take him and pick him up so that he could see these 'friends' he was missing whenever he wanted to go out with them, but he screamed at me that seeing them was "impossible" and that I didn't understand. He was right - I didn't understand - there was no logic whatsoever to what he said. No sense that I could identify; these people only lived 20 or 30 minutes away - that hardly seemed challenging to me. However, he scoffed at my solutions and stormed off when I proffered anything that seemed like a practical answer. To say I was baffled was an understatement. Perhaps I was being an idiot? Was there something obvious that I was missing? I tried to think.

So it should have come as no surprise when he angrily told me one day that it was no good, there was nothing for it, we were selling the house. He didn't like it there, couldn't settle and didn't want to stay. No debate. No compromise. No attempt at trying to make it our home. We were going. In fact, he screamed as he banged his fist on the kitchen counter, "I'm leaving this house whether you come with me or not!". It was like watching a child have a tantrum. When I took myself upstairs to avoid him seeing the tears that had inevitably flowed under the torrent of his fury, he sought me out only to yell, "And I might have known all you'd do is fucking cry!".

We finished the work we'd been doing to the house, which he was desperate to bring to an end, so the decorator was as amazed as I was when I shared with him how Simon didn't want to stay.

"I've been lucky enough to work on some amazing projects during my career, but I have to say this house is about the most beautiful I have ever worked on - how your vision has come to life is stunning," he said.

We both stood in our hallway admiring the sweeping staircase and pondered how anyone could not be happy to live there. He liked Simon, I could tell, but even he was stumped by this decision to sell.

All of this raised a thorny issue that had begun troubling me and I was preparing myself to tackle with Simon. His other house had sold several months prior, but despite this, he'd made no indication of paying me the half of the deposit money we'd agreed. I was paying an equal share of all the costs of the renovations. One of the other options we'd discussed was that he'd put his share of the deposit money into paying off some of the mortgage, which would reduce the monthly repayments; that hadn't happened either. As time passed and the silence grew I became more concerned that I was contributing more than my fair share, whilst he sat comfortably on a stack of cash. A stack that he checked up on with a regularity that I found staggering; he logged in to his online bank account on an almost daily basis.

It was notable too that all the talk of marriage had evaporated, which, unfortunately for him, had a light shone on it when his ex-wife announced that she had got engaged. He knew that I would feel like it had rained on our parade; he'd have been aware that he'd made promises on that front that he'd not delivered on. In fact, despite all his dreams and words and promises, he seemed not to have made any further investment in our future together - emotionally or financially.

I picked a day when he seemed in a better mood and calmly brought the subject up, wanting an honest conversation to see where he was at. It became another excuse for him to have a gargantuan rage at me, watching him switch in seconds, from being in a good frame of mind to an angry monster. He launched at me verbally about how wrong I was, how I was being "selfish", "unreasonable" and "money-grabbing", about why he shouldn't do what we'd agreed (which made no sense at all), that the money was better left in his account, and that he couldn't believe that I was even raising any of this. I defaulted to my oft-employed mode of trying to keep the peace, saying that I wasn't wanting to fall out, just to be reasonable and to discuss if things had changed for him so that we could look at our options. My words were to no avail. I was unable to appeal to his better nature as he dissolved into a silent brood and resorted to banging around the house in a physical display of his displeasure; whatever button I had pressed on this topic, it felt like the nuclear one.

A day or two later of obvious rumination and he went mental again - without provocation. He was outraged that I had dared to mention the money or question his intentions. This was becoming a regular pattern: explosive rages, then emotionally cutting me off as he disappeared into himself. He prided himself on being able to cut someone out as if they were dead; he'd done it more than once with his own family.

I decided to confide in John, despite Simon's streak of jealousy about him; we spoke as friends regularly these days even though we were now divorced - something else Simon had requested. He reasoned that he couldn't ask me to marry him whilst I was still married, but (of course) only if I "wanted to get divorced". I trusted John's financial acumen, so I shared with him my situation. He was quite worried that I had no proof about investing my money. At the time I'd not thought twice about it - why would I? I began to feel I was in an impossible situation and it was clear that any attempt to talk about it was going to incur his wrath. He had me exactly where he wanted me on this one: paralysed.

Meanwhile, Simon was actively looking at houses again and all his conversation became about moving; places that were convenient to him, but not for me. He only saw his viewpoint, and my suggestions of buying somewhere nearer my work for me to stay at a few nights each week were met with accusations of not wanting him and his children: "How will I ever explain to the kids that you don't want to live with them anymore?".

It was exhausting, the permanent knot in my stomach from walking this tightrope was making me ill. We already had a cleaner to manage the house, so I suggested we might need to arrange a bit more support when we moved as I wouldn't be able to manage it all myself if my commute was going to increase. He went ballistic, telling me I was deeply selfish and couldn't want family life. I tried to explain it was precisely the opposite, that when I saw him and the children I wanted to spend quality time with them, not, as he used to complain, be stuck behind the ironing board! Yet when he'd dug himself into a position, it was impossible to pull him back out.

Whilst he saw his brother as inferior to him intellectually and socially, and loved nothing more than lording it over him, he did talk to him and would (sometimes) listen. So when I'd organised a birthday party for the youngest one and invited Simon's brother and family, I took the opportunity to express my concerns about his desire to move again, the perpetual unhappiness, and about how he felt about me.

"He's never felt about anyone how he feels about you - he's always said that to me", his brother tried to reassure me whilst his wife nodded enthusiastically. "He's not been with anyone how he is with you".

I tried to see this in the positive way that it was intended. I explained my worry that he was so restless.

"He's always been like that - a bit flaky", he said awkwardly and told me not to read too much into it.

They couldn't understand why he would want to leave our house either: "This place is amazing, you've made it gorgeous, it's like a dream home. We say that every time we come here, we love it. I don't know what he's thinking, but our Simon is never satisfied".

I shared my worry that at some point his dissatisfaction was going to extend to me: "Someone younger, shinier than me will come along and I think he'd just be gone", I confessed for the first time to anyone.

"Never! No way! You're the best thing that's ever happened to him; to him and those kids".

I was so grateful for their words and support; I felt better for having said my concerns out loud. They knew him best. I just had to trust that we'd catch a break and things would get better.

❧

TWENTY-SIX:

CRY ME A RIVER

It was early October when Simon first noticed that something wasn't right with him. Well, it was the first time he indicated to me that he was a little concerned about his genitals. Given his propensity for negative attention-seeking and over-exaggeration, it was never easy to get a decent perspective on how bad anything was. Even when I thought I did, it often turned out that my perspective was different (less dramatic) than his. So when he shared that he had "a spot" on his manhood I wasn't sure what to think. That's not entirely fair. I do know what I thought because, after a week of him talking about it, I asked him: "You've not been putting that somewhere you shouldn't have been, have you?", nodding towards his crotch as we walked towards the local pharmacy to find some kind of remedy. I wasn't sure what kind of remedy he was looking for, I'd always failed to notice the aisle dedicated to 'knob-rot'... perhaps I'd just been unobservant all these years. He was horrified at my question, even though I felt it was the sensible thing to ask: "How can you even think that?!". "Well, if there is a problem we just need to be honest", I said. He seemed genuinely put-out. Oops. I'd sort of thought it was funny, even if my reason for asking was to establish if we needed a serious conversation.

Having left the children in the car we were under time pressure, so Simon and I quickly scanned the shelves for some kind of lotion or potion that might help him. I had no idea what I might be seeking, but felt that 'looking busy' about the task at hand was the best strategy given his demeanour. He picked out some cream and we went to the cash desk with him feeling embarrassed, but happier that he was purchasing something that might provide him with some relief from whatever was occurring in his pants.

I knew that things hadn't improved, in fact, had deteriorated, from what he told and showed me (hmm, sexy) by late November. I knew enough to understand that, for a guy, this was fundamental. I also had sufficient life experience to tell him that he needed to put on his 'big boy pants' (no pun intended) and make a GP appointment. This was met with noisy protestations, but I told him that I wasn't qualified to help him with his concerns so he needed to seek professional help, not that from the internet, which I was certain he'd have been consulting at length. Crikey, everything had become a pun!

It had been a tough day at work already when Simon called me in tears. I ducked into a meeting room so that I could have a proper conversation to understand what the matter was. He'd been to the GP who had given two possibilities for what Simon presented on his genitals: either a 'significant' sexually transmitted infection (were there 'insignificant' STIs??) or cancer. "I do not like the look of that", the doctor had said. My heart began to pound. Whichever one of those it was, neither was welcome news; there was little I could say in comfort. I tried to get him to tell me what else the GP had said, but he was too distraught and under time pressure to collect the kids from school; as much as I adored them, having them this weekend was the last thing we needed. "I'll get in the car and come home as soon as I can", I said, knowing that several meetings stood between me and my ability to make good on that promise, "we'll get the kids settled down with a film and then we can talk about it properly". I certainly did not feel as calm as I was conveying, but I was at a loss to know what else to say.

I tried to make it through the rest of the afternoon with some semblance of productivity, even though my brain was scrambled. If it was cancer then goodness only knew what that meant. If it wasn't, well, I had to be honest that option was just as scary; that would mean that either I had given him something or there was a chance that he had passed something to me. Christ! I honestly didn't think I had anything to pass on. I'd been poked (see, more puns!), prodded and tested so much over the years thanks to my hormones that I couldn't imagine that it was me. My brain was spinning trying to contemplate something that up until that point had not been of the remotest concern. Simon and I had been together for almost two and a half years, a fact that I'd pointed out to him on the phone when I'd felt the finger of suspicion being pointed at me. "The doctor said these things can lay dormant for years", was his curt reply. Right. Ok. Time for some tough conversations.

By the time I got home, I was already exhausted; Simon's pallor showed he felt the same. Having occupied the children we sat in the kitchen with a glass of wine and addressed the issues in front of us. We each told the other that we'd not been unfaithful to our relationship and concluded that, if indeed it was an STI, then it was something from one of our pasts that we were just going to have to get tested and treated for. We'd just accept that this was something that we'd gone through together. Cold comfort, but at least we were being mature about it; I suspected that any results that didn't fall in my favour might elicit a different response from him, but for now I would accept what we'd agreed.

We had no option but to discuss the 'C' word. He unravelled at this point and, in an increasingly rare acceptance of any physical contact, allowed me to put my arms around him. "Let's get the facts first and then we can deal with whatever it is that we're presented with", I tried to reassure him. I knew from what Emma had been through that the premature contemplation of possible scenarios was grossly unhelpful. Although neither of us slept well that night as we each reflected what this could mean for us.

The following day he went, as advised by the GP, to the local genito-urinary clinic. I'd heard repeatedly the previous evening how horrified he'd been at the indignity of having to show his manhood to a stranger (a point that, I have to say, is lost on a woman as we have to get used to it; now was not the time to say that), so I knew that he was dreading this experience for several reasons.

I stayed at home waiting and tried to present a scene of normality to the kids.

Having been given such stark 'options' by the GP I wasn't prepared for what came back through the door a while later. The clinic nurse had disagreed with both of the doctors' conclusions; she said she'd seen a lot of STIs and was very confident it wasn't that (selfish or otherwise, a huge sigh of relief from me) and thought cancer was unlikely from what she saw. She wanted him to return the following day to see the specialist doctor, but what she'd said had to be a little reassuring at least. Not that this translated to how Simon was speaking about it, but I was positive and tried to buoy him up.

The specialist GUM doctor was a huge help. He was certain that it wasn't an STI or cancer, but something else entirely. Something treatable. Not uncommon and not life-threatening. Don't get me wrong, not great, but neither of the horrors we'd been preparing for. Topical treatment with a steroid cream was suggested, so that's what happened next.

I'd like to report that that was the end of that, but nothing with Simon was ever that straightforward. I'll keep explaining how this unfolded and come back at a later stage about what else happened in our lives in between.

It was mid-December when I took a day off to wrap

presents for the children whilst they were at school. My family were coming for Christmas and we had big plans to enjoy it in our beautifully refurbished home. I had busted my backside getting Christmas trees, decorations, stocking-fillers and presents ready. Simon still wasn't 'right' despite the steroid cream and was feeling miserable. I'd been as constructive, reasonable and upbeat as I could, but his perpetual 'sadsack' demeanour was a little wearing. I did understand from my bladder cyst how much this stuff could impact you mentally as well as physically, so I was advocating patience and providing lots of reassurance. This day I did the school run to give him a break and to fetch some supplies, before returning to the mammoth wrapping exercise.

When I got home he challenged me about how long I'd been so I knew he wasn't good. I often got shouted at for being 'late', not being home soon enough... which meant 'not there to pay him attention'. This day was one of those, but it took a different turn as he started to cry. I didn't want to see him upset, so I tried to console him and understand what was causing the extent of this meltdown. I expected it to be that he was impatient for the steroid cream to do its thing and for his penis to heal. Quite the contrary, he began talking again about having cancer; to say I was surprised was an understatement. The specialist had been clear what it wasn't and absolutely no tests along that route had been suggested. To start with I affectionately gave him a cuddle saying, "Don't be silly! It's all fine. The doctor told you what it was and it's not cancer, not even a hint of it". That, I quickly discovered, was not going to cut it. I don't know how to describe the hours that unfolded, all thirteen of them, as I carried on and tried to complete the task in front of me. He sobbed all day. He talked about death and cancer all day. I ran out of positive things to say or words of constructive comfort. Nothing seemed to even make a dent for more than a few minutes.

I understand about worry. I understand about mental health. I know how the need to stay strong and keep going can wear you down. I have to say, though, that this was a whole other level. In the end, I stopped saying anything, not just because I was struggling for new things to say, but because I was worried that I might yell, "For fuck's sake!". This was unnecessary wallowing of a different magnitude. What I wanted to say was that when I was told that there was a threat of cancer in my bladder I had got up every day for six months - in constant pain - and kept going. I had gone to work, I had done more than my fair share around the house, we'd moved, I'd seen to his sexual needs (something that he wasn't currently doing in return I might add). Then when they'd been able to tell me that the cyst had dissipated, it was only to deliver the news that the scan had instead identified a shadowy mass on my liver and that I needed to go straight to my GP to get an immediate referral for tests! I will admit that at that moment I had a major wobble - it was quite a shock - but it lasted an hour, maximum, after which practically sorting out a diagnosis had been the main priority. Action was required, not emotion. Keeping calm and carrying on. I'm not looking for a medal, or point-scoring and I'm not refusing to acknowledge that we all handle things differently… but some perspective is needed as to what I was handling here.

He cried on and off ALL DAY about something that he knew WASN'T AN ISSUE! People out there actually had cancer. I was beginning to lose patience with this interminable attention-seeking. It horrifies me to say that it was almost as if he WANTED it to be something more serious. At the end of thirteen hours, I slumped at the table, exhausted from trying to make an amazing Christmas for everyone else, and wondered how to make this better for him.

My mind crept uncomfortably back to that morning and why I had been out so long. I'd been standing in a card shop trying to pick out the more 'special', family Christmas cards that I always sent; I needed to select a card for Simon. That is what took the time, but not for good reasons. I'd realised in the shop that I had tears running down my face. Not because of the beauty of the words, but because none of them explained how I felt. Sending a card that said how loved and cherished I felt, how blessed and excited I was to spend Christmas with him…the words rattled around my soul, creating an unnerving echo that I'd not faced into before. I could have just picked one, it was only a card, it'll get thrown away come January…but I couldn't bring myself to do it. Given how he'd been over the last few months - longer - it felt like a lie.

What had happened to the guy I'd met? The smart, funny, charming, attentive one. The one that was so captivating that even the below-par sex hadn't mattered. I loved and wanted to be with that guy like nothing else had mattered. I wanted him back and I felt like I tried constantly to make him return. Sometimes I succeeded. More often lately, I didn't. He'd been ill. We'd had a lot of work done on the house. It had been tough on him. A good Christmas and it would all be better. I wiped away the tears and got a grip of myself. I bought a card with the least-worst sentiments, something that I felt I could stand behind without too much dishonesty, and then lied about why I'd taken so long to get home.

In January, he wasn't any better. He was thoroughly desolate. This medical condition was coming and going, but not with any real trajectory of improvement; believe me, my opinion was being requested frequently enough to state that with certainty. I understood why it was getting him down. At least he had accepted it wasn't cancer. The problems in his pants, however, had to take a back seat for a few weeks whilst he developed and dealt with an abscess under one of his teeth. He'd needed root-canal surgery, which was (inevitably) another drama, but neither of us was prepared for what ensued.

As he screamed in pain and paced the floor one night, I was again faced with something the likes of which I had never experienced. As always I was given chapter and verse of what was documented online, which included the various ways people had killed themselves due to the relentless pain. At one point, I contemplated assisted suicide…. Joking aside, I appreciated that what he was going through was excruciating, but he'd refused to let me take him to the hospital. I wasn't sure why given that it was offering a solution; he didn't seem to want to take it.

The morning after, the pain had eased a little and he insisted I went out to do some chores as he intended to get some sleep anyway. I was grateful for a couple of hours of respite from the screams. Within a couple of hours, he called me from his car - he was searching for an emergency dentist because he was, once again, beside himself with pain. By the time we both got home I failed to stifle a shocked laugh, "Oh my God, you look like Buzz Lightyear!". He had, in the short time I had been away, developed a very large jaw. My humour was misplaced and he burst into tears. I apologised profusely. Not the moment for my comedy genius.

A couple of hours later as his face continued to swell, I insisted that we went to the local A&E; I was genuinely worried now. They dosed him up on painkillers that gave a bit of relief and allowed us to make the trip to the emergency dentist with at least a little sleep. This turned out to be the intervention that was needed. At last, some rhinoceros-flooring drugs that would put this to rest. They wiped him out and made him nauseous, but desperate times called for desperate measures. From the first issue with a cracked tooth to the abscess healing, it had taken nearly a month end-to-end. We were both exhausted. Now we were just back to worrying about his nether-regions. They didn't improve his mood any, but we must surely now be through the worst? Wishful thinking.

TWENTY-SEVEN:

SIMPLY SAUSAGES

I wasn't sure quite what combination of stresses had aggravated him on that early February evening as I drove home. I tried my best to look after him, to play more than my part with the chores, parent the kids, create a beautiful home... but what I received was complaints about how pointless my efforts were and how late I got home. I started recording on my phone what time I got in as evidence against his claims that I was "never home before 7pm". Apart from the one evening a week I went to choir, his assertion was blatantly untrue. He continued to tell me how I was "no use" as he was "basically a single parent"; I tried to reason that I did what I could around my demanding, full-time job, but reason never even chipped the surface of his victim mentality.

Driving home this particular evening I was looking forward to having friends come over, so I gave him a call from the car as I travelled along the motorway. My call was answered with his screaming rage. My heart began to pound as I tried to understand what had happened. What was articulated was a singular issue for which I was responsible: discarding some sausages from the fridge. Apparently, these had been his plan for the youngest's dinner, and I had ruined it because I had cleaned out the fridge before work that morning and thrown them away due to the lack of an identifiable use-by date. The concept of "feed him something else", was not welcome. Instead, I was going to pay for my mistake.

The rage that was streaming down the line at me was unprecedented; it was of the type that I recognised from that night when his eldest son was muddy. It was beyond that. Never, personally or professionally, had I heard anything like it. I have difficulty finding the words to describe quite how it was. Apoplectic anger, seething, disproportionate, unreasonable, without the hope of placating. It might not even convey the gravity of the situation when I say that he then, in our voluminous kitchen, put his phone on speaker and started crashing about the room: doors and drawers were slammed, metal trays banged, shouting and swearing. The cacophony was deafening. Shocking. My only comfort was that I knew that he wouldn't let his little boy suffer this; he would be secured away somewhere else because heaven's above that Simon should ever let himself fall from the pedestal on which his youngest held him. Meanwhile, I knew, as did he, that I was driving towards this fury - nowhere to go, no chance of avoiding it; I was careering towards it at seventy miles-per-hour. When he finally decided I was clear about how angry he was with me, he abruptly hung up.

I went into the house and the all-too-familiar aura enveloped me. Hostile. Volatile. I could hear Simon talking to his son in the children's TV room, so I plastered on my best smile and went in to say hello. Normality for the children was always my top priority. As I went in his youngest looked up and called out my name with a smile and his usual excitement. In contrast, Simon glowered at me and turned away. He did what he always did - he circled the wagons around his children, the youngest in particular; it was designed to let me know that they were not mine, I was not part of their unit. I was an outsider. Isolated. He liked me to know that he could take them away from me at any time and I would have no recourse; he gave no thought to what that would mean to the children.

I was not welcome, so I went and sat in the front lounge. It was a beautiful, peaceful space decorated in deep jewel colours; it was my favourite room in the house. Aside from its extensive use at Christmas, it was rare that anyone else came in here apart from me, so I relished a few minutes of solitude on the plush sofa. My mind and heart were both racing. I knew that the second wave would be coming. I was already tired. Mostly, I was tired of placating him when I didn't mean it. Who had I become? At work, I was strong, not afraid to stand up for myself and others; clear in my opinions and values. At home, I was turning into everything except that. I guess my need to be loved by my co-workers was significantly less than the need to be loved by my partner. I could find another job. I knew that finding another partner was far harder. I'd not had the best of luck and in Simon, I'd found a smart, funny guy and a ready-made family. It couldn't have been better. Where had that gone? All the ingredients were there, but somehow these last few months we'd been unable to concoct the lavish banquet on which we'd feasted in those early days. All I tasted now was fear - of being alone.

Simon barged into the room. When he was minded, everything about him was bullish: big, loud, brash, harsh. I winced. It made me become the antithesis. He threw words at me like arrows - darts of hate and criticism - as we prepared for our visitors. Once they were with us we ordered take-out; he and I got in the car to collect it. As we pulled up he spoke once more with words coated in attitude and I couldn't hold it in any longer.

"You don't even notice me", I said calmy. "You're so consumed with you that you don't even look up and see how unhappy I am. How much I try, how hard I work, what I do for you and the children, how much I have tried to nurse you and stay positive. When I was ill I was just expected to pick myself up and keep going; moaning wasn't an option. I have supported you, loved you, helped you, but you don't even think to stop and look at what this is like for me. I am desperate, unhappy and lonely. And you don't care".

I wasn't angry. I didn't raise my voice. I was just… sad. All I wanted was to be acknowledged; to matter. He silently got out of the car, picked up the food and drove the short distance home. Back on our drive he stopped the car and apologised. I was surprised but pleased. At least he had heard what I said. I didn't realise that the apology had a cost attached.

The following morning he unleashed his wrath. We were in the kitchen when he started to scream at me. The rage. There it was. He was in full flow with our guests still upstairs. I went and closed the door to stop them hearing - ashamed of his outburst and mortified about what he was saying to me. I was humiliated that this was how I lived. He'd lost it. Livid and telling me it was all my fault: my behaviour, my attitude, my inability to do what was needed, my selfishness that I insisted on having my "own life". Putting him and the children second. I'd spoken up and out of turn.

It brought to mind a question Jen had posed at Christmastime: "Has he ever hit you?". Without missing a beat I'd replied, "No, but I'm ready". My answer had shocked me; it came so easily that I knew I must have subconsciously been contemplating that possibility.

At this moment I braced myself for things to get physical. His temper was so incandescent I could see how it would ignite into a flash that would be a punch. I was shaking with shock, fear, adrenalin. Would I let him hit me? Would I fight or run? I didn't know - right in that instant, I felt rooted to the spot as his temper continued to rain down. I was compelled to hear what it was that I did that evoked this response. It was like running the steel of a knife blade along my arm to see how much pain I could endure. It was like self-harm. I was determined to know what I did that was so wrong, so bad. Maybe I deserved this. Perhaps I had been unreasonable. I'd probably communicated badly. Sometimes he made me feel small, contained, controlled, so I wondered whether last night I'd behaved like a scolded, petulant child. The injustice of how he spoke to me did press my buttons. I had likely let that frustration show. It was probably my own fault, of my own making.

I believed I'd been the one who had gone too far. I should have kept quiet, ridden the waves. This relationship was over. I was sure of it. Once our visitors had left, Simon went out of the house without saying a word to me; I watched him drive away in a cloud of furious gravel dust. I didn't know if I was desolate or grateful. He hadn't hit me. Maybe going out was his way of preventing that. Maybe he would store up his anger for when he returned later: the dreaded second wave. My brain was foggy with the possibilities and the fatigue that living on my nerves created. I was desperately trying to make sense of what his actions meant. Then he called. I leapt to answer, holding my breath in anticipation of what he might say.

"I am going to take a drive to look at some furniture for the holiday cottage, I wondered if you wanted to come with me?", he said.

It was brusk, but it was his version of an olive branch. The storm hadn't passed, but the thunder was now rumbling further off in the distance. My relief was palpable; I sat down on the sofa. "If you'd like me to", I tried to sound 'light' in my tone, amiable. Placating.

"I'll come back in 10 mins and get you", he said. Then hung up.

I'd swerved the end of the relationship; that was a relief. We could pull this back around.

I blamed his health; it must be impacting how he felt about himself. I encouraged him to go back to the doctor. He knew it needed to be done, so he faced his fears and saw the GP. Alternatives were not forthcoming, so he took matters into his own hands. He took to the internet and found himself an 'expert'. I didn't ask what he googled to come up with that.

Off he went to expose his genitals to someone else, which was personally a relief - it gave me a day off from it. When he returned home he was delighted to have found someone that he viewed as a specialist in this area and who was able to answer his questions about causes and treatments. The recommendation was surgery, quite radical surgery at that. I think my face might have said it all. He let me cuddle him briefly.

So now we were on a path towards his surgery. It would take place under general anaesthetic. He'd been told that he'd struggle to walk or get out of bed for the first two weeks; it could take up to 6 weeks for him to be able to drive again. Managing the care of the kids (not least because Simon wasn't minded to share with their mothers exactly what the issue was) whilst ensuring their ongoing contact with their father was going to be tricky and important to get right; we'd just have to play it by ear. Understandably, he was anxious about the surgery itself, but also hoped that this would allow him to get back to 'normal'… although we'd had to discuss that 'normal' would look and feel a bit different on the other side of his surgery. Simon was especially worried about this part: about how much 'care' I was going to have to provide for his most prized possession. "We're just going to have to get on with it", I said, "We'll just have to keep our sense of humour and do what needs to be done to get through it". It was the best I could offer.

Don't get me wrong, none of this was pleasant, but I was trying to focus on the other side of it all and believing that once this was sorted he'd start to go back to his old self. Sometimes being with him was like I imagined it to be living with someone with dementia: the feeling of loss like you were living with a stranger, and then suddenly they'd burst back through the darkness. The wonderful man I met and loved would show himself. It was as though he recognised who I was, remembered 'us'; the rush of happiness I felt would give me hope that it was all going to be ok, that the halcyon days were coming back.

One such moment came in April. With a month to go until his operation, Simon told me that he wanted to book to take me away for a long weekend to mark my birthday. "We have to accept that we won't be able to celebrate your actual birthday, because I'll still be recovering. I'm sorry", he said, "So I'd like to take you away when I'm recovered to make up for it". I was so touched that it mattered to him that my eyes filled with tears; that for the first time in what felt like a very long stretch he was thinking beyond himself. It gave me faith that we were indeed on the path to better times.

First, we had to get through the surgery. His consultant reassured us that this was, for him, a routine procedure.

It was what he said when he returned after the operation that I paid more attention to. I was grateful that at that stage Simon was still heavily under the effects of the anaesthetic.

"We had to do more than I had originally anticipated", he began.

"Right", I heard myself saying - shooting a glance at Simon to see whether he was taking any of this in. He was barely conscious. The surgeon went on to advise me about hygiene, care and the stages of healing. It was, in particular, his articulation of what to expect that held my attention and filled me with horror: "In a couple of days time it will look like he's been ravaged by a wild animal", he said very matter-of-factly. Simon, I could tell, wasn't tuned in to this. The surgeon reassured me that this was normal. "Right", I repeated, not able to find any other words and hoping that the wincing I was feeling internally wasn't showing on my face. I'm not sure why I wanted to look like I was taking all of this in my stride.

We were, eventually, sent away with a stack of wading and bandages, some pain killers and a set of instructions on how to dress and care for whatever it was that lay beneath Simon's surgical dressings. As awful as it was I was sure that as a shared experience it would bind us as a couple and bring us closer. This day was the start of the journey forward. As I drove him home I told him the worst part was over; it wasn't an intentional lie.

The surgeon knew his stuff. The wild animal turned up a couple of nights later, and what we woke to was swollen, bruised, bloody and weeping. Simon yelped in horror when he saw it. "You poor bastard", were the only words I could find to say. It was no point trying to tell him it wasn't so bad. My only hope, I joked, was that the swelling was a permanent fixture, "if the doctor has made it bigger then he really is a genius!", I said to elicit a laugh. He smiled at least. Many a true word is spoken in jest.

The days and weeks that followed were tough. I spent as much time mopping tears and being encouraging as I did changing dressings; it was a slow process, but signs of recovery were definitely, progressively there. Believe me, I spent that much time with it being offered up for my inspection I was starting to think I knew it better than he did.

Several weeks later after the last of the stitches

worked their way out - yes, I winced too - he was left with a raw-looking wound that now just needed to heal. The surgeon didn't want to see him again for nearly a month, so patience was necessary - a virtue that Simon was not flushed with.

ॐ

TWENTY-EIGHT:

TRUTH OR DARE?

Work was increasingly creating more angst for me, I was being bullied by my boss and it was not subsiding; I was picked on every day either in the office or over email. I felt that sick sensation form in my stomach each Sunday evening; it had turned into a knot to which I now seemed to be waking every day. Yet here I was, facing into this daily battle, and having a similar fight at home. The contrast was that in the latter I felt completely unable to say what I felt. It was one day when I caught myself agreeing with Simon, pacifying him, taking the blame for something, trying to keep his voice down so that the children couldn't hear the altercation, apologising for being wrong, that I wondered where the hell the real me had disappeared to - again.

What I needed, what Simon and I needed, was some time away. I needed to forget about work for a few days, and he and I needed some quality time together. The fact that we were going to Europe for four days was both exciting and a god-send. Simon had organised a trip with every detail taken care of - beautiful hotel, flights, excursions; I was hugely encouraged by his thoughtful behaviour.

I'd been eagerly putting ready my clothes and toiletries for packing for several days, as well as making sure that Simon had everything he needed washed and ironed. I was due to finish work at lunchtime on Friday and meet him at the airport, so in the preceding days, I put most of my items in the case, ready to put the finishing touches in on the morning of our departure.

We had been continuing to debate our living situation and had indeed been looking at alternatives to buy now that our house had sold. It had, I'd admit, led to some difficult conversations because all of the places where Simon was prepared to live meant significant journeys and changes to my life, with no compromise from him. The only house on which we had agreed, he had got very excited about and then inexplicably had gone cold.

I think it was possibly concerning this debate, although I wasn't entirely sure, that led to the text message I received just after I arrived at work the day before our trip away. I looked at my phone before going into a meeting and was shocked to have received a lengthy diatribe; it detailed the type of despicable human being I was and how hurt and disgusted he was by my selfishness at not wanting to put aside my needs for those of him and his children. I was stunned by the venom of the language and the fact that none of it had been hinted at that morning at home; it was delivered only an hour after I arrived at the office.

What had provoked this? Why had he sent it now? He signed it off saying that he no longer felt able to go away with me because of my attitude. What the hell? I was dumbfounded. I tried to hold it together as I responded, expressing my surprise and the fact that it would be preferable to talk about it. When I took an opportunity to call him, I was met with the same bile and tirade about how I wasn't prepared to prioritise him or the children - not just with regards to the house, but in general.

By the time I returned home that evening, we were no longer going away. I got ready for bed and slid in silently beside him. He didn't speak to me and there was no chance that we might touch; I'd begun to wonder whether the fact that his youngest now seemed to be allowed to sleep in our bed every night was an excuse not to come near me. It would not be lost on him, however, that my little buddy invariably cuddled into me. I often felt, despite his considerable encouragement initially, that his children's love for me, especially by the youngest, was a source of irritation.

I got up for work the next day and got ready as usual. I was trying to formulate a plausible reason to tell my colleagues about why I would no longer be going away. Simon appeared in my dressing room shortly before I was due to leave and with a semblance of softness that had been entirely absent the previous day said, "So do you still want to go away then?". I was lost for a moment as to what to say. I was completely confused by yet another U-turn. "Well, if you think you can still go", I proffered. I was minded not to be incendiary in any way. I stood still, looked at him straight and feigned calm that belied how much my heart was racing; I had no idea what reaction to prepare myself for, so I tried to be ready for everything. Nonchalantly he said, "It's all booked and paid for, it would be a shame to miss out on it. I'll see you later at the airport, ok?". He walked out of the room and got in the shower. I allowed myself to exhale. Perhaps he'd realised how disproportionate his behaviour had been. Who knew. I hurriedly put the last bits into my open suitcase, hoicked it into my car, and drove to work still not entirely convinced that we might get on the plane later.

He arrived at the airport a few minutes behind me. He smiled across the crowd as he walked towards me, and as he reached me he dropped his bag, grabbed me round the waist and nuzzled my neck. "Why don't you want to come and live with us you little bastard?". He pulled back, grinning, licked his lips and then kissed me hard on the mouth, "Come and live with us! We want you with us!". I let out a laugh: surprise, relief, unease. I wasn't sure what to make of it, but right now I was just ready to embrace the good mood that presented itself and aimed to do everything I could to maintain that in the days ahead.

The trip turned out to be amazing. Everything we did, but mostly just how we got on; it was like old times. I basked in the feelings of yesteryear as they came flooding back into the here and now. We explored, we ate, we talked and laughed. We made memories that I felt I would cherish for a long time. The weather was great and the location was stunning. There was only one fly in the ointment - Simon continued to be worried about a sore that stubbornly refused to heal; it was shown to me and spoken about with increasing frequency over the days we were there. He was due to see the surgeon the following week, and that's all the comfort I could offer him: "Don't try and second-guess what that might be". My words didn't seem to be making much headway.

Well, maybe it wasn't the only fly in the ointment. As we sat a couple of days into the break, waiting for our lunch at a beautiful restaurant - outside and shielded from the sun by a parasol - we began talking, as we so often did, about the children. He spoke about his eldest and we mused about how fast she was starting to grow up, turning into a young woman in front of our eyes. He then did something he'd done on numerous occasions previously: he chose, in talking about her physical development, to tell me about how his ex-wife "had great tits". I felt my hackles rise, not because I felt any jealousy in respect to his ex, but because of the blatant insensitivity of his comment. Did he honestly think I wanted to hear that? I didn't think I ought to have to put up with it at any time, but especially when we were away on holiday; a holiday that was meant to compensate for my non-birthday. Not least because it had been a non-event because I had been busy attending to the sorry state of his genitals! I couldn't hold in my irritation; I'd promised myself the last time that the next time he said this I would say something.

"I don't like it when you talk like that. You've done it on several occasions. You wouldn't like it if I did the same. If I told you Connor had the biggest knob of any man I'd ever met, would you think that was ok? Would you like it if I told you several times?".

I was calm, but I was firm. It needed to be said. He rarely said anything positive about how I looked these days and certainly hadn't touched me sexually in the last 6 months. In fact, only once in at least the last 9 that I could even recall! So to hear him wax lyrical about his ex-wife's breasts (again) was just too much. He went silent. I guess there wasn't much he could say in response. After a few minutes, he made his excuses to go to the gents. When he returned I said, "Look, sorry if I was a bit harsh, but when you do that it's hurtful. We've been having a really lovely time, so let's just agree that we're not going to say anything like that to each other ever again and move on. OK?". He nodded just in time for our food to arrive.

The following day was our last; he seemed more agitated about his sore and vociferous about his desire to go home, but we made the best of it. I arrived home on a high, feeling like we were back to where we had been at the start of our relationship and that we might just be turning a corner. The house sale was progressing; we were looking at options of where to live and I had reconciled that I was going to have to make compromises regarding our location. Most promising of all was that he and I had re-connected during our time away.

Work, however, was my own personal sore that seemed unable to heal. In the 10 days that followed our trip, suffice it to say that the situation unravelled. Despite my best efforts to look at ways to mend our relationship, my boss had confirmed that he intended to make me redundant. He'd put that fact on record to me without any of the required procedures being followed. I felt shattered - both by the outcome and how it had been conducted. So I was faced with being jobless by the end of the month after all my hard work, achievements, and the progress of my team.

"Don't worry about it. Don't worry about money. I'm right behind you", Simon said as I paced the kitchen floor distraught about my team, the house sale, a house we were as yet to find or purchase - we'd only been able to secure our current mortgage due to my employment! I now felt a huge responsibility to him and the children. He was calm and reassuringly supportive; it eased my anxiety a little. Yet in the days that followed it was, as the cliché goes, a rollercoaster of emotions - although more 'downs' than ups as I came to terms with the injustice of what was happening to me at work.

I began the search for a new job. Reaching out to those I trusted in my network, ensuring my CV was up-to-date, and trying to get my thoughts together around what I might find and where. Perhaps this was an opportunity. Simon hated the work I did, the hours he felt were unreasonable, the fact I had to travel so far each day and not help him out enough with the children; this might be the change that we both needed to reset our lives to one that we wanted.

I shared my thoughts with him as I tried to contemplate what the future would hold - he was spending so much more time on his properties lately because he'd been making the most of the run of good weather we'd had to sort out the garden. He'd even been staying late in the evenings or sometimes overnight more recently to have a bonfire of all the debris with the guys he was working with; he said they'd sit by it with cans of lager and watch the flames for a while. He seemed to be working so hard and was there so often that I was concerned he was overdoing it, especially when I was worried he was still healing; there had even been a few occasions when he'd been there most of the weekend whilst I stayed at our house with the children. A new life with greater balance and perhaps where we finally fulfilled our property development dream, started to sound increasingly attractive.

&

TWENTY-NINE:

GOODWILL & BAD FEELINGS

It's not easy to capture everything that goes on in the dynamics of a relationship, and certainly not in a linear fashion, because life doesn't work like that. So before I can go forward with my story, I need to temporarily go back because it will, I hope, add texture to some of what was happening.

I've mentioned Christmas in our home already, but I now want to say a little more about this time; it would have been a distraction from what I was trying to explain previously. That time was quite pivotal for me. My family were coming to stay as I previously said. It's worth saying that we had a great time, our extensive home was ideal to host our guests and I pulled out all the stops with decorating the rooms; I enjoyed that kind of thing and I could lose myself in it. Christmas had always been a big deal in my family, so I wanted to make sure it was really special for them, especially as they were travelling so far and we were all upset that my parents couldn't join us; they were staying behind to care for my elderly aunt.

What I learnt later was that, as my sister put it, "We only came because of you". I was humbled, but I also

319

understood. We had, the previous April, all been on holiday together - my parents included. The trip of a lifetime to Florida - a huge villa with private pool. We'd unveiled the trip to the children in both families to great excitement. It was a trip that Simon and I agreed we'd pay for - all anyone needed to bring was spending money and to cover the cost of food. Simon had never been to Florida, so he didn't know what he was letting himself in for really, apart from my description. Yet as we walked away from the travel agency he skipped and ran and hugged me, "We're going to Florida!". He knew how much I'd loved it when I'd been previously: "It's just wall-to-wall happiness whilst you're there", I'd told him.

It was as we approached the holiday that his tone around it changed. He'd told several of his 'acquaintances' that we were going and those that had been all said how amazing it was. Everyone told him how much he was going to enjoy it. Therein lay the issue. Simon hated being one of the pack - he liked to be different, special, "superior" as one of his family had once described it to me. Before we even went I started to get the awful feeling that he wanted to be the exception to the rule - the one person who came back saying he'd hated it. So that's what he did. Right from the outset, he was morose. He complained about everything even before we got on the flight. I was on edge for the entire holiday - walking on eggshells and working relentlessly to try to ensure that his pervasive misery didn't ruin it for everyone else.

My family marched on regardless and ensured they had a great time - their glass-half-full attitude to life and love of the whole experience meant that, for the most part, they had a great time. Simon's children, I was told by their respective mothers after the event, also seemed to have a fantastic time. There were occasions with the eldest two that I wasn't sure; they seemed short on engagement and definitely on gratitude - something I had observed regularly over the time I had known them and tried to rectify as much as I could. I think the extended time together brought the difference in attitude between my sister's children and his own into sharp focus for Simon; he started taking pot-shots about my niece and nephew because he didn't like that they were polite, mature, thankful kids.

I ended up in tears early on in the holiday because I was distraught at how he'd spoken and behaved towards me in front of my father in particular: "He shouldn't have to see you treat me like that," I'd explained. He did apologise to my parents, but none of his behaviour improved. What astounded me was that he couldn't see beyond himself enough to think that this holiday was really about the children and that he needed to put aside any of his discomforts to ensure that they had the best time possible; he just didn't have it in him to do that. It was all about how he felt, what he wanted to do, how it was impacting him - and being the centre of attention. In short, he made himself look like a total arsehole. My mum picked up how he spoke to me, how he did the 'circling the wagons' around his children to isolate me. Yet he claimed, "I'm completely isolated whilst you're here with your family". He wasn't accustomed to me having 'back up' and it destabilised our usual dynamic.

Suffice it to say, he destroyed that experience for me. My memories of it are not of any of the things we did, because the only things I enjoyed were the ones without him. Everything else is a memory of anxiety and embarrassment. He reduced my mum to tears (something that he shouted at me for when they were out of earshot) and my sister very clearly drew the battle lines with him. "Twat," was her summary; at least she could make me laugh. What it did provide was much merriment amongst my family as they passed around photos that showed everyone else smiling and having a good time, whilst his face was often tense and his lips pursed.

This was why Emma said what she did when they came to us for Christmas, it was to see me. It was probably why I worked so hard to make it go well - I wanted to mend fences and create some positive memories of us as a group. Simon almost put that at risk, however.

We agreed that we wanted to make catering for everyone as straightforward as possible (I need to explain that I only had a kitchen because it came with the house!), so we decided to go out for Christmas lunch, which I sorted and paid for. For everything else we brought in pre-prepared vegetables, salads and meals as much as we could; Simon agreed he would pay for this (roughly half ordered each ordered from two separate supermarkets) as it was the equivalent amount to the Christmas lunch.

In the days immediately before Christmas, I went to collect both orders. In the second supermarket, however, they advised me that all that had been paid was a small deposit and that the balance of the order needed to be paid at the till. I was a bit surprised, so I called Simon to check whether he knew this so that we weren't inadvertently paying twice. He was as surprised as me, but checked online (of course, constantly in touch with his bank account!) and confirmed that yes, we had only paid a deposit. "Ok", I said, "I'll go and pay for it and I'll just need you to transfer the money over to me". That was the agreement we'd had. What happened next stunned me. I started to get a series of furious text messages from Simon - aggressive 'shouting' words about what a terrible person I was. He couldn't believe that I was asking him for money, expecting him to pay for things; he was putting in all this effort and expense for my family and yet I dared to ask him for cash.

Now, I don't want to keep going on about money, but I do feel the need to put this incident into context so that I can convey the feeling that I was perpetually being 'fleeced'. I had bought and filled stockings for his three children almost entirely out of my own pocket. I'd bought presents for him - good presents I might add - for him from his children. It is worth noting that, whilst you absolutely don't give in order to receive, I got nothing from his kids on Christmas Day (or on any birthday for that matter even though I always ensured he had gifts from everyone). Anyway, as I said, it wasn't about the money - I didn't care about that, but I just wanted to put his comments into perspective as to what I had contributed. It was the wave of abuse that I was now getting for daring to suggest we should stick to our agreement. It was just lucky for me that he had the kids with him so he couldn't call and scream at me. I just got reams of abuse; it was relentless. I had worked so hard - remember, he was spending his time crying that he might have cancer whilst I'd been wrapping presents. Once again, I found myself in tears in my car - mostly because of the injustice of his words. I'm afraid that I lost my cool at one point - when he said that he'd (temporarily) covered a couple of thousand pounds of costs for the last of the decorating of the house, I did respond with, "What, like the £180,000 I covered for the deposit on the house?". His half of which I still hadn't received. I just couldn't help myself. Cheeky fucker.

I was greeted by the usual brooding punishment when I got home, although he was, miraculously, able to pull it around in time for our guests to arrive the following day. Once he could show off playing the 'host' and taking credit for the festoon of outdoor lights and roaring fire ready to toast marshmallows on, he was suddenly 'happy'. I could tell from Em's expression that she understood where the lion's share of the effort had come from, even though I was allowing him to enjoy the full glare of the spotlight. I knew that she knew that I knew, so we both just let him get on with it.

It was one evening whilst she and I were together on the sofa in front of the wood burner enjoying a rare quiet moment that she broke the silence and asked, "Can you see yourself staying with Simon?". It wasn't quite the conversation I'd expected, so it pulled me up short. "Umm, well", I stammered as I tried to gather my thoughts, "he has said he wants to marry me", I said. Although I didn't tell her that we'd discussed it when his ex-wife got engaged and whilst he'd agreed we should (ironically with this very Christmas being our planned date), and swept me off to bed (oh, those happy days before knob rot set in!), he'd then told me after sex that he didn't think it was the right idea. To say I'd felt used was an understatement.

"Yes, I do. I think now the house is sorted he'll settle down a bit", I continued. I'm not sure either of us was convinced by that last statement. "It's just that Rich and I don't think it's much of a life for you", Emma said. She wasn't about to let it go. "You seem to do loads to look after those kids and then every other weekend you're just going to watch the football - for two people with the money and resources you have you don't seem to spend much time enjoying life".

To have someone acknowledge how much I did, in the face of so much criticism for the lack of it from Simon - I just wanted to hug her. I don't think anyone had noticed on Christmas morning how I had to leave the room after he gave me his card: 'You to me are perfect' it had said on the front and, true to form, he'd written some loving words inside that supported this sentiment. My eyes had filled with tears because when he'd shout, "You are of no use to me!", during yet another meltdown about his responsibilities with the children, I felt so far away from 'perfect'. Yet once-upon-a-time, it had been perfect; beyond amazing and happy. I'd felt filled with love and joy and thanks every single day - like I was the centre of the universe and deserved this awesome life after all I'd been through. He'd been the one to do that, to take me to those heights, to make me feel loved and valued in a way I hadn't done before. Without him, I'd have none of that; at my age, I'd probably never experience those feelings again. And sometimes I still got them back - that man returned and swept me along in those memories.

Yet far from the season of goodwill, it seemed to be the season for tough questions. Simon and I took his youngest to stay with my family for New Year. I took the opportunity for us to meet up with Jen and her husband as I missed them so much and got to see them so infrequently. When we were alone I knew Jen well enough to understand that her questions were seeking a deeper discussion than the polite one we were having; she was worried about me and trying to establish how I truly was. Simon was out of earshot so little that I couldn't open up and tell her. It was a couple of weeks later when we spoke by phone that she confessed that, after we parted company that day, she sat in her car and cried. "You just didn't seem right", she said, "like he's taken you away, suppressed you". That's when the killer question came - the one about whether he'd hit me.

The one where I'd not missed a heartbeat in my response.

THIRTY:

UNLUCKY FOR SOME

Before that digression, I was at the point where, in the 10 days since my employer decided that it was me, and not my bullying boss, who needed to leave the organisation to resolve the leadership differences between us, I went through constant turmoil from the grief I felt regards my team. It was compounded by the worry I would create for my family, how we would manage the house sale/change of home for the kids, the options it would present for Simon and me, and, bluntly, the loss of income for me - who knew for how long. Simon reassured me of his support for me and said that I didn't need to worry.

I wasn't sleeping well. I was distressed and exhausted - everything tumbling around my mind all day and into the night. Waking up in a cold sweat, feeling the injustice of how the work situation had been 'resolved' and worried for what it might mean for the future of the lovely people that I was honoured to have led. The pressure felt immense. I was trying to put some structure around my days and my approach to thinking about life on the other side, but bluntly I was struggling to gather my thoughts due to the fog in my brain.

It was Friday 13th July. I woke up naturally as there had been no need to set an alarm; I wasn't intending to go into the office under the current circumstances and we didn't have the children to get ready for school. It was still fairly early because I was conditioned to get up and out, but the sun was already out - it was a glorious day. Quickly the reality of my situation pierced my consciousness, the anxiety washed over me and I sighed as I lay back in the bed. I tried to steady my breathing and not let the panic overwhelm me. Simon stirred next to me, looked over and saw that I was awake, before getting out of bed to use the toilet in the adjacent bathroom.

I was sitting up in the bed trying to get my thoughts around how to tackle my day when Simon walked back in the room. He strode over to the bed as he began to speak.

"When the house sale has gone through, this is over and we need to go our separate ways", he announced.

My heart began to pound and there was a hollow, whooshing noise in my head; I felt myself go hot all over - like I was burning from the inside out. It was adrenalin; the sensation you get when the body senses it will imminently need to make the choice between its fight or flight responses. I sat still for a moment as he looked at me. My brain had not yet processed this unexpected news.

"I cannot come back from what you said when we were away. I can't bear to lie next to you anymore. I cannot bear to be near you. It's over".

Just like that. Devoid of emotion. Although the stride into the room, I realised now, had been his preparation to make sure he said it - now or never. Don't bottle it. For all his rage, he was just a coward - not very adept at confrontation.

So it was all my fault. I had caused this. A few misplaced words amongst a myriad of support, kindness, sacrifice, love and encouragement. This ultimate punishment was my reward. He seemed to forget that the only reason I'd mentioned Connor's manhood was to make him think about how much he hurt me with his words. I tried to reason with him, but he waved me away. Nothing he'd ever said had warranted my words, he claimed. Nothing I could say now would change his mind. He was cold. He was accusatory. He was final. This was my fault; I only had myself to blame.

I began to cry as the news started to sink in - why now? Why, when he already knew how much I was suffering? What about promising he'd support me? And, my biggest concern of all, what about the children? He shrugged, "We'll work something out so you can see them sometimes if you want". It was unthinkable, unimaginable, that this would be it - not just for me, but for them! What would he say? How would he explain to them? To the littlest one in particular. I was

329

his "other mummy". Just weeks ago they'd all bought me Mother's Day cards. The first time I had ever received one - and I had received three. I recalled the words in each of them: the eldest had thanked me for the last three years and hoped there were "many more to come". The middle child had made me cry by writing: "Thanks for being like the mum at dad's house. I love you", and Simon had told me himself how much trouble the littlest one had gone to in picking out my card. The tears caught in my throat as I remembered cuddling him and thanking him for the beautiful card; he always went a bit coy but hugged me back when I told him how much I loved him.

I started to beg as my heart began to shatter into pieces: we could fix this, I told him. After everything we'd been through, especially after the last few months of his illnesses and surgery, we could rebuild this. Start again. My lack of job meant we had options: could move anywhere, carve out the life we wanted, how we wanted it, no more long commutes and late arrivals home, no more 'single parenting' and taxi services for him. I pulled out every moan and complaint he'd thrown at me over a long period and offered a solution. He began to cry. That gave me hope - perhaps he wasn't finding this as easy as I first thought. Maybe he wasn't as certain as he'd seemed. We talked round and round for the next hour, to-ing and fro-ing about what we'd been through and debating the end of our relationship.

The scale of the loss was devastating - the children, my partner, my job, my home - it was too much to even contemplate. He even told me about how much he'd loved me. How he had wanted to marry me. How I'd been the one that had made him happier than anyone ever had. How that first holiday had been like a fairytale; he even mentioned a love letter he'd written for me afterwards to tell me how he felt. And yet he was letting one comment, made from a place of hurt, bring all of that to an end. It was like torture. Eventually, he simply said, "It's over. I'm going up to the cottage". As I sat on our bed, crying, shocked and drained as he got showered and dressed. He couldn't even look at me as he left.

I showered and let the water wash over me, trying to rub the salty tears off my face. As I stepped out and stared in the mirror, I realised how pale and tired I looked. I wouldn't want to be with me either. Jobless, infertile, old, ugly - what did I possibly have to offer anyone? He'd not slept with me for months and looking at me I couldn't blame him. I didn't fancy me either.

I couldn't stay there. I'd tried to fight for him, to convince him he was wrong. It hadn't worked. Now I wanted to run. I didn't know when he'd be back, but I couldn't face him.

I did the only thing that I could face. I called Jen.

The best place for mobile signal in the house was the littlest child's room. As I sat on his dinosaur duvet cover and picked up one of his soft toys, I had started to cry again before Jen even picked up the phone. Here I was again, I was well aware, crying a bad relationship story down the phone to her. True to form, she was unfazed by any drama. "Lovely, are you well enough to drive?", she asked. "I think so", I gasped between sobs. "Then put some things in a bag and come to us. Just get out of there", she said. We put down the phone and somehow I managed to get my thoughts together enough to gather some belongings; I threw my bag in the car having breathed a sigh of relief as I locked the house up behind me. Whilst I drove to Jen's on autopilot, I tried to process what had happened in the preceding hours. The pain was physical. It was all-consuming. It left me numb.

In the following two days, Jen did what she did best: she cared for me, held me whilst I cried, tried to feed me and asked me the questions that needed to be asked. As I sat on her sofa with my phone in my hand and the tears coming down my face, I tried to understand why he wasn't getting in touch; he was constantly online, I could see, but there was no news from him, not even to see how I was. She spoke out loud my fear:

"I hate to ask this and I know you might not want to consider it, but you don't think perhaps he might have someone else?".

My immediate reaction was to dismiss it. No! He couldn't have. After all, I'd spent the last 9 months supporting him through a horrific abscess and surgery in a place that didn't lend itself to a relationship! How could he possibly be seeing someone else? Where would he have met them and how could he find the inclination given everything that had (or hadn't) been going on 'downstairs'? Yet as I sat there and watched his uninterrupted 'online' status, I remembered the outset of our relationship and how, had anyone been watching him then as I was now, they'd have seen exactly the same. The sinking feeling took me to a lower depth that I couldn't have conceived was possible.

He did, eventually, get in touch: he hoped I was ok and with my family. No opening was offered for me to respond to. I replied anyway. I asked him about the letter he'd spoken of - the one he'd written after we came back from our first holiday. I asked him to email it to me. As I sat and read it the tears poured down my face; it spoke of how I had changed his life, made him complete, brought him a peace he never thought he would find. I couldn't believe how much the emotions he articulated with such passion matched so much of what I had felt too - like we were two pieces of a jigsaw, made to fit together. If we'd had that once, that strength of feeling, there was no reason why we couldn't find that again - that completeness, that love, that intensity. I wrote a letter back - full of the emotions that now needed to pour out of me - how no-one had ever made me feel how he had, how I couldn't imagine living without that feeling because I was certain that I would never find it again with anyone else. I loved him. I loved his children. I loved that he had given me a family and the chance in some small part to have the one thing I'd never thought I'd have - the chance to be somebody's mummy. His children loved me. How could he possibly throw all that away?

After a couple of days with Jen, who had been kind beyond belief, I got up early on Monday morning and drove back north. My stomach was in knots. I didn't know what I might face or how I was even going to begin to pick up the pieces of my life. I had nothing to focus on, other than how broken it all was. I didn't know where to start. Nearer the truth, I didn't think I had the energy to start.

As I had already begun to do, getting another job had to come first. If I had a job I could afford somewhere to live at least. But what job and where? I couldn't decide whether I wanted to stay in the North (the pull to where Simon and the children were was strong) or to run 'home' to the South where my family were. Once they'd heard my news that was certainly their desire. The reality was I might just have to go where the work was, which could mean a move anywhere. Another move, another requirement to start all over again and to build a new life...the thought of that made me feel even more exhausted.

I was driving back North to meet a recruiter I'd known for years. It was just a speculative discussion to understand the marketplace, get my CV in front of him and look at my options. As it transpired, he was reasonably upbeat and knew of a position at the right level and salary that was, ironically, only 10 minutes away from where I currently lived. Time was of the essence though as they were at the tail-end of the process and the employer had a preferred candidate in their sights; we needed to move fast.

It was going 'home' that was the hardest. Simon had communicated that he was going to stay at his cottage on the coast as much as possible, so I wandered around our vacuous house taking in all the memories it held as the eerie silence overwhelmed me. I felt sick at every turn. The children's drawings adorned the kitchen walls, the washing basket was full of their clothes that always seemed to end up there having barely been worn and the enormous bed I'd shared with Simon stretched out in front of me. I couldn't bear to lie in it. Not alone. Not in that huge space knowing that in the days beforehand he had laid there without me.

I moved into the spare room - at least if he came back we would have our separate spaces and he would still be near the kids. If need be they might not even notice for a few days that our sleeping arrangements had changed. Protecting them was key. Not disrupting them was important. Perhaps he and I could talk and find a way forward. I soon discovered, that as well as not being able to eat, I also couldn't sleep. Every conversation, every nuance, every message went round in my head. And I couldn't stop watching his 'online' presence and thinking about what Jen had said.

What was strange in those next few days was his behaviour. It started with him turning up at the house - randomly, without announcement, in the middle of the day when I would expect that instead he'd be working in the garden at his cottage. He'd turn up, talk to me and then cry. Lots of crying, distress, pacing the floor. When he saw that I was filling boxes with my belongings (whatever happened, we'd sold this house and were leaving it) he'd said, "You're packing?", and his voice had caught, choked on the emotion of the words. Strangely, whilst he was there and during these outbursts, I felt unusually calm. I felt compassion for him; I guess I thought that perhaps he was undergoing some kind of internal struggle with the idea of the end of our relationship. It was like he was trying to communicate something to me, something deep, but that the words failed him and he couldn't quite allow the emotion to come out. After he was gone, however, I was bereft - emotionally drained and overcome with the grief of it all. Desperate to try and reach him, to try and rekindle what we'd once had, keen for him to see who I could be if he'd only let me.

Then things turned again. Messages first and then emails - full of bile and nasty demands. The inability to reason with him returned; there was a threat in his words that worried me. He was becoming more unpredictable: when he'd show up, what mood he'd be in, whether the rage would come. He no longer had cause to keep it civil, to contain it, and his written words had a menace that scared me.

I took to sleeping (or, more accurately, not sleeping) with the lights on. I put keys, the wrong keys, inside every lock so that he'd at least have a struggle to get in if he arrived back at night and I'd have a chance to prepare myself. The fear was real and deep-seated; it was borne of that night with his eldest son, from the questions about what had really happened that school day with his daughter and of all the moments of anger that I'd been on the receiving end of. It was there in Emma's questions at Christmas and it was present in my response to Jen's. I was afraid of him.

I felt my fear for certain when he asked if he could come to the house and speak to me; it was the day I had an interview for the job I'd been made aware of. I expected to be at the company for about an hour and a half, so I agreed a time for us to meet on that basis. My stomach was already in knots - I'd barely eaten or slept now for days. The burden of stress from my entire circumstance meant the weight was dropping off and it was starting to show. Now I had an interview to contend with for a job I really needed. It was a job I knew I could do. The interview went well, in fact, a bit too well. I became increasingly conscious that Simon would, by now, be waiting for me at home; he wasn't a man you kept waiting. The thought started to ricochet around my mind about how he'd be when I did go home; I couldn't deny that now might just become that time when I needed to be ready for him to get physical. Nothing now could come as a surprise.

When I finally got home he was lying on our bed, brooding. So I tried not to show I was afraid. It seemed to work, yet my 'lateness' was punished with the response that he'd decided he no longer needed to talk or had anything to say. There followed a fit of tears, then anger, before he drove off into the approaching darkness. Next came more nasty emails. Then again a face-to-face encounter where he stated that the one thing he couldn't come to terms with was that he would miss my "incredible grace", the witnessing of which "one last time" was what had evoked such strong emotions in him. At times I wasn't sure if he was taking the piss. Whatever this tactic, it was exhausting. This, inevitably, showed on my face the next time I met with some of my amazing friends at the choir I sang in. Two weeks earlier they had consoled the loss of my job and now I was breaking the news that Simon had left me. I struggled to contain my emotions. They were stunned, to say the least, and furious at his timing. I explained a little of how Simon was behaving, which led to one of the most incredible acts of kindness.

My friend Susan, who I sat next to every week, stopped with me by my car at the end of the evening. Seeing that holding myself together for the preceding two hours was taking its toll, she looked squarely at me. "Come and stay with us. We've got plenty of room without the children there". I thanked her profusely for her thoughtfulness, just the mere gesture was so lovely at a time when I felt so wretched. "No", she said, "I'm not just saying it, I mean it. If it were one of my girls, I'd want someone to do the same for them. You need to feel safe, you need somewhere safe to go. Come and stay with us". I was humbled by her kindness and whilst it took me a couple of days and a nudge from a mutual friend, I took her up on her offer. I had to get out of that house. I didn't have the energy to tackle its contents and it's memories whilst simultaneously living with the fear that being there day and night provoked.

Having grabbed some basic provisions - well, perhaps a bit more than just the basics - I was shown to the most beautiful room in Susan's home; it overlooked their garden that was the passion project of her wonderful husband, Graham. I'd met him just twice before, but his ease of manner, intellect and humour - as well as the fact that he'd spent a lifetime living in this female-dominated household and knew the drill - put me instantly at ease. I felt like I breathed out for the first time in a very long while. I slept, finally, with a calmness that had evaded me for weeks, even though my desperate loneliness meant that to start with I still kept the bedside light on for comfort.

Their relaxed relationship and the fact that they kept going about their normal business despite my presence, is what helped me to keep going; they reminded me that the world was still turning whether I liked it or not. The emotional and practical nourishment (I was starting to eat a little) allowed me to face into the packing up of the house with a vigour I'd previously lacked. Knowing that I could go in, get stuff done then retreat to their safety was more empowering; it gave me back some control and removed a little of the fear that had been exacerbated by my exhaustion.

So I went to the house to do some packing. Simon wasn't communicating with me, so I had no idea what I would find.

What I discovered was way more than I could have anticipated.

THIRTY-ONE:
DIAMONDS & DELUSIONS

His car was on the drive as I pulled up, so at least I was prepared that he'd be there. If he was at home at this time in the morning it was likely he'd stayed overnight because he had the children, so I could also be ready to see them and all the heartache that would entail. I let myself in. I had practical stuff to do and I just needed to get on with it.

Despite his numerous impromptu visits whilst I had been at the house, my unannounced arrival was met with horror. I went upstairs as I could hear that the youngest was in the bath; Simon rushed in when he heard my voice, totally thrown as suddenly this wasn't on his terms.

"What are you doing here?", he demanded.
"I've come to do some packing". I felt incredibly calm.

The presence of the small child between us I knew offered me some protection against Simon kicking off.

"But the kids are here. I've told them about us". His words were like a knife through my heart, making the nightmare a reality. I tried to not let it show.
"What did you tell them?".

340

"That I loved them, but that I didn't love you so that we wouldn't be together anymore".

"And how are they?", I said, trying to stay level about the fact that I loved them appeared not to have been conveyed to them.

"They're fine. They understand", he said matter-of-factly.

"Right, well at least they know", I said making my way past him so that I could have a moment to myself to ensure I kept my composure, even though I was dying inside.

His phone rang and he disappeared, so I got the little one out of the bath and cuddled him. The elder boy came in and hugged me. I told him that whatever else happened I wanted him to know I loved him. He couldn't speak, but nodded. I went and found the eldest in her bedroom to say "hi"; she was, as ever, caught up in her technology and distracted. Just like her father, quick to move on emotionally. At least she seemed ok, which reassured me.

Simon was on the phone downstairs. Meanwhile, in our bedroom, I caught sight of his iPad. I picked it up. As the kids often used it, I knew the code. I was compelled to take a look. I feared what I might find, but I needed to know. The ground rushed up to meet my falling stomach, as the internet search history revealed more than I could have imagined. Page after page of evidence that there was, indeed, a new woman in his life: love poems, love quotes, searches for 'romantic restaurants' near his coastal cottage. The best of all, order confirmation for a diamond ring - purchased from the website that I had signposted him to when he'd talked of marrying me and asked where I'd recommend he might find a ring with a large diamond.

I walked downstairs to the study. I went in and shut the door; he was off the phone. I knew I had an incredulous smile on my face. I told him what I'd found. Of course, whenever confronted with logic he tried to outwit you with his own, perverse version of it. On this occasion, he tried to turn it into a matter of invasion of privacy; he said he was going to call the police. His jaw was clenched indignantly. I laughed. "I don't think being caught with your pants down gives you the right to claim the moral high ground, nor is it a police matter", I said. He was furious, but he knew he couldn't deny it. The evidence I had was too damning. He had to confess that he'd met her up at his cottage; she worked at a local hotel as a chambermaid. I knew it would be all about finding someone to do the chores and relieve him of his children. "So you're marrying the nanny", I said. He tried to protest, but his words fizzled out; he looked at his feet as he fell unusually silent. He'd only just met her he said, in the last couple of weeks since we'd been over. I snorted, "Well then that makes you sound like an even bigger idiot if you're getting engaged after knowing her for only a fortnight!". I was starting to enjoy myself - he hadn't been prepared for this. "And what about the children? How are they going to feel now that I am being instantly replaced with a new stepmother?".

The rage began to take hold of him now; he was losing his composure: "This is my life and I can do what the fuck I want!", he screamed.

"But it's not just your life though is it?", I was incredibly calm, "It's three other little lives that you are also responsible for".

The decibels increased. "It's my life and I will do what I want and everyone else will just have to get fucking used to it!".

That said it all. None of us mattered. What harm he did, even to his children, was irrelevant. He was like a spoiled child, totally self-centred.

"What's happening to you - you did this! It's your fault! This has happened to you because you wouldn't do what I wanted!", he shouted in my face.

There. That was it. In that sentence; that moment. I'd not complied. Not given in. He wanted the 'nanny'; someone who would subjugate themselves to his needs. Someone to take away his need to care for his children on the basic level, so that he could do what he wanted and only do the 'fun' parts of parenting. I smirked as the scales fell from my eyes. Then he really lost it.

He started crashing around the house yelling about the need to take every piece of technology out of it because I couldn't be trusted. The children got screamed at to get ready to go out. He stuffed every laptop, iPad and phone he could find into a bag as he stormed around the house, failing to realise two things: that it was already too late because he'd been caught with his pants down (and boy, had I seen enough of him with his pants down to last me a lifetime!) and that he'd neglected to take the largest piece of IT equipment we owned. The family computer remained on the kitchen counter. He was unravelling and it now just amused me. The kids were my protection, or rather the littlest one was; he wouldn't want to be seen to fall from grace in his presence.

Before they left the youngest called out for me; he wanted my help putting on the new shoes I'd bought him. He sat a few stairs up from me and we chatted whilst I tied the laces. When I'd finished he got up to go, then hesitated. He turned back and threw his arms around my neck and gave me a huge hug; he was a smart boy - he knew. I realised he'd known for months, way before I had. It dawned on me that the less his father had loved me, the more he had. It was why he'd clung to me so much these last few months, been like my shadow, slept next to me whenever he could; he'd been making up for his dad. Simon appeared at the top of the stairs just in time to witness the hug; I could tell the sight infuriated him. I tried not to let either of them see my tears.

"You will never fucking see these children again!", he hissed at me before slamming the door. The house shook. I watched him screech away down the drive.

I called his ex-wife. She already knew about this new

woman and apologised profusely that she'd not known what to do about telling me. I reassured her it was fine; she was in an impossible position. He'd already told their eldest about her, apparently; there'd been a card sent with him for her birthday.

"Now that's a woman angling for an introduction", his ex said knowingly. "Apparently, she's 'The One'", she continued, "I mean, as if! He's only known her five minutes and, without meaning to sound harsh to you, he says that about every woman. To be honest, you lasted longer than I thought and I thought perhaps he might mean it with you. I have to tell you my kids adore you - I had to give them a big cuddle after Simon told them it was over. I said, 'You're gonna miss her, huh?'. He's just a narcissist, he's why our daughter is in therapy. You just have to accept that it's how he is. One thing I learnt was that he'll never let go of one branch until he's firmly got hold of another. All I can tell you is that I am so much happier now that I am not with him".

There spoke the voice of experience. She'd been there and she'd seen it come and go on several occasions since. Those words, combined later with the perspective of the youngest's mother, helped me know that I was not alone in my experience and that I hadn't been losing my mind - despite his best efforts to convince me otherwise.

THIRTY-TWO:

SELFIES & STIs

In the next couple of weeks I'd managed, despite his venomous emails, to reach an agreement that he wouldn't come to the house for a week; that he'd allow me to move out uninterrupted. He wouldn't agree who would take what, so I resolved to take as much as I could given that he had plenty of my previous-life's belongings furnishing his other properties.

Emma and Rich came to help me for a couple of days; we moved mountains getting things packed up or taken to the skip. I was immensely grateful as much for the emotional support as the physical help required to bring this complicated chapter to a close. As I cleared out the house and packed away my life, curiosity would often get the better of me. I'd realised that through the family computer I could get a glimpse into his life: photographs, calendars, internet search history - all of it was synced to this computer; it made fascinating reading.

The best were his photographs. This new woman, it turned out, was considerably his junior and of the 'selfie' generation; her Facebook page was full of pouty pics. So he'd taken to doing these too. I could see, much to mine and my family's hilarity (oh come on, I couldn't

NOT share them around!), all of his attempts. Thanks to 'live' photo mode, you could see him preparing his pout! He looked like a teenage girl. It was so unattractive and mortifying; I was embarrassed for him.

More challenging amongst the pictures was the one he'd taken of his youngest son alongside this woman's child. From the date of the picture, I could see that almost as soon as he'd originally told me it was over they'd all gone out for the day. That poor little boy had been suddenly thrust into this new family set-up and was standing alongside a new 'brother' who was about the same age as him; he was no longer the baby of the family. Displaced. His sad, awkward little face said it all.

Then there was the slo-mo video of Simon and her - dressed up for the races (she owned a horse, so Simon was obviously doing all the things she enjoyed and pretending he did too). She was swigging from a can of cheap lager as they sat around a table on the train with their drinks in a carrier bag. As one of my friends said, "He's quite literally gone from Champagne to lager!". Suddenly the evenings of supposedly drinking lager around a bonfire up at his cottage, the ones that had made him late home, made sense; he hadn't been with the lads at all. I remembered a day when I'd challenged him about why he was wearing the expensive watch I'd bought him with his scruffy gear to go and work in the cottage garden. I realised now that he'd clearly been taking her out and not working at all.

The best was the naked photo she'd sent him the night

before he'd told me it was over - all sultry and tattoos - she looked like she knew her way around the bedroom and would probably, based on my experience, frighten the life out of him. I smiled wryly. When my nephew saw that picture he asked my sister, "Mum, is she a hooker?" - Em and I roared with laughter at that one.

I won't deny that I was angry. Was I angry! I felt so betrayed, so used, so stupid, so heartbroken...the list went on. I'd be the first to admit that I had some 'fun' with some of his belongings to vent my spleen, which, I might add, I did ultimately compensate him for. But he'd played dirty too - he accused me of harassment (weeks later, which didn't seem much like harassment it must be said), and tried to get the police involved by accusing me of stealing his belongings. They weren't much interested and adopted a much softer tone when I mentioned about our involvement with social services and the incident with Simon's son; he had far more to lose than I did if things turned nasty in that regard. They said they'd advise him to be sensible and I heard nothing more.

In truth, much of what I was finding out about him was helping me. The more I saw and heard, the less I recognised him. I realised that this chameleon of a man was a hologram - to me and everyone else. How could I love someone that wasn't real? He'd been an illusion, morphing into whatever I needed to ensnare me and now he was off doing it with someone else: pretending to be an animal lover when they frightened him. And there's nothing like a horse for attracting flies

- I smiled to myself wondering how he was managing to contain his urge to squeal due to that phobia to impress this woman!

Little did this new woman know that in the background of his ardour, one of his greatest terrors was playing out: a medical terror. She, I discovered, was a carrier of a sexually-transmitted condition. He was a man with a newly-delicate manhood. In his efforts to win her, he'd placed himself at risk. Whilst he would have been presenting her with a picture of happiness and sweeping her off her feet, I could see that he was repeatedly researching this situation and looking for genito-urinary clinics nearby. At least he had some prior knowledge of these to draw upon. I knew enough about him to know that this fear would be occupying his every thought and unravelling him under the surface. I wondered if he'd cry on her for 13 hours...

There was a final nail in the coffin of my feelings; it came in a chance finding on that same computer. It was a letter. The file name was saved in the same format as the infamous letter he'd sent to me after we'd broken up: the one that he'd written after that first year together. I'd found the letter he'd written to me on the computer and reassured myself from the date stamp that he had indeed written it that first Summer. I opened this other letter - the one saved with her initials where once there had been mine. It turned out that was not the only similarity.

As I sat and read 'her' letter, my jaw began to drop.

He'd copied and pasted 'my' letter (which begged the question now whether it actually was mine!) and rehashed it for his new love. In places, it was word-for-word the same whilst in others the sentiments were strikingly similar. I began to laugh. Then I called Jen. "You will not believe what I have found now!", I shrieked down the phone. I'd thought nothing about his audacity could surprise me any longer, but this - to give him credit - this surprised me on another level. It was my email to his new lady containing both these letters that prompted him to complain to the police. It was worth it just to imagine his apoplexy when those turned up in her inbox! I'd have loved to have heard how he explained his way out of that one. How I would have loved to have been a fly on his wall.

Having secured his commitment in writing to the solicitor handling our house sale that he would pay me back my deposit money as well as my half of the remaining proceeds, I took everything that I thought I was owed from that house. In trying to resolve who got what I was indebted to a friend, who started out acting as my lawyer for the work situation, but later, because of the lovely guy he is, ended up getting embroiled in the personal stuff; as the wave of the home situation hit me I could no longer separate out my emotions about the two events: loss was loss, grief was grief. Either way, I was going to take a long time to heal.

This friend, in particular, helped enormously to reassure me of my sanity after he spoke to Simon whilst trying to broker an arrangement regarding the remainder of our possessions. I was worried about him speaking to Simon, I warned him that he was very charming, would seem very reasonable and would seek to convince my friend that I, in the way that he often spoke about his previous ex's, was a "nutjob/psycho/maniac". When my friend called me after speaking to him I held my breath waiting for him to tell me that Simon had been a complete gentleman. What he said shocked me:

"I don't know what else is going on with that guy, but he is totally unhinged. He screamed and shouted and carried on at me when all I was trying to do was help him".

I was stunned by this turn of events, if not shocked at all by Simon's propensity to behave this way. What had happened to the icy-cold manipulator he prided himself on being?

"I had to ask him three times to stop shouting and swearing at me. How he has never ended up in trouble with the police I will never know", my good friend continued. Then the words that changed everything for me: "I've never not believed what you told me about his temper, but I honestly couldn't have imagined how bad it was. All I can say is that you've dodged a bullet. I no longer feel sorry for you, I now feel sorry for this new woman he's with because I promise you, with a temper like that the next thing that would have happened was that he would have hit you".

The weight lifted from my shoulders was incredible. I

was not mad. I had not imagined it. The vindication of my feelings and fears was absolute.

&

THIRTY-THREE:

THE ART OF BEING SELFISH

I couldn't have told you that was what I'd needed to know in order to be able to move forward, but it turned out it was. I ceased questioning myself and started to believe myself. I began to confront what I had endured and to share it with others.

I'd be lying if I said that was easy.

I felt so ashamed. Ashamed that I had let it happen to me. Ashamed that I thought I was smart, but that I hadn't seen what he was. Even worse was that my whole career was based on 'people', that I prided myself on being good at really seeing and reading them, but here I had failed to spot the signs, even when Jen had asked me whilst Simon and I were still together whether I thought that he could be a Narcissist. My best friend could spot it from hundreds of miles away. I felt like such an idiot.

Yet somehow I couldn't hide away. I had to let those around me know what had happened. I felt the need to explain why I'd been who I'd been throughout that time, even though in reality I think I'd done a remarkable job of hiding what was really happening. My truth was that it had altered me. Initially, I only saw that as being in a negative way but over time I learnt that I gained so much in my survival.

My greatest concern was that I didn't become a 'victim', not just to what Simon had done, but also all the other episodes in my life where I had been manipulated, controlled, 'abused'. At home. At work.

Not for a moment do I want to absolve any of my perpetrators of their responsibilities; they ought to be held to account, even if only through me saying what they did out loud. However, the brutal truth was that I couldn't change any of them and, instead, I realised that I had to start with me.

The implosion in my life was so catastrophic this time that I had to sit up and take notice. In the aftermath I was forced to stand naked in the desolate landscape of my life and survey the wreckage; there was nowhere to hide this time. A bit like in the story of The Emperor's New Clothes, I similarly had to accept that I was exposed. Basically, I was going to have to 'style this out'. Embrace it. Because in actuality there was freedom in everything being scrubbed clean. It was an opportunity, even though it was a long time before I saw it as such.

There was much that I went through in the days, weeks and months that followed Friday 13th July that it took me some while to reflect on and see the lessons in. Or the positives. When I thought I had lost everything, it was hard to see the gains because they seemed so minuscule. Yet when you've experienced any devastation in your life, you have to count the victories, however irrelevant they might seem: a smile, sleeping, eating - a particular one for me as this was always my Achilles heel and I lost half a stone in those first two weeks. For my size this was significant and, for the record, I looked awful. Other 'successes' included breathing in and out without intense emotional pain, managing not to cry for absolutely any period of time... you get the picture.

Bizarrely, the predominant thing that I made peace with was the crying. I cried every day, sometimes several times a day and often for long periods at the start. I cried every day at some point and in some small way for over a year. What changed was the nature of the crying and the reasons for it. At the outset it was huge, body-wracking sobs of grief and desperation...but, rather surprisingly, over time they turned to tears of gratitude. I became so grateful for what I had escaped, what I had gained and for the chance to start again in re-carving out a life and the person that I wanted to be. I had been given choices where previously I'd felt like I had precious few.

Some of the choices I took were stupid - too much to describe here! - yet they too taught me so much (as well as creating some great comedy material! and I became thankful even for those.

This wasn't about 'finding' myself. The key was that I had to re-create 'me'. I was inspired when someone very kindly gave me a copy of the George Bernard Shaw quote, which I felt could have been written especially for me:

"Life isn't about finding yourself. Life is about creating yourself."

For so long I had tried to conform. To do what I 'should' or 'ought' to do. To please others. To fit in. Be liked. To try to be lovable. None of it had worked. It was time to press the re-set button, tear up my blueprint, go back to the drawing board...however you want to describe it. I had to rebuild myself from the ground up, starting with selecting on which patch of ground I wanted to start my (re)construction.

The next step was to put my hands over my ears and sing "la la la!" anytime anyone tried to tell me who I should become. In the past I had allowed myself to be so easily swayed by those opinions because I didn't trust my own judgement. This time though, I had to do this. Me. My way. In my own time. How I wanted. It was time to learn the art of being selfish.

Only then could I fathom out who I was and start to put the disparate pieces of myself back together.

෨

A FEW WORDS ABOUT COERCIVE CONTROL AND NARCISSISTIC PERSONALITY DISORDER – I.E. WHY I WROTE THIS BOOK...

It is wonderful that so much more is being spoken about with regards to coercive control: in the news, in the media and even being tackled by soap operas and other TV drama series. We must cultivate a greater understanding of the subtleties of this odious behaviour and make it easier to spot, challenge and eradicate.

Because it is subtle. As a 'victim' it is really hard to fathom that's what is happening to you and, like any form of abuse, even if you have an inkling that something isn't right, you feel ashamed - too embarrassed to speak up. Who do you tell? How do you convey how these many tiny, innocuous incidents that are so easily explained away add together to make you feel like you are going mad? How do you articulate that you are being abused?

It took me a long time to accept that what I had suffered was emotional abuse. Not least because, in different forms, I had endured aspects of negatively controlling behaviours across many relationships. I'd held that deep belief since childhood that I was unworthy, unloveable, and going to be left alone in this world. The belief that I 'should' be nicer, especially as it transpired, to the men in my life, which is why I attracted the kind of men that I did. That belief had shaped pretty much every relationship encounter I'd had.

Yet this last one left the deepest scar. How could I - a smart, intelligent, successful woman - be allowing herself to be diminished, manipulated and bullied? Was my need to be loved and not be lonely so great that I would let myself be treated in this way? In short: yes. The idea that no-one would want me, and a succession of relationships where indeed they didn't because of the self-fulfilling nature of that belief, meant that I was filled with nothing but gratitude that this man might want me. I would endure anything to prevent him from leaving.

My fundamental strength of character meant that I held on to enough of a semblance of who I was before we'd met to ensure that I could recall some of who I'd once been. I was fortunate that I had other pursuits in my life that I felt so strongly about, as well as wonderful people that I'd met through those activities, that meant I refused to give them up - even when placed under tremendous, often insidious, pressure to do so. Once I opened up to those people they provided the perspective that I wasn't 'mad' or 'insane' as was often levelled at me from within the relationship. Not everyone who suffers coercive control is so lucky to have those people left in their lives by the time their abuser's work is done.

Accepting that you have been abused (and giving it its proper name) is only the start. We need to level-up our attitudes to emotional abuse and see it on a par with its equally horrific sibling: physical abuse. Only then can society change and improve, allowing those who need to, to speak up without shame.

For me, I had the added complexity that it is highly likely that my abuser had Narcissistic Personality Disorder. It is not unusual to find either this, or something on the spectrum of psychopathy, within abusers - they have to operate somewhere outside societal norms so that they can behave as they do. I was embarrassed that I didn't recognise the narcissist in my life, especially given I had briefly researched them at one stage during my studies. However, I now accept that when you are at such close quarters to something, your vision tends to become blurred. It took people other people to spot it initially and name it out loud.

This suggestion led me to research and read articles on the subject; the accuracy of their words versus my experiences made me weep. Sometimes the phrases quoted that those with NPD use towards their 'supply' (victims) was word-for-word what had been said to me. It was uncanny - like someone had transcribed my life.

What I learnt was that the deep self-hatred that a narcissist has is like an internal empty vessel that can never be filled. It's what drives a narcissist to treat people so badly and with such rage when their self-loathing gets too much or the mirror is held up to them. It is why they are perpetually unfaithful as they try to find that special someone that will finally put an end to their emptiness; it is a fruitless pursuit the fact of which makes them progressively unhappy - and dangerous.

We need to spend more time talking about these behaviours rather than allowing them to lurk inside the homes and minds of the people who have to live like this. Like I did. Only then can we end their suffering and prevent others from falling foul of the narcissist's charms.

That is why I wrote this book.

Doing so was a risk. Narcissists are vindictive. Along with those who practice coercive control, they have boundaries outside of accepted norms, which means they are likely to seek revenge if their will or world-view is challenged. Yet I decided that it was a risk I had to take to show how easy it is to be sucked into the vortex of their world and to have your own perspective tipped off its axis.

The point of this book is not to highlight the individual characters - who they are is not of interest; it is about explaining the lessons they teach us. It is about the fundamental tenets that form an abusers mindset, as well as the way in which our society currently views abuse such that it provides opportunities for them to practice their methods, often in plain sight.

This book is designed to educate about how it can happen to anyone; that the profile of a 'victim' is not what we might first imagine. It is to show that abuse can be found skulking behind the doors of the 'haves' just as much as it can the 'have nots'. It is to share that those that endure it may not be shrinking in the shadows, but may well be standing in front of you in the coffee queue or sitting next to you on the train. They may be working with you or for you and may even be leading you - looking for all the world like they have it all, have it all together and all the while doing an additional daily job of work to hide their reality from you.

That's why we have to see with different eyes. We have to create a space for dialogue. We have to see the vulnerability to speak our truth as a strength. Let the scales fall from our eyes about what form an aggressor may take as much as we shift our perception of victims. In a world of endless possibilities, we must understand that the possibilities are endless; we must lift our gaze and truly see.

Because twats are, after all, everywhere.

అ

EPILOGUE

I t was the second weekend after my world imploded that I went back to my parents' home that was the pivotal moment for me.

As I said goodbye to them my dad started to cry. He could see how broken I was and was at a loss to know how to make it better for me. I could appreciate how desperately hard that was as a parent and, in our relationship, I felt appalled that I had done this to him. I was responsible for this pain and I didn't have the strength to prevent it. I wasn't sleeping. I wasn't eating. I was tortured by the fall-out of everything that had happened over the last 18 months. I had no reserves left with which to fight my own desolation and, therefore, none with which to reassure him. I didn't feel like it would be fine. I couldn't see how this would ever get better. I had no hope to share round.

I was used to my mum crying sometimes. That's not to say it was ok when it happened, but it was a feeling I was more accustomed to. But this, my dad's grief, no. I'd not thought I could break any more, but I was wrong; there was a further depth to which I could plummet.

I got in the car and drove away. I don't think I had ever felt so sad. The word itself doesn't seem to even cover it, but in its simplest form that's what I felt. Sad.

Somehow I had to find the strength to drive several hours back North. It was still, technically, my 'home'; I was compelled to go back there to sort through the ashes of my life and pull out my possessions because they were now, in my mind, all the stability I had.

As I drove I kept turning up the volume on the radio. It took me a while to understand that I was trying to drown out the noise in my head. It took longer still, too long, for me to realise it wasn't working. Gradually the noise, I noticed, wasn't in my head anymore. It was a vibration in my body that was oscillating persistently and the frequency was increasing. It had turned into a physical pain. It was a pain like nothing I had ever experienced. It was becoming more acute with every mile. It was starting to affect my breathing, my ability to concentrate, my focus. As I joined the motorway for the final leg of my journey it became so overwhelming I began to feel afraid. It was so all-consuming that I could no longer deny what it was. It was a pain that needed to stop. It was designed to incite drastic action to make it end. The kind of feeling where you would stop at nothing to be rid of it.

I wanted to die.

I needed to die.

It was the only solution to this pain. To make it stop.

It was unbearable.

I was driving faster and faster. I knew I didn't have

proper control of the car. I knew that in an instant I could manoeuvre this speeding hunk of metal to catastrophic consequences. It was like a compulsion - a passionate desire. If I just did that I could bring this pain to an end.

Something in amongst the cacophony in my head made me aware that I needed to get this under control. To do… something. Maybe I knew I needed to prevent those around me becoming collateral damage. I'd like to think so.

I knew that I couldn't keep going like this; the feeling was mushrooming now and filling every space inside me. No matter what I tried, I couldn't suppress or deny it any longer.

I was out of control.

I needed help.

I still can't tell you why I called Charles. All I can say was that the compulsion to contact him, out of all the numbers in my phone, was intense. I wouldn't even at the time have put Charles properly in the category of 'friend'; he was a work contact who had done some coaching with me and my team. I'd always really liked him, but he was most definitely more of a 'business acquaintance'. Yet he was kind, mature and, possibly of key importance at this moment, had worked with mental health charities. Of everyone I knew he was the least likely to panic when I told him I wanted to die.

That call was the most important I'd ever made in my life. I cannot even contemplate what would have happened that day if Charles had done something as simple as not pick up my call, to have been busy doing… something else.

But he did pick up. He knew it was me. He sensed intuitively by my inability to formulate a sentence that I was in trouble. He knew what to do - that must have been why I called him. I needed someone to take over and tell me what to do because I had, almost literally, run out of road. I had nothing left to draw on, or so I believed at that moment. I had to ask for help.

It turns out that I didn't even have to ask. Charles knew. Just my act of phoning had sent out that distress signal, it wasn't important for me to articulate why.

He spoke so that I didn't have to. He talked me in, to where he was waiting. He told me he was there for me. He stayed with me on the phone whilst I drove there. He met me at my car. He put his arms around me. He didn't try to make it better with words. He made it better by being present. The solid presence of another human being. When he did speak, it was to tell me that he wasn't going to speak. We sat each with a cup of tea. No pressure. No judgement. "I'm going to just sit here", he'd said gently, "and whenever you're ready to say something, you speak".

I felt like it was the kindest thing anyone had ever said to me. It was the most powerful gesture. For so long

I'd not been 'heard'; for someone to make me feel like my voice was the most important one in the room was incredible.

We sat in that silence for many minutes during which time I felt my heart rate start to return to normal and a calm exude from Charles that was like a blanket wrapping around me. I had not felt calm in a very, very long time. Stepping back from the edge on which I suddenly realised I had been standing for many months was immense; it was a relief that I'd forgotten existed. I didn't know it then, but learning to live without the adrenalin of relentless fear was going to take a while to re-programme. Thanks to Charles, there was going to be that opportunity to re-educate me.

I don't recall what words first came out of my mouth to break the silence that sat patiently between us. I knew that what I said didn't matter, it was that I indicated that I was ready to speak that mattered. From there, Charles could help me find some equilibrium. I have no idea what he had planned that day, what tasks that my call had disrupted, but none of that was remotely conveyed. I had his attention, in full. He showed up for me with every part of himself. When I'd reached a point of feeling like my purpose on this planet was pointless, he made me feel like I mattered. Just by being there.

He saved my life, just by picking up his phone.

I didn't know it at the time, but in that moment, in the myriad of lessons Charles was teaching me about humanity, MayDey was born - a business focused on responding to the needs of those that want to, for whatever reason, change their lives. Changes big or small, that's not what matters - it's not a matter of someone else's judgement - but just to know that whatever the change and whoever you are, you are not alone.

Charles did more than just ease me enough for me to get back in my car. He gave me that first step to recovery; it was to understand that to ask for help is as powerful to the person whose help is sought than it is to the person who seeks it; it started a process of saying 'yes' to where help was offered, or of asking for it where I saw a need that someone could fulfil.

What I learnt is how willing people are to help. How positive it is for them to learn that they have something that is of value - a skill, a trait, a contact, some knowledge - something that you need. We are pack animals and we like to feel like we are contributing to our tribe. It is that which gives our lives purpose.

I didn't die that day, or on any of the days that followed, even though some of them were unspeakably difficult, because I had someone who was walking alongside me. As I continued to put one foot in front of the other I began to see - to allow myself to see - how many others were also walking with me. That I wasn't just a burden to them, that sometimes I was a benefit. By showing them how they mattered to me, I also mattered.

My life had transformed, initially by circumstance rather than design, but now I was starting to consciously build a crew that would allow me to once again set sail in my boat.

For the first time in my life it was a boat that I had designed and built.

છે